So Much Nearer

Essays Toward a World English

Other Books by I. A. Richards

The Meaning of Meaning (*with* C. K. Ogden)
1923

Principles of Literary Criticism
1925

Practical Criticism
1929

Coleridge on Imagination
1935

The Philosophy of Rhetoric
1936

Interpretation in Teaching
1938

How to Read a Page
1942

Speculative Instruments
1955

"A Leak in the Universe" (*in* Playbook)
1956

Goodbye Earth and Other Poems
1958

The Screens and Other Poems
1960

Tomorrow Morning, Faustus!
1962

I. A. Richards

So Much Nearer

Essays Toward a World English

HARCOURT, BRACE & WORLD, INC., NEW YORK

First edition
Library of Congress Catalog Card Number: 67-20318
Printed in the United States of America

Chapter 1 is reprinted from *The Times Literary Supplement,* by permission. Chapter 3 is reprinted by permission of the Brooks Foundation, Santa Barbara, California, from *The Computer in American Education,* Don D. Bushnell and Dwight W. Allen, eds. (John Wiley & Sons, 1967). The first part of chapter 4 appeared in the *New York Review of Books,* April 14, 1966, and is reprinted by permission; the second part has been printed in the journal *English Language Teaching,* Vol. XXII, nos. 1 and 2, published by Oxford University Press. Chapter 7 is reprinted from *Style in Language* by Thomas A. Sebeok by permission of MIT Press. The lines from "Desert Places" are from *Complete Poems of Robert Frost,* copyright 1936 by Robert Frost, copyright © 1964 by Lesley Frost Ballantine, reprinted by permission of Holt, Rinehart and Winston, Inc.

Preface

The essays that follow will be found to be—from different angles and for different audiences—converging treatments of a common theme: what man collectively could be doing for himself and what in this he should be doing first. Little explicit reference is made to how he is, as yet, using his vast new powers, so recently acquired and so swiftly growing. Some threatening sides of these developments are being recognized and despaired of. The hopeful possibilities, the great practicable steps, receive less attention. It is toward construction that the reflections here encouraged turn.

The first essay, "From Criticism to Creation," serves as a Prologue, introducing and linking the central ideas which are later discussed, and telling something of how the writer became concerned with them. The second piece, "The Technological Crisis," sketches some of the inescapable outcomes of our ever-accelerating technological advances. The third, "Computer-Conveyed Instruction," takes the arrival of the greatest of man's new powers as an occasion for looking closely at the resistances and obstructions which may prevent their sane employment. Since uses of computers pressingly raise some very practical questions about language, the fourth paper, "Some Glances at Current Linguistics," considers at some length why so little present readiness to provide useful advice appears there; and the fifth, "Meanings Anew," attempts to restore semantics to its due dominance in language control. The central question, How can utterance defend itself from misconception? is then explored in "The Future of Poetry." This same matter—the separation of mistakes from acceptable differences in interpretation—is taken further in "Variant Readings and Misreading." The most threatening instances of miscomprehension and distortion of meanings—those fostering and arising from the needless and deadly antagonisms between Chinese and Western traditions—are discussed in "Mencius Through the Looking-Glass" and "Sources of Conflict." The long-term dangers that must here be acknowledged lead to a final paper, "Toward a World English," suggesting inquiries and developments that—if pushed with a tenth of the energy now being devoted to space projects—might help with our presently mind-numbing situation. The collocation here of inter-planetary and other gulfs comes from Robert Frost, who gives me my epigraph and title.

> They cannot scare me with their empty spaces
> Between stars—on stars, where no human race is.
> I have it in me so much nearer home
> To scare myself with my own desert places.

I cannot adequately convey my gratitude for the generous, thoughtful and prevenient care which, through tranquil months at Middletown, has allowed these reflections to be gathered and arranged.

I. A. R.

The Center for Advanced Studies
Wesleyan University
Middletown, Connecticut
May, 1967

We all recognize—more or less unsystematically—that quotation marks serve varied purposes:

1. Sometimes they show merely that we are quoting and where our quotation begins and ends.

2. Sometimes they imply that the word or words within them are in some way open to question and are only to be taken in some special sense with reference to some special definition.

3. Sometimes they suggest further that what is quoted is nonsense or that there is really no such thing as the thing they profess to name.

4. Sometimes they suggest that the words are being improperly used. The quotation marks are equivalent to "the so-called."

5. Sometimes they only indicate that we are talking of the words as distinguished from their meanings. "Is" and "at" are shorter than "above." "Chien" means what "dog" means, and so on.

There are many other uses. This short list will suffice to show how heavily we overwork this too serviceable writing device. Some of these uses accordingly are taken over by italics, but there again ambiguity easily arises. We italicize for emphasis (of several kinds) as well as to show that we are talking about words themselves or about some special use made of them. In speech, of course, many of these subtleties can be handled by intonation and pauses, though not with high uniformity or equally well by all speakers.

At places in these essays, quotation marks will necessarily be given an inordinately heavy task to perform. This there is no avoiding. In all interpretation work we have to be able to hold up words and phrases for separate and special attention, and we have to do our best to indicate what our attitudes to them and to their meanings are. It is somewhat absurd, indeed, that writers have not long ago developed a notation system for this purpose which would distinguish the various duties these little commas hanging about our words are charged with.

I have therefore experimented in my *How to Read a Page* and *Speculative Instruments* with a range of special symbols to take the place of the usual quotation marks. They will be small letters placed, as quotation marks are, about the words, the phrases, and the sentences they single out. I continue this experiment here. A key to this notation follows. It will be found in practice, I believe, that two glances at the key are enough to prepare the reader to recognize, without consulting it anew, what I suppose myself to be doing when I use the notation. It gives us a compact means of commenting on the handling of language—more comprehensible, less ambiguous, and less distracting than the usual devices of parentheses, qualification, and discussion. I believe it will abridge both the optical and the intellectual work of the reader.

KEY

^{w}____^{w} indicates that the word—merely as that word in general—is being talked about. The marks are equivalent to "the word." For example, ^{w}table^w may mean an article of furniture or a list.

^{r}____^{r} indicates that some special use of the word or phrase is being referred to. The marks are equivalent to, "Please refer to the place in the passage we should have in mind here." For example, ^{r}Nature^r for Whitehead is not Wordsworth's ^{r}Nature^r.

$^?$____$^?$ indicates that our problem is, What does this word say here? Not whether anything it seems to say is acceptable or not. The marks are equivalent to "Query: what meaning?" There is no derogatory implication. Most ?important? words are, or should be, in this situation.

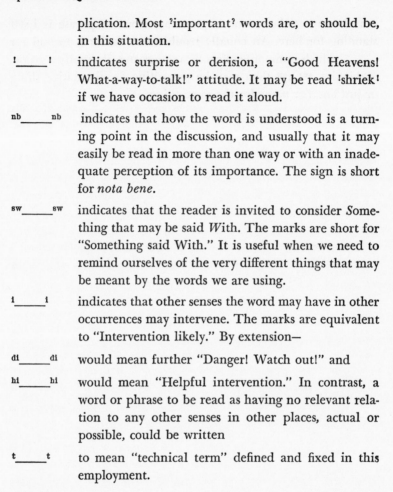

!____! indicates surprise or derision, a "Good Heavens! What-a-way-to-talk!" attitude. It may be read !shriek! if we have occasion to read it aloud.

nb____nb indicates that how the word is understood is a turning point in the discussion, and usually that it may easily be read in more than one way or with an inadequate perception of its importance. The sign is short for *nota bene.*

sw____sw indicates that the reader is invited to consider *Some-*thing that may be said *W*ith. The marks are short for "Something said With." It is useful when we need to remind ourselves of the very different things that may be meant by the words we are using.

i____i indicates that other senses the word may have in other occurrences may intervene. The marks are equivalent to "Intervention likely." By extension—

di____di would mean further "Danger! Watch out!" and

hi____hi would mean "Helpful intervention." In contrast, a word or phrase to be read as having no relevant relation to any other senses in other places, actual or possible, could be written

t____t to mean "technical term" defined and fixed in this employment.

Lastly I will use the mark =, equivalent to, to indicate that the words or phrases it links are to be taken as having the same ?meaning? for the purposes in hand. This escapes the unfortunate suggestion that whatever the first is talking about !really is! the second. The usual device is to write (*i.e.,* ____), which too often carries the suggestion that somehow we have no need to ask

ourselves what the second explanatory word or phrase is itself
standing for here. An equally troublesome device is to add (or
____), which commonly offers us a dangerous, if usually a crude,
ambiguity. ˢʷOrˢʷ then may be presenting an alternative thing
or just another *name* for the same thing.

Contents

xiii

So Much Nearer

Essays Toward a World English

1
Prologue: From Criticism
to Creation

At the beginning of their momentous discussion of education Socrates asks Plato's brothers this question:*

How would it be, since we are not very able people, to do as though we were trying to read small writing at a distance? If someone told us that the same letters but much greater were to be seen in a different place, wouldn't that be a godsend? [1]

So they turn from what justice is in an individual to what it is in the state and go to and fro between them "looking for what is like the greater in the idea of the less." The outcome, it is arguable, was, as Werner Jaeger put it, "the invention of man." [2]

Such comparisons can be—to use Coleridge's phrase—"speculative instruments" of extraordinary suggestiveness.[3] It is well, however, to recall that Socrates tells Glaucon again and again that they will never get to the real truth via this parable but will have to take a longer and harder way round—by a labor in dialectic which some would say has barely yet begun.

A modern equivalent, a contemporary guiding parallel for a design for education, would be biological. The great letters in a different place would be present-day theory of evolution: the

* References and comments will be found in *Notes and Glosses* at the end of each essay.

3

small letters would be speculations as to how we may best try to help minds to grow. Dialectic, however, in Plato's sense, "the continuous attempt to audit an account of the meanings used in a discussion," would come in from the start. It would ask us to reflect as self-correctively as we can, and with all the aids that present-day computer-handled data-processing can supply, on how ideas, ambitions, pursuits, quests for being and so on, compete within as well as between minds, and on just how selection among them may be taking place. We should be considering—against the biologic background—what should be happening and what we can do to favor it.

L. L. Whyte's recent *Internal Factors in Evolution* [4] lucidly and compactly summarizes the crucial distinction: [5]

It is now being suggested that beside the well-established external competitive selection of the "synthetic" theory of evolution, an internal selection process acts directly on mutations, mainly at the molecular, chromosomal and cellular levels, in terms not of struggle and competition, but of the system's capacity for coordinated activity. The Darwinian criterion of fitness for external competition has to be supplemented by another: that of good internal coordination. Internal coadaptation is necessary as well as external adaptation.

Major analogies work both ways. Plato's parallel has structured both theory of government and psychology. Hosea's comparison of religion and marriage remade them both. Taken crudely they can be distorting commonplaces. But there are delicate uses too in which they can help both studies to realize how much (and how little) is known about either and in what different modes of knowing.

Here both the great letters and the little belong to biology. In both, recent focus has been on minute structure and serial order: at the molecular, chromosomal, and cellular levels and at morph, phrase, sentence in the linguistic hierarchy. In both, the interdependencies of parts and wholes [6] become ever more evident as skill in conceiving them improves. For both, the prospect of man's being able to extend constructive control has recently been leaping closer. The look of the future has been changing almost as much in education as in genetics. New invitations to pioneer investigation and fruitful design are opening. What was prophecy—a willful, painful hope—thirty years ago is now as plainly attainable as a mere landing on the moon. Meanwhile the losses and dangers we incur through the needless world shortage of effectively capable people rise like the cost of living. As Michael Roberts in *The Estate of Man* [7] showed so clearly, this is the gravest of our shortages, the one in most need of remedy. In 1948 the situation was both worse and better—worse because what could be done about it was not yet in sight: better because the ablest people were not yet being siphoned off on such a scale into technologies which may be multiplying rather than decreasing the risks. Plainly, if a larger proportion of capable people can be produced, this task has first claim. And what other means to this can be suggested than the redesign of instruction?

"Something must be done!" was the conclusion to be drawn from the studies of misunderstanding reported some thirty years ago in my books *Practical Criticism* and *Interpretation in Teaching*. In England and in America alike people selected by the current system as those most qualified, those who had benefited most from the most expensive literary educations obtainable, were, it had to be recognized, far too often incompetent—deficient in ability to comprehend. Later experience has confirmed this finding. Literary studies, as at present conducted, do not produce enough capable people. Better instruction must be provided. And this redesigned instruction must start with beginning reading. Only thus can it clean up main sources of the failure to comprehend at what should be the highest literary levels. Malformations due to early misdevelopment are its probable cause, as studies of grosser failures in reading—the "underachievement" in literacy that leads into delinquency—are now bringing out.

One of even Coleridge's most seminal hints [8] suggests how crucial the introduction of its first notation can be to a mind: as a means of re-examining, rearranging, reshaping the outcomes and the methodical habits of its first and greatest intellectual achievement: the acquisition of speech. We recognize easily enough in the history of cultures how era-making an invention writing has been—the shift from Homer to Plato,[9] now, in this past decade, spreading through the remaining illiterate majority of mankind. We have not deeply enough realized how often what happens in the process of learning to read can make or mar the learner, and thus become era-making for him as well as for his society. A new notation is an opportunity for review, an offer of a new means of coordination— chances that are lost if it is learned as no more than a Morse-type code, a mere transcript of speech. We lose all the greater values if we limit reading—by whatever devices—to a process of matching sounds and marks. It is far more than that. It is the growth of an instrument for comparing and controlling meanings, for holding up and looking into the miraculous but fleeting achievements of oral utterance. It can also be an occasion for mind-breaking failure, for stultifying confusion, for confirmation of misconception and misdirection. Which it becomes may depend, so it seemed when I let Coleridge lead me [10] out of literary criticism, upon the minute design of the invitations to exploration and exercise therein presented to the learner. These were the possibilities (summarized twelve years later [11] in "Responsibilities in the Teaching of English" in *Essays and Studies by Members of the English Association, the 1947 Annual* (London: Oxford University Press), now reprinted in *Speculative Instruments*) that drew me out of criticism into creation, out of comment on endeavors into a new endeavor. Despite the disdain for Education, then all but obligatory among the cultivated, a new attempt had to be made. To go on writing with such prospect [12] had come to seem silly; better to turn from criticism to a more remedial way of serving its cause, to turn from appraisal to construction, specifically, to attempts to construct more effective, because more carefully designed, instruments of instruction.

Only a few features in this design may be sketched here in this prologue. Or, rather, only a few type-specimen explorations may be presented: enough to show its concern with sequence, with intellective-linguistic opposition, with association, with interdependence and coordination and with the concept of ordered growth that holds all these together.

Sequence, and sequencing, are apter terms for the purpose in hand than program and programing. The reason has to do with (and conveniently illustrates) opposition: the key operating concept of linguistics. *The Program,* for any series of events, normally stands in linguistic (and intellective) opposition to what actually happens. It is a prediction, a proposal, a plan for something. And the something may or may not accord. *Sequence,* on the other hand, reverses this opposition: it points to the sequence itself, not to a prospectus or blueprint for it. *Prospectus* goes with program; and so, of course, does *design* itself. Having *program* and *design* to take care of this duality (of prognosis and outcome) we can use *sequence* simply for the series—in opposition to any account or prescription or formula, given either before or after.

It is true that the unfolding of the sequences which matter most to us seems to require a pre-existing program of some sort, which the sequence may or may not fulfill. In the zygote, somehow or other, the series of transformations which are to produce the mature embryo must, it is widely thought, be represented. Within this representation, somehow or other, are encoded, chromosomally, the directives by which daughter cells behave like their mother. As Whyte puts it: "The concentrated microhierarchy of the genetic system thus becomes manifest as the macrohierarchy of the adult." As Psalm 139:16 has it: "In thy book were all my members written . . . when as yet there was none of them." But a book does nothing without a reader, and talk about "cracking the chromosome code" can easily mislead. This word *code* is a mind-trap. I try to show why in "The Future of Poetry" and in "Variant Readings and Misreading," where more on these themes will be found.

G. W. Corner's *Ourselves Unborn,* which quotes the Psalmist, reminds us that "at its beginning the body consists of one cell, by the time of birth it has two hundred billion cells." The story of that growth presents the best instance we know of the importance of sequence, or serial order. What can happen depends throughout on what has happened, and most depends on the earliest stages. Let this be our image in trying now to reflect on the place of sequence in the growth, microhierarchically conducted too, of a skill, or an art, of a concept in a mind.

This takes us back to *opposition.* Let me present now a type-specimen of a fundamental piece of elementary *structuring* that can be conducted under conditions which allow it to be fully observed and recorded for analysis. It is the introduction, strictly at the start, in the learning of English as a second language, of the representation of space-time discriminations. The first opposition used is between *here* and *there:*

> It is here.   (x)
> It is there.   (x)

A fundamental biologic opposition of situation is paralleled by a linguistic opposition of sentences. Neither situation is meaningful except as in opposition to the other, nor is either sentence.[13]

The second opposition used is between past, present and future:

> It was there.   (x)
> It is here.   (x)
> It will be there.   (?)

Again each of these sentences has meaning only in relation to the others, and only so can it be understood.

These are the initial space-time divisions: the first divisions that the seed of the new language can be invited to make, its first steps in growth. They are oppositions of situations that can be enacted in the classroom (in myriad fashions) and depicted in ways which can make them—for cultures which do not use pictures, in Africa, say—equally an introduction to a pictorial notation for situations. The further steps on from this initial structure are as obvious. In opposition to *It* we have *He* and *She* and, under this new division, proper names. As specifications of *here* and *there* we have locating phrases using names of observable objects: *at that window, on this table, in this room,* etc., with *this* and *that,* which support, because they parallel, *here* and *there.*

An essential point will perhaps have been sufficiently illustrated. Entrance to a language can be so sequenced that it is *intelligible.* It is understood through the correspondence in opposition of its sentences, as they come, with the oppositions of the situations which give them their meanings. In this way the primal opposition in the world of THOUGHT: *intelligible-unintelligible* (*clear-unclear* is for meaning what the *here-there* opposition is for space) can be given its proper role, whereby (to use Whyte's phrasing), "An internal selection process acts directly upon mutations" (mainly at the morph, phrase and sentence levels) "in terms not of struggle and competition" (winning teacher's approval or not) "but of the system's capacity for coordinated activity." That is how a language grows healthily in a learner. With enough care in the design-sequence the intelligibility of every fresh differentiation and connection can be maintained throughout by joint use of depictions and of the language taught in preceding steps. This planned instruction can be conveyed via film-strip, film and television with progress for the learners [14] equal to that obtained by chosen teachers handling small groups. And its filmed television lessons can reach millions or, rather, billions. What is notable too is that children coming into English as a *second language* through such intelligible sequences often do better in English composition than comparable native speakers.

Consider to what an extraordinary society a morph belongs. As the minimal linguistic form [15] *combining* distinctive organization as sound with distinctive organization of meaning it has a bi-mundane existence. The morphs are our bonds between the sensory structure of speech and the intelligential order of utterance. They are the grounds, the hold-fasts, the sanction of the interdependence of form and content, matter and spirit, which have always made language so good an emblem, at the least, of the body-soul relation. A morph serves as belonging to two orders: one phonologic-syntactic, the other semantic. Phonologically and syntactically, it is in a very rigidly ordered system indeed—that "grammar of the language" which the child, according to Noam Chomsky, "has in some sense constructed for himself." This is an order which, with stern inflexibility, rules what formations the morph (say *struct*) may enter: *constructive, instructive, destructive, instruments*—a fantastically complex system, the built-in residuum of thousands of years of competition and cooperation. And none of all this need be consciously known to a speaker, till the linguist (or Eric Partridge, with his wonder-working *Origins*) turns on the light. On the other hand, continually, whenever something is being said that is not quite routine and obvious, something we care about saying, innumerable semantic transactions between morphs are being tried out in these or those oppositions, alliances, conspiracies. A diplomatic struggle between possible meanings and modes of achieving them is going on, of which the speaker is very often *highly conscious*—though how it can be reported on is quite another matter.

Turn now to *association*. People have been hearing about "association by contiguity" and "association by similarity" [16] through centuries. But not until Jakobson and Halle (*Fundamentals of Language*, The Hague, 1956) was the centrality for linguistics of these polar operations clearly recognized. By contiguity, missing bits of a cluster or sequence can be restored: $abc - e$; and parts can act for wholes (metonymy); given a voice on the telephone you respond to a speaker. By similarity (analogy, proportion, sameness in difference) what is needed to complete a structure [17] is supplied: $a:c::d:-$; and an aspect can act for a whole (metaphor). A stick-figure man is very different from any man but *is* a little like his silhouette or his shadow on a screen. In general, the auditory channel is metonymic; the optical, metaphoric. Contiguity and similarity, however, are joint operators, mutually dependent, as these instances show: $abc - e$ has a serial order, a linear structure which must be recognized if d is to be filled in correctly; conversely, if the proportion, $a:d::f:-$ is to be rightly solved (with i), contiguity must come in to maintain serial order. Nonetheless these operations are polar.

As Jakobson points out:

A competition between both devices, metonymic and metaphoric is manifest in any symbolic process. . . . Thus in an inquiry into the structure of dreams, the decisive question is whether the symbols and the temporal sequences used are based on contiguity (Freud's metonymic "displacement" and synecdochic "condensation") or on similarity (Freud's "identification and symbolism").

He cites also Frazer's division of charms and concludes, "The question of the two poles is still neglected, despite its wide scope and importance for the study of any symbolic behaviour, especially verbal, and of its impairments." We must grieve for this neglect while so much else of no consequence is being so sedulously pursued.

In sequencing which is designed to encourage interdependence and coordination in the growth process (*Justice* is Plato's word for all this) whether Contiguity or Similarity is dominant in their cooperation is indeed important. A Contiguity programing, using redintegration as its bond, builds up (brick between brick) a "Give the answer!" attitude to a question. A Similarity-difference programing, using contrastive procedure as its gait, induces a "What's the question?" attitude. Contiguity conforms; Similarity explores. Both are exercises of structure, but Contiguity reproduces while Similarity extends and develops. Differences in *learning-sets* as great as these may well decide much in the growth of a mind. How, it will be asked, may dominance by Similarity be assured? Chiefly by taking full advantage of the resources of critically controlled depiction. In the early stages at least, joint use, in lock-and-key combinations, of the verbal and pictorial channels, seems to be the answer. Opposed situations, enacted and/or depicted, call for sentences with corresponding oppositions, and provide continuous exercise in analogy. Leaf through a few pages of advertisements (the most influential and often the most skillful compositions we encounter). You will probably find it easy to sort them into those primarily Contiguity (the stock response being touched off) and those that are mostly Similarity (the customer being invited to follow up a comparison). Someone should be doing this sort of survey study via television to wake up the audience. Inevitably (but unluckily) programs in which Contiguity is dominant are far easier to write, needing much less invention and imaginative exploration. Correspondingly, such programs are likely to generate, in the learner, mere mechanical procedure, boring and dehumanizing. You just fill in a missing word from what you have been reading. It is routine retention that does the trick. Any real interest in the topic need not enter. In contrast, Similarity programing calls for resource and constructiveness, for activities that are enjoyable and restorative. It is regrettable that the sect of psychologists most responsible for the promotion of programing and the teaching machine should have been—by their own self-denying ordinances, by the very limits they themselves set on their own concepts and procedures—those least well placed to take such all-important over-all considerations into account.

Intellectual fashions are inconstant; occupational slants are more explicable. Experimentalists opening up a new field—

whether preparing to place man on the moon or to take over education for the reflex—are to be encouraged in a "scrap and start again" policy, if that helps them. They should not mind if the next inquirers follow suit. Compare:

(A) Hundreds of puzzling questions and obscure propositions about verbal behavior may be dismissed while the new questions and propositions which arise to take their place are susceptible to experimental check as part of a more unified pattern. (B. F. Skinner. *Verbal Behavior,* p. 456.)

(B) The questions to which Skinner has addressed his speculations are hopelessly premature. It is futile to inquire into the causation of verbal behavior until much more is known about the specific character of this behavior; and there is little point in speculating about the process of acquisition without much better understanding of what is acquired. (Noam Chomsky reviewing *Verbal Behavior* in *Language,* Jan.–March, 1959, p. 55.)

What may strike us first is the high confidence of both pronouncements.[18] How does Skinner know—if they are so puzzling and obscure—what these questions and propositions are that "may be dismissed"? How by his own theories does he do it? And in what way do the new questions and propositions "take their place"? Do they attempt the same tasks or just absorb the time available? To change the subject is a well-known way of dodging an inquiry.

Of Chomsky's comment we may ask whether speculations, speculations of all sorts, even those found to be futile and pointless, are not usefully part, by opposition, of the very process of developing "much better understanding of what is acquired"?

Disputatious assertions such as these—especially when their manifest content appears to spring from concern for correct method—have in certain lights a queer air. It is as though the price of a percipience were a blindness, or as though what they see must, like any screen or filter, occult or distort by selection what they are professedly examining. Here both speak with deservedly great authority on verbal behavior—on which who else has a better claim to be heard? Both are dedicated to scientific rigor (of very different brands, it is true). Both are famed for an exacting and regardless respect for fact. And yet each, in his own way, cultivates his own neglect of the processes by which his facts are obtained. The behaviorist doctrinally disallows the consciously and critically directed activities by which he selects his observations. His opponent, though admitting and indeed extolling intuition, remains startlingly unconcerned about its operations.

Look, for instance, at these two sentences of Chomsky. We can "see" innumerable things about them. We can "see" that the second sentence is explaining and justifying what the first has said. Of any word or phrase in either of them we can "see" that some substitutions of other words are possible (in various ways and with varying outcomes) and that other substitutions for varying reasons are not possible . . . and so on indefinitely. Any discriminating and reflective user of language can "see" illimitably much about it—by which he guides his use. In his choice of a word or a sentence form, or in his interpretation, he exercises enough knowledge about how language works to amount—could he describe it—to a sufficient theory. But how different these actual operating modes of knowing are from those that occupy the working hours and the produced pages of the linguists! It is as though we had here one of Niels Bohr's Complementarity situations: as though the employment of linguistic understanding and the attempt to formulate it were incompatible. Try to say how we "see" any of these things. What sorts of "seeings" are they? Compare

1. "seeing" that *It* and *is* are different words;
2. "seeing" that *It* must come before *is;*
3. "seeing" how *speculations* differs from *speculating;*
4. "seeing" that there is a big and peculiar sniff or snort behind these words here: *speculations* (Ha!), *speculating* (Hum!).

How are these "seeings" all different? Are they hierarchic—some dependent upon others? Must we see which word a word is before we see how it interacts with others? And just what interactions with *addressed* and *hopelessly* must we have taken in before we can see that *speculations* is derogative in its use here?

On such matters competent users of a language achieve a truly remarkable agreement—so perfect in some instances as to appear preternatural. I am not inviting anyone to doubt that. Indeed it is half my point here. The other half is our failure to agree at all on how we do it. What most clearly needs to be recognized is that the practical linguistic knowledge through which so much agreement comes about is of incomparably more importance than the explanatory theoretical constructions on which there is such strange failure to agree. It is improvement in the practical skills with language which is immediately needed, not in the theoretic accounts which have yet to show that any of them can help anyone to speak or write or understand or read any better. All use of language—all agreement and disagreement on further matters which arise through language—depends upon these "seeings," these prehensions of the facts of linguistic structure, facts, however, which are dismayingly far from being systematically accountable for. In brief, we can talk without being in sight of saying how we can do so. It may be comforting to recall that the same is true of walking on the one side and of thinking on the other.

Pause for a moment longer to consider how odd it is that linguists in general pay so little attention to these seemingly direct prehensions which are prerequisites to all further thought. It is as though a student of physical vision were to say: "Don't let us bother about the eye and brain and how they work and all that! We need only care about WHAT we see, not HOW." So people have thought—inadequately. The instruments of any inquiry enter and become part of the problems. There is, it appears, an analogous gap or lag in the study of communication. We are so busy with WHAT we may have to say that we under-consider both how we shape what we say and how we shape our understanding of what we take as being said. And yet it is through these considerations, through watchful enough attention to our dealings with *signans* and *signatum,* that the only road to improved competence must lead.

There is, however, another set of questions of deep interest and of possibly practical concern to designers of instruction. They have to do with the development of language in the young child. On this Chomsky has four remarks which deserve the closest attention:

> The child who learns a language has *in some sense* [my italics] constructed the grammar for himself on the basis of his observation of sentences and non-sentences. [1] . . . Furthermore, this task is accomplished in an astonishingly short time [2] to a large extent independently of intelligence [3] and in a comparable way by all children [4]. Any theory of learning must cope with these facts. (Noam Chomsky. *Op. cit.,* p. 57.)

On these, I will agree to (1), remarking only that *in some sense* is perhaps the most powerfully protective phrase in any metalanguage. On (2) we have to recall how much the child did in its prenatal nine months and how much it has been doing how swiftly since. On (3) let us note that "intelligence" refers to test results hardly commensurate with the feat of learning to talk. On (4), how suggestive it is that languages regarded by good judges as very different in difficulty should be acquired by children, whatever the linguistic environments of their ancestors, at much the same pace! What all this suggests is that learning to talk may be, as many have surmised, more like other post-natal growth achievements than like most things we call learning. Our brains preternaturally triple in size in the year following birth. Perhaps—to become perilously more speculative—abilities to learn are, in a more general fashion, continuations of *internal selection* processes tuned-up and set for the child by his early social triumphs? Perhaps these abilities, with their illimitable promise, survive as a rule only long enough for their bearer to learn to talk. It is often alleged that thenceforward his abilities, as opposed to his acquired skills, decline. If so, might this be a consequence of the chaos:

> a universal hubbub wilde
> Of stunning sounds and voices all confused [19]

—the sea of unintelligible vocables through which, once he has learned to talk, he has henceforth to swim? True, we all learn to survive, indeed to ride upon, its waves! Busy learning *that*, is it surprising if, too often, decade by decade, we grow less capable of learning how even to attempt anything more?

That, however, was in a pre-dawn 1950-ish mode. Why should not man, taking to heart a lesson from his unborn self, divert a little of his spare energy to trying, scientifically, to make the best of himself? The tested linguistic-intellective means are ready for development, the intelligible sequence waits, the mass media are available, the unappeased desire burns . . . to transport the whole planet's population, before the second millennium, step by step, from wherever they may happen to be, into a joint conception of what they would like to become. The obstacles, well we all know them! But recall how impossibly man's possibilities have in one lifetime expanded, and consider what his new design-potential already enables him to do.

I have to add a word upon my title. *Creation*, as used there, is participation in a design beyond any we can conceive:

> So be you not neglectful
> Of incompassability.
> We ARE because we went to school
> To views we could not see.[20]

Prologue: From Criticism to Creation

(1)   The phrasing used is from my version of *Republic,* Book II, 368D (Cambridge University Press, 1966), made for people—in all countries—coming for the first time to Plato through English. The vocabulary and constructions are as simple as I could keep them without distortion of Plato's meanings. This main gateway for all the world into the Western mind needs a channel, freed from all unnecessary and accidental obstructions.

(2)   Jaeger is, of course, thinking of Western Man. *Paideia* (New York, Oxford University Press, 1939.)

(3)   The phrases *speculative instruments* and *practical criticism* can be found in Coleridge's *Biographia Literaria.*

(4)   *Internal Factors in Evolution,* Lancelot Law Whyte (New York, George Braziller, 1965), p. 14. An account of resistances to changing ideas in theory of evolution which illumines parallel resistances to developments in educational design.

(5)   Other formulations are frequent. The contrast may indeed be almost as old as thought, and have been a preoccupation of many cultures. Needham, for example, remarks that for the Cambridge Platonist, Cudworth, "Each individual thing had an indwelling formative organizing 'plastic nature,' the unconscious deputy of God within it. As Cassirer has well said; for Cudworth, all events in the universe depended not on forces operating from without, but on formative principles acting from within (how strangely Chinese the doctrine sounds)." *Science and Civi-*

lization in China, Vol. II, "History of Scientific Thought" (Cambridge University Press, 1956), p. 503. Needham notes the attraction of this line of thinking for modern biologists.

At many points in what follows, the instances and comparisons presented in Needham's great work have deep relevance. In this connection, describing the exaltation by Hsün Tzu (c. 270 B.C.) of *Li* (rites, proper observances) into a cosmic principle, he remarks: "Not in human society only, but throughout the world of Nature, there was a give and take, a kind of mutual courtesy rather than strife among inanimate powers and processes, a finding of solutions by compromise, an avoidance of mechanical force, and an acceptance of the inevitability of birth and doom for every living thing." *Op. cit.,* p. 283. (See Note 2 in *Notes and Glosses* to "Sources of Conflict.")

(6)   *Parts and Wholes,* Daniel Lerner, Ed. (New York, The Free Press, 1963). A discussion of part-whole relations from physics through to poetry; see especially the contributions of Edward Purcell, Ernest Nagel, Roman Jakobson and I. A. Richards.

Cf. Needham, *op. cit.,* p. 567: "There is 'law' implicit in *Li,* but this law is the law to which parts of wholes have to conform by virtue of their very existence as parts of wholes."

(7)   *The Estate of Man,* Michael Roberts (London, Faber and Faber, 1951).

(8)   *Coleridge's most seminal hints:* "When we consider, that the greater part of our success and comfort in life depends on distinguishing the similar from the same, that which is peculiar in each thing from that which it has in common with others, so as still to select the most probable, instead of the merely possible or positively unfit, we shall learn to value earnestly and with a practical seriousness a mean,

already prepared for us by nature and society, of teaching the young mind to think well and wisely by the same unremembered process and with the same never forgotten results, as those by which it is taught to speak and converse." (*Biographia Literaria*, Chap. XXII.)

(9)   *the shift from Homer to Plato:* Eric Havelock in *Preface to Plato* (Oxford, Basil Blackwell, 1963) very fully discusses this transition showing the depth and extent of the changes that can occur in a culture as an *oral* tradition is replaced by a literature. In the Greek case the outcome was singularly happy. But with the cultures, say, of Africa, there are grave reasons to fear that values now carried in speech will be swept away without compensating gains for any but an unhappily separated few. On how this world-wide transition is managed (or mishandled) the mental and moral quality of living of the majority of human beings, *for many generations,* will depend. But how many competent people are thinking about this—compared with those competent people who are devoting themselves to ʾwinningʾ some local and ephemeral war?

(10)   *let Coleridge lead me:* It was not easy to decide to leave the secure and highly approved as well as delightful purlieus of Literary Criticism to pursue doubtful ends in Education. People at that time were pointing derisive fingers at Russell: "Go into Education. Why, of course, when he has nothing more to offer as an F.R.S.!" It was a recognized thing that interest in Education was a sign of failing wits. Coleridge's support at this time was a great comfort to me. I can recall consulting friends I revered. I learned something from their patient—but distrait—poses. T. S. Eliot, however, was one of the exceptions.

(11)   *summarized twelve years later:* I have never had any evidence that anyone—beyond the proofreader—ever paid any sort of attention to what this piece tried to present. If an

utterance may be compared with a radar beam, the absence of reflected waves would suggest that its path has been entirely unoccupied.

(12)   *To go on writing with such prospect:* R. P. Blackmur, that abstruse and gentle wizard, in what seems to me by far the most readily intelligible of his immensely resistant books, the posthumous *A Primer of Ignorance* (Harcourt, Brace & World, 1967), finds (p. 77) the results reported in *Practical Criticism* "stupefying." He adds later: "The protocols turned in showed gross failures to understand, to appreciate, or to judge: that is, they had failed to *use* the poems at anywhere near the level the poems required or deserved." His report on all this is continued through his Section 9 (pp. 160–172) and is evidence of the difficulty of helping the new man not to lose all touch with those earlier men from whom most of his virtues must be derived.

It is worth noting that Blackmur was among those who misconceived Basic English, supposing it to be intended to replace full English. "Richards is the supreme methodologist, in the good and the bad sense, of the situation of the loss of unconscious skills in the use of words which constitutes the new illiteracy. His counsel of desperation was the Basic English which would debase us all until we could rebuild our vocabularies" (p. 163). It was this misconception which Winston Churchill attacked in the House of Commons, November 4, 1943: "I have tried to explain that people are quite purblind who discuss this matter as if Basic English were a substitute for the English language." But the notion dies hard. As to "unconscious skills in the use of words" is it not perhaps better to regard them, with Coleridge, as "the representatives and rewards of our past conscious reasonings, insights and conclusions"? This assumption at least offers us means for remedying the sad situation, through exercise in these very reasonings, insights and conclusions—for which exercise Basic English provides a convenient and a powerful device.

(13)   *Neither situation is meaningful except as in opposition to the other, nor is either sentence:* In this simplest primordial instance the role of opposition is peculiarly evident. But the same holds true throughout: Any situation is for us what it is by differentiation from other situations; it takes its distinctive character from being otherwise than they would be. The range of situations we can recognize reflects the differences we can apprehend. The recognition, however, need not be explicit or clear to consciousness. Much of our thinking is our attempt, as here, to make the implicit more explicit.

Opposition may be highly specific and precise, or general and indefinite. Among the most specific instances of opposites are enantiomorphs (A form which is related to another as an object is related to its image in a mirror, Oxford English Dictionary Supplement 1933). For example, rotated letters *b d*, triangles ◺ ◿, right- and left-hand gloves, helices. Such opposites may be alike in all respects *except* in the strictly definable regard that can be stated in terms of rotation: turning a right-hand glove inside out gives you a left-hand glove. On the other hand (= in opposition to the enantiomorph) the expression on a face may be palpably opposed to other expressions it can take on—without anyone being able to see what the differences and similarities between them are. See C. K. Ogden, *Opposition*. This exploratory and provocative little book, now republished by the Indiana University Press, summarizes much of the history of this confusing but centrally important topic and makes valuable suggestions toward its clarification and development.

(14) *progress for the learners:* With such film and film-strip sequences, "the Bureau of Educational Research of the New York City Board of Education carried out controlled evaluation of both the Spanish and the English instruction which indicated that the teaching of English to non-English-speaking children by TV was at least as effective as conventional teaching; that the teaching of Spanish to bright children by TV was as effective as conventional teaching in the year 1959–60, while the teaching of Spanish by TV was more effective than the conventional teaching in the year 1958–59." (Report on CCCTV, The Story of the Chelsea Closed Circuit Television Project. Findings and Guidelines, p. 8.) The Report adds: "These programs consisted of televised sound motion picture film series prepared by Language Research, Inc. Each series included 24 self-contained, 30-minute language lessons involving carefully regulated syntactic and lexical elements exemplifying the Graded Direct Method. The audio portion was a sentence chain; the video element, stick-figure cartoons.

"The instructional films developed by Language Research for the Chelsea project are readily usable in other settings, at other places and other times.

"This report was written by A. Barnett Langdale. . . . Until the supply is exhausted, copies may be obtained from: Bureau of Audio-Visual Instruction, 131 Livingston Street, Brooklyn 1, New York."

To this it may be interesting to add a report on the long-term effects of a *designed* entrance to Reading.

A short report on the present standing of matched groups of 1958–59 first-grade beginners in the Delmar Experiment (near Albany, N.Y.) is quoted here in full, as issued by Mrs. Doris Flinton and Professor Morris Eson of State University of New York.

Comparison of Honor Grades in Grade VII
of Original Experimental and Control Groups in the
Language for Learning Experiment

In September, 1958, experimental and control groups in the Bethlehem Central School District were started in the first grade. Three first grades in three of the schools constituted the experimental group of seventy-five children using the "Language for Learning" reading and English program. Three first grades in three other schools in the system constituted the control group of seventy-five children who used the reading approach which had been standard in the school system for many years. One of the hypotheses proposed at the beginning of the study was that effects would be best evaluated when these children entered junior high school.

In September, 1964, the pupils who still remained in this school system and who had been in the first-grade study group there, entered Bethlehem Junior High School. There were thirty-three experimentals and thirty-seven controls left of the original 150 pupils. Since these groups had been equated on the basis of reading readiness and intelligence and sex, and groups had been heterogeneous in nature, a survey was made of their distribution in the seventh-grade groups. In the junior high pupils are assigned to sections according to ability levels. Table I gives the numbers from each of the study groups in each of the 12 seventh-grade ability levels.

Five honor rolls (Dec. 1–May 7) were examined for the number of times each pupil was represented there during the year 1964–1965. Honor rolls are made up of all those who received grades of A or B in all subjects during a marking period. All ability levels were represented on the honor roll. The experimental pupils had a chance of placing on the honor roll 33 x 5 or 165 times. The controls had 37 x 5 or 185 possibilities. Investigation showed that the experimentals made 46 entries on the honor rolls compared to 19 entries by the controls.

The results show that the experimental pupils had 27% of their group on the honor roll compared to 10% of the controls. These figures are not biased by the distribution among the various ability levels. (Table I)

Table I

ABILITY GROUP	EXPERIMENTAL	CONTROL	TOTAL
1 & 2	12	7	19
21 & 22	5	7	12
31 & 32	2	7	9
7	4	5	9
8	2	3	5
9	3	3	6
10	3	1	4
11	2	3	5
12	0	1	1

$$N \quad = \quad 33 E \quad + \quad 37 C \quad = \quad 70$$

From this long-range study it may be concluded that the pupils of the experimental group are using their abilities better in their studies than the control group. It will be pertinent not only to follow these children further through school but also to make parallel studies of the next year's seventh-grade which contains the remainder of a second study group equated in 1959.

The emphasis upon what has sometimes been called a "meaning first" approach to reading in the Language for Learning program, in contrast to the "discrimination first" emphasis to be seen, for example, in Bloomfield and Barnhart's *Let's Read* and in courses using Pitman's i/t/a (Initial Teaching Alphabet) can account to a large degree, we maintain, for this "using their abilities better in their studies," by the experimental groups. The compact, high-utility vocabulary develops the defining resources of Ogden's *Basic English,* from which it is derived. The grading of sentence structure and the operational analysis of semantic-syntactic relations have been implemented by use of the cartoon language films based on *English through Pictures,* Books 1 and 2. A characteristic of the Graded Direct Method approach at every stage is its cultivation of sentence sense.

(15)   *minimal linguistic form:* What we call its ˢʷformˢʷ can also be described as "its oppositional relations to other morphs."

(16)   *"association by contiguity" and "association by similarity":* Aristotle in *De Memoria et Reminiscentia,* 451B, 18–20, speaks of these as "having started in thought either . . . from something either similar, or contrary, to what we seek, or else from that which is contiguous with it." This gives us three modes of association: Similarity, Contrariety and Contiguity. Later thinkers—I do not know who began this—came to regard Similarity-Contrariety as one mode, positive and negative, and Contiguity, juxtaposition in space and/or time, as another. The interplay between them, the necessary mutual support, the varying oppositions . . . offer a vitally important field of inquiries still awaiting development. Some further discussion of some aspects of it will be found in my work in progress, *Design for Escape: World Education, Through English, Through TV, Now.*

(17)   *to complete a structure:* a phrase which here is challengingly ambiguous. The completions for Similarity steppings are very different from those on which Contiguity steppings depend. To distinguish them we need, at present, sustained *practice* for which there is, as yet, no clear

theoretical and explicit guidance. As we easily discover by watchful experiment, attempts to describe and thereby distinguish Contiguity and Similarity linkages run great risks of being mistaken for one another, and thus of generating a Comedy of Errors. Nonetheless, Dromio of Ephesus is not Dromio of Syracuse. Contiguity's "missing bits" are restored as your forgotten umbrella may be. There is nothing about *it and you* which requires you and it to be together. On the other hand, when Similarity is at work, the part supplied may be as much required by the rest as your heart is for you—if you are to be you.

(18) *high confidence of both pronouncements:* At this point it may be not amiss to append a discussion in another medium.

VERBAL BEHAVIOR

Hundreds of puzzling questions and obscure propositions about verbal behavior may be dismissed while the new questions and propositions which arise to take their place are susceptible to experimental check as part of a more unified pattern. (B. F. Skinner, *Verbal Behavior,* p. 456.)

The questions to which Skinner has addressed his speculations are hopelessly premature. It is futile to inquire into the causation of verbal behavior until much more is known about the specific character of this behavior; and there is little point in speculating about the process of acquisition without much better understanding of what is acquired. (Noam Chomsky, *Language,* Jan.–March, 1959, p. 55.)

I

Confidence with confidence oppose:
Knowledge ducks under in between two *No's*
So firmly uttered. Look again. You'll see
Uncertainty beside uncertainty.

May be dismissed indeed: who've seen, done, been,
And meant their share in what it all can mean.

To *be dismissed,* poor thankless servants, so,
Who still command the words that bid them go!

To take their place: crowd up their space, perhaps;
There'd be no places should their duties lapse.

Puzzling, obscure: how else appear (for whom?)
Being the reed itself on the uttering loom
Whose warp and weft, in all their endless play,
Are ordered but while they its rede obey.

Susceptible to experimental check:
Who was the first caught sticking out his neck;
Trying conclusions with the sustaining word?
Who saws his branch off, he must fall absurd.
What can be, will be tested—and the test.
What cannot, all the all-supporting rest:
The insusceptible, the puzzling, the obscure,
Hid premises of all we take as sure—
Are checked by use, or nothing could be checked.

High Clarities that may, can, do select
What we dare take as safe, dare take as seen,
The Intelligible raying through the Screen,
Ah, MAY, CAN, DO, Calm Goddesses of Heed!
Who'd worship You must reconceive his creed;
Must straight divine which One of You in turn
His prayers address; accurately discern
Which of your Vehicles before him stands;
Or, rather, holding out unmeddling hands,
Invoke Your power to settle for him who
Inspires him now in what he may, can, do.

More unified: There are, You let us know,
Two ways to unity: Do not let go
A jot; or else: dismiss all but
The patterning maze that constitutes our rut.
There press our bars and reel on in our race,
Swallow our pellets and maintain our "face,"
To the prescriptions of the groove conform.

This humbler unity wears uniform;
Its votaries—of each especial brand—
Feel most at ease when marching in a band,
Taking a shrunken view of *understand*.

Until much more is known: again by whom?
And with what manner of knowing? No doubt, this doom
Confines itself here to no more than some
Of the modes of doubt whereby we may, can, come
Some way toward that other Unity.
How to Behave Ourselves! Both Have and Be!

As a child learns his language, learning then
"His language" isn't "the language"; and again,
"To have learnt how" is not "to have by rote"
(To tell you what was said I need not quote),
At a thousand million points he grows aware
(Enough to make whatsoever account despair)
Of what he DOES and why. He could not DO
(No action there) unless into it went,
Beyond mere outcomes of experiment,
The mutualizing influence we call
EXPERIENCE: control of each by all.
Nor need, nor should, we often recollect
These past awarenesses, though they select
What's said and how we say it (feeling, tone,
Cadence, content, implication)
Balancing claims in the verbal commonweal.
This constitutes the check and the control
By which each phrase flies subject to the whole.

Process of acquisition: how we learn to talk;
We gain our portion as we learn to walk,
Some worse, some better, uneven here the score:
Shakespeare began while crawling on the floor.

Better understanding of what is acquired
Must span the range from "dolt" through to "inspired."
But walking too's an art. Into a stride
Flows the free balance that's the body's pride;

As shuffling shows the locked rigidity,
The stiff old price that's paid to move the knee.
As every phrase is linked in some degree
Through context, rhythm, near synonymy,
By metaphor or by metonymy,
With countless others, im- or mediately,
So every step must balance what your eye,
Ear, head and hands are doing, to get by.
Each sentence we may utter takes its tone
From many another, no one of them its own,
Each served and serving; and from its tone its sense
As often as not ensues through prescience.
These are no histories of the relative strength
Of isolate responses. So, at length,
(It has been long!) we shoo these artifacts out
And wake—to entertain another grade of doubt.

Much more is known: but not as science knows.
Its schemata will no such sights disclose.
Fabric of formulas derived, distilled,
Abstracted from the on-going: moments filled
With much irrelevant to enquiry's end,
With much from which, ?truth? must itself defend,
Science must simplify, clear up, reduce
To principles, define, align, produce
In terms that to its purposes submit.

On no such terms is living language knit.
But, as the system of our former deeds,
Grasping or speaking, as a web which needs
No inventories stored on neural shelves,
Being the temporal figure of our selves
In act across, above, the gulfs of time
(To lend a word or mitigate a rime),
What is acquired is more than may be known
Or understood—except wherein it's shown:
Our various achievements with the word
Conceived or uttered, heard now or unheard.

II

No sense in fretting to be off the ground,
There's never hurry whither we are bound,
Where all's behavior—and the rest is naught,
Not even rest, but void beyond all thought.

Ponder what plausibilities we may
Our ponderings impond'rables obey.
Swayed by a breath, a balance never still,
The will forespent to guard us from our will,
We hang in stays. Stay now to seem to see
I.e. (*e.g.*) not what it seems to be.
Id est, that is: tune in and focus sharp
Upon the string on which I have to harp.

Identifying *id*'s one task; its mother,
Identifying *what it's said to be*'s another;
Uniting two such ventures is a third.
To make these three all one would be absurd
Were it not general custom of the tribe
To which all viable thinkers must subscribe
Or give away that they don't know the ropes
By which are raised and lowered all our hopes.

Nor are *e.g.*s, for example, any better
Or less in need of checking to the letter;
In need of charity, the kind blind eye
Ready to let disparities slip by;
In need of easy openness of mind
To let whatever will make up a kind;
Let things be things, be all alike in that,
All other sorts be sort of from a hat.

Look close, be choosy, test, assay, appraise,
And clear-cut limits thin out into haze;
The actual dissolves, the formulas extend,
Advance, combine, replace us as our end.
The principle how clear! How plain the rule!
Until—what can possess the fool, or school,

To clamor for examples! Be content
If somehow, wordless, you divine what's meant.

What YOU—beyond the rivaling webs of the word?
A YOU who are no speech, uttered or heard,
Nor tell, nor show—but in yourself assured.
Consider. Though the quivering vocal chords,
Their echoing outcomes, be indeed the swords
That cut all knots, divide and conquer all,
Carve out our universe, exalt us to appall,
Win all our victories, lose all our wars,
Create all values, settle so all scores,
Behind a sword a hand, behind the hand
The intelligential hierarchies stand.

?Seraphic? Yes. The Seraphs are a sketch
THEY made long since to comfort the sore wretch
Cast out of Paradise he knew not why
To start his long climb back into the sky.
A sketch indeed! Where missive, messenger,
Intercommunicants . . . commingled were:
Minds dreaming of themselves as elf of elf;
Mind picturing Itself before Itself.

It was not strange the sketch should give them wings,
Platonic emblems of celestial springs;
That Amor's bride too curious should be
And learn in exile what's the penalty;
The coming day rays up its light ahead,
Lights you whichever way you would be led.
So, though Psychologists disdainfully
Tear off our wings, crying, to set us free:

"These gleaming sails are but the flattering means
(Theologic gear, Pythagorean beans!)
Whereby grubs flit and feed and lay their eggs,
By metaphor, beyond the reach of legs.
No Psyche more! Homunculus-theory, out!
Verbal behavior's all it's all about."

Yet nonetheless for that, indeed, the more,
New growing wings these vaulting words outsoar.

Be it not forgot, if we'd conceive a mind
The purest model in our speech we'd find:
Speech whose swift beat is borne upon our breath
Doing its best to mitigate our death,
Taking the breezes blowing where they list,
Settling when they lapse, biding the tryst,
Weeting unwitting of the how and why
Within the WHAT its words are wielded by.

(19)   *voices all confused:* part of Milton's description of limbo, *Paradise Lost,* Book II, line 951. It is tempting, and might be instructive, to take Satan's journey and its outcomes as an image of the adventures of the young mind.

(20)   *views we could not see:* adapted from my poem "Complementary Complementarities" in *The Screens and Other Poems* (Harcourt, Brace & World, 1959).

2

The Technological Crisis

This essay was originally a speech given at the University of
Alberta, Calgary, on March 17, 1962. The title-question was:
What Future Educational Needs of Society Will the Teaching
Profession Be Called Upon to Meet?

This question is openly an invitation to prophesy. "Future
educational needs of society"—what are *they?* What else can
they be but far bigger supplies of reasonably adequate people?
And what is education but our only conceivable means of producing such people?

It is appropriate here to set our demands and our hope high.
Before I have finished you will be saying, I expect: "How optimistic! What a dish of dreams to set before us!" I will remind
you, though, of three dreams that in my lifetime have changed
our conceptions of human possibilities, three dreams that have
come true: the dream of the automobile, the dream of the air-
ship and the dream of space travel. I can remember when all
these were no more than dreams. We have seen them become
technological necessities, presuppositions of the current human
endeavor. And I will remind you too of that terrifying line
from Yeats:

In dreams begin responsibilities

The "educational needs" we have to conceive are direct outcomes of such changes: responsibilities thrust upon us by man's
recent growth in power of all kinds. But chiefly in power to
change his conditions and means of living and to change himself. All *power*, I need not remind you, has its attendant perils.

Think now of the tasks of *control* which every new accession
of power brings with it. Today we can save babies and prolong
life as never before—another very ancient dream indeed come
true. Result—the *population threat* [1] to the human attempt.
Here is a new and very representative educational need. As the
world emerges from its current dangers, it will have to face up
to the still harder problems of regional over-population and
under-nourishment. And that well within this century. Already,
annually, more people are suffering from starvation than ever
before, both in sheer numbers *and* in proportion to those who
have enough. And this situation is going to get much worse
before it can get better. Here, in Alberta, of course, you are
about as far removed from the representative world condition
as to population-pressure and food-production as it is possible
to be. But that does not in the least let you out of the world
dangers or of the educational need for people able and ready
to take their share in what will have to be done. [2]

A few small steps of technological advance—in medicine—have
flung the world into this enormous and increasing biological
difficulty and hazard. There are many other technological fronts
on which steps of advance are going to have barely foreseeable
repercussions creating *educational needs that the teaching profession will be called upon to meet.* The "call" won't be perhaps very articulate but don't doubt that it will be strange, bewildering and urgent. And every such call will increase the need
for bigger supplies of reasonably competent people.

In brief, with the rate of technological advance accelerating as
it is, there is no longer any escape. Education must meet these
mounting emergencies with technological advances of its own—

with technological advances commensurate with the growing need.

And what specifically should these be? Here is where that dish of dreams I spoke of has to be served to you and I realize that it may not be easy to swallow or to digest. And there is another difficulty: "Give a dog a bad name!" and, well, you know the rest. I have to give my technological recipe three bad names. I have to mention three labels: "Programing," "Audio-Visual" and "Teacher Training." For reasons that I suspect are good ones, nobody cheers up much at mention of any of these things. And yet what I have to sell you is a new combination in a new DE-SIGN of these three.

I have brought out the big new name here: DESIGN. That is the technological answer: better, more effectual, design of instruction.

To be specific, we need: (1) improved design in the *Sequencing,* the *serial ordering,* of what the learner is invited to do (that is *Programing*); (2) improved design in the joint *collaborative* use of eye and ear—our two complementary cognitive channels (that is *Audio-Visual* presentation); (3) improved design in combining what the teacher can do and what really well-designed audio-visual presentation can do for the learner (that is *Teacher Training*).

Let me take this last problem in design first: What are we currently asking of the teacher? We are asking her to: (1) run a class, to keep it reasonably and profitably (and, if possible, happily) employed; (2) design and present a lesson—effectively organized within itself and effectively related to the lessons which have come before and those which are to follow after; and to (3) observe the class—each member of it—with a clinician's eye, to *diagnose* each learner's difficulties, to *prescribe* and to *administer* appropriate treatment to all the patients.

That is a set of demands that should only be made of supernaturally able beings. It is absurd to ask a human teacher to try to perform all these tasks simultaneously and efficiently.

What then should we do?

We should take the burden of Task (2)—the design and ordering of the sequence of instruction—off the shoulders of the individual classroom teacher and make it the concern of special groups of designers adequately equipped to do it.

In point of fact—you will have been thinking—we do NOT put the responsibility for design of instruction so heavily on the individual teacher. There is the classroom text and behind that the "literature of the subject." We only expect the teacher to mediate between the subject and the pupil. She is a retailer—a retailer who is not, at present, being given a fair chance because the subject, or what has to be taught, is not often properly prepared and arranged for the learner.

The technological answer to this is *Programing*—or, better, *Sequencing*. Programing isn't a very propitious word; we are too familiar with the contrast between what the program says will happen and what in fact does actually happen! Sequencing, then, which does not neglect the full, collaborative use of eye and ear, is the answer. It must be a sequencing that is so *designed* that it puts the job of understanding where it belongs, on the *learner:* hands it to him in such a skillfully adjusted fashion that he can't help doing it and doing it with delight. The learner's reward, his reinforcement, his incentive, his inducement can and must come to him through "the inward glory and triumph of mind" that is the conscious growth in him of his ability to learn.

To secure this, for almost everyone in all fields, is a manageable problem of design.

There are many devices under development converging on the service of this task. They are likely to seem in competition. It isn't really so. For example, those who are chiefly working for and through what used to be called *Teaching Machines* are likely still to misconceive the work of those who are designing sequences for learning through sound film and TV. What a teaching machine does is to supply to a learner a sequence (or program) of challenges to think and then act. It is so contrived,

as a rule, that if his action is "wrong" the problem comes up
to him again; if it is "right" he steps forward to a new problem. With these Teaching Machines (or "Learning Servers") the
learner works at his own tempo. That can be excellent. He has
to find out for himself just what he understands and what he
doesn't. But he also has to learn how to work when the tempo
is not left to him but set him from without. And he has to learn
when he must himself select the aspect to be attended to. And
these are the conditions under which he works with sequenced
film and TV. The resources of film make this possible for him.
The two techniques of presentation are not in conflict but
complementary. They can and should—in any adequate over-all
design of instruction—work together.

It has often been said that film and TV cannot engage the
learner's participation. This is a mistake due to misinformation.
The heart of good design is to induce and maintain alert exploratory activity properly combined with confirmation. Cooperative
use of eye and ear—with appropriate timing and due returns
of contrastive situations—can elicit any amount of active participation. It can do more. It can train the learner to select the
aspect of a task most useful to him. In elementary second-language work, for example, the very same sequence can offer students with different needs different exercises. One may be improving his pronunciation while another is strengthening his
grasp of syntax and yet another is clarifying his semantic discriminations.

I have taken this example from elementary second-language
teaching—a field in which sequenced instruction through film
and TV has gone further than in any other. No one who has
not worked in this field—with English or French or Spanish presented through sequenced situations from zero knowledge on
up—can have adequate ideas of the power and delicacy of this
procedure. It must be realized, however, that the sequencing is
radically linguistic. It uses throughout contrasts or oppositions
of situations requiring contrasts in the sentences which handle

them. The learner is led to see how, as the situations vary, the sentences vary with them. Working with actual speech that carries actual present visible meaning, the learner can be taken through a compelling step-by-step display of the structure of the new language. He can be given optimal conditions whereby, in Chomsky's phrase, he can have, "in some sense, constructed the grammar for himself." The return of the essential structural oppositions (with variation) challenges him to apply the distinctions he is developing. He learns not by rote but through understanding. He is being given, in the simplest, most immediate fashion, an exercise in the elementary procedures of scientific observation and induction. He is not only learning a language, he is being taught how to compare, select, and apply.

For all sorts of reasons the sequencing of second-language learning is the key problem for design in instruction. Acquiring a second language can be and should be acquiring a skill, a science, an art and a code of behavior—all together. Development in a language can and should be a perpetual exercise and discipline in the conduct of discernments and choices at all levels. Therefore language learning can and should exemplify all the problems of sequencing and be typical of all learning. *Of course, as a rule, elementary French, say, is nothing of the kind.* I might put my point here by saying that the world's chief educational need is the further development of techniques of sequencing, of programing—those, namely, whereby learning a second language can become all this.

How about evaluation? We haven't yet realized what powerful instruments for presenting tests and recording performances film and tape and teaching machines provide when the needed analysis is handled by computer. That clinical concern I spoke of as the third task of the teacher can be given, with the computer's aid, the resources of a pedagogic hospital to help him with it.

If sequencing can teach and test a second language so—from zero knowledge on up—it can teach anything. Whatever it teaches, certain over-all principles hold. The most interesting of these may be named the *Principle of Use*. To put it briefly, what should be learned first is what the learner can most *use* in learning more. Another name would be the *Principle of Growth*. Think of any plant or animal. All its growth, from the very start, comes about through what it has already. The whole plant grows in each step of its growth. The seedling can *grow* only because what it already *is* can take in and *use* what it needs—to become what it will be. We don't help it by giving it things it cannot use.

Every subject, every art, every science, every study—from mathematics right across the whole spectrum up to poetry and religion—is initially such a seedling. That is why initial stages in any study can be so important. What happens there can set the patterns of inquiry through which it can go forward, or through which it must fail.

Most attempts to learn throughout history have become rancid with human frustration through lack of suitable serial ordering. This subject, the art, science, study of sequencing is itself—we do well to remember—a seedling. It could, I am trying to convince you here, remake man and his world. It could also, I am afraid, wreck us. There is no power, as I began by reminding you, without its perils. But let us remember that this new technology is self-correcting. With it every student can become a laboratory experiment, offering us the chance to compare what works well with what does not, and redesign accordingly.

The Technological Crisis

(1)   *the population threat:* as reported, for example, in the Report on the International Planned Parenthood Federation World Conference, Santiago, Chile. At present rates of increase (over 2% per year) today's 3.3 billion world population will multiply to almost 7 billion by 2000 A.D. At 2% a year it doubles in 35 years, at 3% in 23; at 4% in 18 years. In Western Europe the present rate is about 1%; in the United States about 1.6%; in Latin America 3% and possibly more (*Time,* April 21, 1967). It may be added that in 1952 UN demographers thought the 1980 population would probably be about 3.6 billion. They now put it at between 4.1 and 4.5 billion. And 1980 is only 12 years away. These portentous figures are usually balanced against estimates of probable food supplies. They are still more frightening and more awakening if we consider the educational resources that must be developed if a ghastly and helpless chaos is to be avoided. The technological reconstructions required will everywhere need a far larger proportion of highly and variously able people than we are currently producing *anywhere.* This world situation into which we are heading is being more widely apprehended, but the depth and extent of the educational reforms necessary and the scale of the design effort called for are not yet recognized; nor has the recruitment of the highest ability to this task begun.

(2)   *what will have to be done:* or "What could we build if we worked together?" as U Thant has put it. "It is obvious," he points out, "that a small part of the ingenuity,

effort, expertise and resources deployed in building an intercontinental missile system, for example, would almost certainly, if applied to the more immediate problems of human misery or of future human development, produce a series of breakthroughs which might well illuminate and inspire man's whole concept of his own future." And he asks: "Why do these totally obvious and desirable developments fail to come about—fail, moreover, in an age which prides itself on its new mastery of communications of every kind?" His answer: "We have been, perhaps, too anxious to define and agree, by force if necessary, upon the ideal to be pursued before making a practical start in cooperation on fundamental problems. . . . If we could start pragmatically by working together on the problems which urgently concern all peoples, differences of ideology and other apparently insoluble conflicts might be seen in a new light as wasteful and unnecessary, and may thus work themselves out over a period of time." (A contribution to man's search for answers to today's challenges, presented by ALCAN Aluminum Limited, *Time,* April 21, 1967.)

3

Computer-Conveyed Instruction

Recent advances [1] in the technology of the use of computers for mediating instruction are sufficiently startling to generate and excuse a considerable succession of doubts. Doubts not as to the feasibility of what seems to be coming to us but as to its possible effects. Indeed daunting would seem a better word than startling as these doubts develop. They build up to a first order appeal for a concentration of the best-poised and most various thinking obtainable on a new and very likely crucial, and certainly imminent, turn in earth's history. What is promised us is new power, power of a far more central and commanding kind, and far more transforming, than has ever before been offered to beguilable and Adamically irresponsible man. This power is nothing less than an indefinitely great *multiplication* of the efficacy of our thought.

This formulation is designed to excite a grim series of questions. What is this "our" so lightly used? *Whose* thought is to be made so much more efficacious? Who is to be trusted with these new super-powers, if they are in the least as they are described? What accreditable supervisor's decision can intervene to prevent such facilities from being used merely to maintain and perhaps establish the routines and conventional acceptances of this not-too-enlightened decade? As with such things as railway and other gauges, slot-machines, etc., hitherto, what can stop casual decisions from committing invincible investments to the perpetuation of radical mistakes? What guarantees can we hope for that the best thought extant or on the way will not be barred by whatever step-in-quick effort first gets an inside track to the control panels and plugboards? Why should this new incalculably increased power not follow an only too well-known pattern?

Outcomes of technological revolutions are probably unpredictable. Foresight, at least, was in short supply as to what would happen with each of the sudden unheralded accessions of power which have divided human history through our last three centuries into periods: (revolutions, goings round)—more charged with strange hope and familiar despair than even those due to the advent of fire, agriculture, metallurgy or writing. What was done with steam? If it gave us an enviably reliable, convenient and harmless transport facility, did it not wound labor so cruelly that the scar-tissue in most industrial societies is even yet a crippling embarrassment? What was done with electricity? If it gave us handy light and heat and communications, did it not give us, besides, a centralization of decision-making which decision-makers have been disastrously unable to carry? What was done and is still being done with the automobile? If that "plague of vast mechanical toys," as Wyndham Lewis called it, has rendered us familiar services, and given many almost their only discipline in regard to the rights of others, has it not also half dissolved the family, reinvigorated crime, and confronted the regional planner with problems now growing evidently beyond him? And what loss has it not entailed of walking ability, contact with nature and of time available for reading and undistracted meditation? What was done with radio? If it gave us a means of distributing music, has it not also supplied anodyne and distraction addictively (not to mention Hitlerian mass hysteria) through periods in which widespread reflection has been more needed than ever before? What was done with TV? Though it began to return a little authority to visual perception (enough to dispose even of a McCarthy) and though it has made great public ceremonials once again—even for communities on the modern scale—a unifying force, what has been the price in scatter and trivialization of interests, despite gallant efforts of academics who had hoped they might have things of use or importance to convey? What has been done with the airplane? Are touristic successes or confrontations of statesman unable to do more than routinely recall what they came so far for, are these enough to compensate for Coventry, Dresden, Hiroshima . . . ? What is being done with nuclear resources, with missile capacities? What is likely to be done with weather control? Comments on these transformations of human possibility can obviously be no more than invitations to you to compare them with your own. We all know how what may look like blessings can, as the consequences unfold and grow and come home, seem little else than afflictions. Why should we think that a means to the increase of human power in many ways surpassing and transcending all of these together will in fact be more intelligently, humanely and wisely used?

"Surpassing and transcending"? The claims behind these words perhaps need support. All the above-mentioned epochal steps may be regarded as extensions of familiar specific human capabilities. Steam replaced and transcended men's and horses' muscular energy. Photography and telephony surpassed and extended the range of our distance receptors. So, more widely, did radio and TV. But the offerings of the computer go behind all such services; they extend the resources of the central nervous system itself. They invite developments in that (whatever it is) which uses our distance, and all other, receptors and effectors: that which is, however little we know about it, most ourselves. The computer can supply inexhaustible skilled service, aid beyond belief in whatever we have the wits or the heart or the ruthlessness or the stupidity, to instruct it to do for us. Suddenly, we have a Caliban-Ariel attendant, adviser, executant which will do for us even more than we, in our wisdom or folly, can contrive to tell it how to handle.

Wisdom or folly? Some among computer aficionados can almost persuade themselves that their monster servants can be taught to tell them which is which. Computers can, no doubt of it, tell us any amount which may be helpful: what many of the circumstances are, what decisions have been taken in similar circumstances and with what outcomes. They can be made to show us—with more exactitude than our imaginations can compass—what someone or other has told them will be relevant to our problem. But of the WHAT ELSE that may be relevant they are uninformed. It is up to us to be somehow cognizant of, susceptible to and judicious with that illimitable WHAT ELSE. That is the testing point. Here comes in the difference between living by the book of rules (and the computer is but a book with a built-in selective reader) and living by the judgment-instinct, that ultimate responsibility which is seen in all true action and most clearly in the creative arts. Another way, this appeal to the relevant WHAT ELSE, of reaffirming the concluding declaration of Shelley's *Defence of Poetry:* "Poetry is the unacknowledged legislation of the world." [2]

But, someone may reply, will not computers, by taking immense intellectual burdens off our shoulders, free us for precisely these tasks of ultimate choice, these legislative acts? While fearing that they will not, we may hope so. It is obvious that the great slave-based communities and others rich in service have owed much of their accomplishment to their servitors. A man or woman alone, doing his-her everything for his-her self, commonly does little or nothing else, noble or nefarious. We are almost all of us products of the assistance we can accept. Equally, we are potential victims of those who, for whatever motives, high or low, would like to run things for us. These are reflections to be borne in mind now that we are so soon to come into competition with those who will have intellectual instruments of a million or a billion mind-power at their disposal. Like all power sources, the computer is not going to lessen responsibilities but increase them.

These may seem gloomy prognostications. They can equally, with a small shift of policy, become a summons to the highest of imaginable endeavors—the reconstitution of man in the new image we can now conceive for him.

Probably everyone livelily aware of what the computer can make available toward such efforts is haunted by such thoughts. As probably we are haunted as much or more by recollections of the deadly possibilities of all new power in the hands of the apprentice sorcerer:

> And since man cannot use or spend aright
> The little time here given him in trust
> But wasteth it in weary undelight
> Of foolish toil and trouble, strife and lust,
> He naturally claimeth to inherit
> The everlasting Future—that his merit
> May have full scope, as surely is most just.[3]

What James Thomson set down of the individual and his personal future we have to read, in a computer context, of the entire human venture. And on every scale and in every dimension. Men have, I suppose, on the whole used and spent their energies well (as compared with what the ants and the octopi have done). They have perhaps of late disappointed the naïver angels by behaving worse than most could fear with their new means of maltreating their fellow men. On the other hand, they have unquestionably developed new virtues with the coming in of those techniques of scientific inquiry which have given them these new means. They can now practice extensively, almost universally—as professional conduct—a lofty if also a prudent rectitude in the handling of evidence and calculation. This does not, it seems, go back, professionally, beyond the founding of the Royal Society. Cognate, perhaps, with this are sympathies with the disasters and triumphs of others which Dante, let us say, or Milton would have found unintelligible and inexcusable. It is with this new impartiality, this new "hate of hate," [4] this new curbing of pride, this new enlargement of sympathies that we must ask what there may be about the powers of the computer which can protect its employment from becoming yet another example of a means which beclouds and prevents attainment of its aims.

Not forgetting how much of computer technique we owe to incentives of dream warfare, the preparation of a universal shambles, we can yet stress that its development has been under the control of an increasing complexity in required operations. Man's activities have shot up in scale and in connectedness. His rapid enlargements in numbers and in mutual dependencies have imposed necessities to which the computer world is the response. Thus there is a severely practical side to its arrival. The computer is the technical means by which man can handle intricacies otherwise beyond him—beyond, that is, his available supply of able-enough persons. There is naturally the economic side. Computers are not inexpensive, nor is the time of those competent to brief them for new undertakings. This again may, to a hopeful eye, look like a useful restraint upon doubtfully valuable employments. But, as so often in the record, the new means have rapidly overtaken the original needs which called them into being. The *instructional* uses, with which the rest of this essay will be concerned, have followed with alarming suddenness the calculation and administrative uses. What is disturbing is that neither the superb ingenuity of the technologist nor the purview of the educator fits either of them at all necessarily for the reflective choices, the discriminative judgments, the legislative acts above alluded to. There is, however, this comfort. Computers can be made to be exactly observant and critical of their own routines, able to collect the evidence of the inefficiency of a program, analyze it and indicate the needed redesign. In short, computers, suitably instructed, can become in an important degree self-corrective in their procedures. It is this last feature which affords us our best hope as to their service to education.

At this point two fresh sets of doubts will reasonably assail us. One concerns the resistances which educational procedures can put up against innovations, however necessary and well accredited. The other comes from certain limitations which may appear as to what may be expected of even the most cunningly briefed computer. The first are practical, professional-political obstacles; the second are theoretical objections. Let us look at the two sets in turn.

Franklin D. Roosevelt, writing to Cordell Hull in June, 1944, remarked, "If in regard to Basic English we get the views of 'competent government specialists' we shall certainly sound the death knell of Basic English or anything like it. I never knew any group of such people to agree to anything really different from the existing system or for that matter anything new. Basic English has tremendous merit in it." [5] These anticipations were more than fulfilled. Winston Churchill, having appointed a volunteer committee of the Cabinet to take care of his hopes for Basic English, was strangely surprised to find it failing to meet; and C. K. Ogden, inventor of Basic English, having refused for years to appear in *Who's Who,* consented, at last, in order to insert "1944–6, bedevilled by officials" as his summary. Basic English, it should be pointed out, was a pioneer prototype for many of the inquiries into symbolic similarities and differences [6] which computer programing needs and engenders. Its explorations of "vertical translation" from unrestricted into restricted language are a landmark in the history of an investigation which will be a major concern of programers for generations to come. Therefore the adventures of Basic English in Officialdom deserve sympathetic study. Not even Churchill and Roosevelt, with all their understanding of such things, could cut through the maze. We should deceive ourselves, however, if we considered this the fault of the officials. It is the consequence of their role. The role remains, however much its occupants may change and pass. Useless to resort to blood transfusions, to restaff Offices with Academics. The Office is still more than the man. Statesmen, moreover, who have to learn so much about

officials are often strangely unaware of the characteristics of
Academics. They are slow to realize that "the scholar's melancholy is emulation" and that his favorite remedy for this melancholy is conspiracy. Once again this is not the scholar's fault;
it is the outcome of his role. Unless he is abnormal—in which
case he is likely to have other disabilities—he must ever be
looking over his shoulder to see who, from whatever angle, may
be about to catch up with him and steal his show.

The statesmanship of the instructional development of computer resources will have to be much occupied with role-psy-
chology, and at a very tricky set of points where academic, administrative, business-hierarchical and teachers' conceptions of
themselves, their work and their duties come into highly sensitive and selective connections. The term "education" straddles
a various field into which have entered in recent years strong
and highly organized interests, among which child-psychology,
learning theory and linguistics must be mentioned. All of these
have for some decades been in a condition of considerable
polemic excitement, launching attacks on and busily conspiring
against traditional positions and one another. As the traditional
defenses seem to weaken, within each of these advancing "disciplines" factionalism becomes the more exacerbated. Some of
the bitterest bouts of contention and some of the sourest re-
pugnancies have been between yesterday's and this morning's
revolutions or revelations, stresses not eased by the way in which
?new movements? not infrequently seem to stem from better
focused attention on what Aristotle or Augustine and their
expounders may have been hoping to mean. Add to all this that
these skirmishings and vendettas occur not only in the pages of
the leaders but are reflected in derived textbooks written for
the use of teachers and for adoption by school systems. And as
business comes more and more into the picture, the famous warfare among publishers hardly seems likely to be replaced by
any more tranquilly discerning rule of reason. And we may bear
in mind that Roosevelt's remarks on "competent government

who, at certain moments and on certain matters, do, in the highest degree, help their pupils to learn, enabling their mental eyes to discern both the general nature of the task and the specific phase, making the appropriate choices of strategy in exploration evident and inviting to them. Having said this much of the rare teacher in his rare hour—salt of the earth bestowing his sweetness and light, the token teacher whence we derive our ideal type—and having paid grateful homage to him, we will be free to note that most teaching tragically falls short of and fights against this ideal.

Why this should be so is a matter due for more study than it has ever received. The means have not been available; now in part they are. Possibly the failure may be due to the degree in which the teacher teaches as he was taught, until he learns better. He does as he was done to. There is no need to invoke depth-psychology in suggesting that a pupil, become teacher, may not infrequently be paying back what he underwent himself. He is normally in a position in which it is extremely difficult for him to know what he is doing. Whatever the reasons, failure, procedure making things harder not easier for the student, is so widespread that the public impression (shared by not a few even in schools of education) that there are those who enter this high profession who might not hold down another job has sadly much justification. It is now recognized that the very grave shortage of persons willing to become teachers and able to give even moderately good service in the role has become already a major threat to the culture.

This contrast between the ideal teacher—radiant cultural figure—and the actual supply may well explain much in the sad ambivalence of the social status of the teacher. The Gown shares with the Cloth a curiously mingled respect and suspicion in the onlooker's speculative glance. Does he or she realize what this profession aspires to? Or how much frustration in other minds any failure entails? Is it surprising that teachers sometimes have a desperate, a brazen or a guilty look and seem riddled with in-

specialists" will apply also to the chosen advisers of the
trial colossi who are hoping to take over the supply and
bution of educational software. They apply as well to t
ditional panels and committees these advisers will seek to
erate with. We may recall Philip Guedalla's description
committee as "an inverted Micawber always waiting for
thing to turn down." It is much easier to get agreement o
sound thing to do" than on the unparalleled. The resul
deprive innovating projects of criticism that might be
to them. They are penalized for having said *purpose* whe
officialese is *objective*. But they are not told to shut up
they propose to meddle with the pupil's autonomy.

This sketch of some of the practical, the administrativ
business and the advisorial resources of obstruction will at
remind us of factors that enter (besides any merits or den
of the project itself) into steps toward finding out what sh
be done. Education, with the exception, possibly, of the e
tainment industries—TV, Radio, the Theater and the Con
is the area of activity richest in examples of a principle v
even than Parkinson's Law—the principle that "probable
penditure of effort in any matter is inversely proportiona
its importance." It is much more likely that we will let c
puters hurry the world onward into every sort of further dar
than that we will concentrate their resources on the produc
of enough good-enough minds to save it.

A computer-borne *instauration* (to use Bacon's word) of edu
tion will have somehow to circumvent all these resistances. I
there is a more deeply rooted source of probable frustration to
considered. Why is so much teaching in an average schoo
waste of time? Here again the answer has to be given in terms
roles: the teachers' roles. We must beware here of the absu
traditional view which makes teaching and learning reciproca
We must replace it with a sufficient recognition that the learn
teacher relation is among the most complex, varied and equivoc
of all. Let us first clearly and firmly agree that there are teache

securities and encrusted, like Glaucus, the sea god (*Republic*, 611D), with disguises and defenses? The penalties of this dismaying position are felt, if not often voiced, on both sides. By the teacher: "Ours is a belittling life," as *Stalky and Co.* has it; by the observer: "Every teacher has a mental odour," in Coleridge's summing up.

It may seem odd to load this essay with such an inventory of familiar failings, such commonplaces of educational criticism. But needs must, while the numbers of children requiring instruction inexorably rise, and the prospects of a provision of teachers adequate to the task as steadily fall. In a clear recognition and realization of this state of affairs are the source of our hopes for better things and our fears of worse: our hopes that a convergence of the highest capacities for design may take over via computer instruction; our fears that the new powers will—as has so often happened—just multiply stalemating mediocrity.

Computer-handled teaching must attempt to match the vastness of its responsibilities with a self-criticism worthy of them. Fortunately, it will be on view, open to analysis and comment, as no instruction hitherto. Its every step in every sequence of them will be on record, reproducible in full actuality, and with the failures and the successes which have attended them. And though the examination of much of this material ranks with everything that is repellent, it is this that stirs an impulse to be optimistic.

In contrast, traditional classroom teaching has been perforce private, observed only incidentally, except by the teacher and his pupils. Inspections, team-teaching, the presence of extraneous witnesses in the classroom, in many ways disturb and deform what most needs to be observed. Nor do they yield the full actual record which is needed. Computer teaching, on the other hand, can compile and analyze its own full record, and undergo the appraisal of those who know most about what it is attempting and are best placed to be guided, in their redesign, by the ways in which it is failing. No doubt it will, for a while, be sprinkled with, indeed deluged by, opinions which enjoy no such advantages. Early attempts to do by computer just what has been done traditionally by select individual teachers are likely. So experimenters with language-teaching by film and TV have sometimes thought they should just put a teacher in action on view.[7] May such underestimates of the new medium not too much discredit the misused means! These things happen whenever new technical resources become available. They illustrate the teacher's genius for yoking up his old oxen before the tractor. Consider, for example, a language laboratory in Africa set up for teachers whose classes had hardly a sentence of viable English among them. It was used to provide the teachers with model pronunciation, on tape, of such things as "Now, Tommy, I don't want to have any more trouble from you!," "Put your hand up properly!," "Go and stand in the corner!" and other samples of the grim appurtenances of classroom incompetence. Such things do not show, however, that tape, when its uses are understood, is not an epoch-making aid in teaching.

Let us turn now from obstacles to objections, to what may be advanced as inherent limitations in computer handling. Some of these are not hard to answer and as they are likely to be often enough heard, answers are in point. Others look exceedingly recondite, but some sort of elucidation may be briefly attempted.

The simplest of these objections perhaps is that since computers are machines, their students will lose much that they might learn from another mind. When so simply propounded we may reply that a computer, however prodigious its performance, is no more than a channel (like a telephone) through which directives put into it by other minds come to the student. These directives are, of course, extremely complex, being hierarchically ordered implications aiming to supply appropriate interactions with the learner who is conversing throughout via the computer, with the minds that have programed that sequence. It is true that the directives enabling all this are put into the machine in code, operated in code, and decoded into whatever is offered for the student's comprehension and further response. But all this internal code-traffic need no more stand between the interlocutors, the programer and the student, than does the telephone, in whose operation too there is transformation from message to signal and back.

A more sophisticated objection can take off from the word *need* in the last sentence or from the word *channel* four sentences back. What can be encoded is a selection only from the resources of language (which again makes its selection from the larger resources of thought). The objection is that the machine must be limited, and so biased, by being confined to the selection. But in this it is not fundamentally different from any other instrument. Whoever has drawn with watercolor and with charcoal knows how "the properties of the instrument used enter into, determine and confine the scope of the investigation"—to quote the Instrumental component of Niels Bohr's *Principle of Complementarity*.[8] The computer *is* so limiting. It cannot understand or respond adequately to most of the points a student may want to put to it. And it is an important part of the programer's task to find means in the sequence of the computer's behavior to indicate to the student what he can and cannot reasonably expect from it. Here of course come in the truly great topic of ambiguity and the problems of the obliquities and equivocations of language, all of which so often *multiply with the importance of the message*. The nub of the objection is that the student and the machine will miss one another's points too often for their exchanges to profit him.

To this there are two answers. The minor one is that communication between live teacher and pupil is commonly not in the least as good as is supposed. Those who resist this proposition have probably forgotten what being taught is like. The more important answer is that there are subjects (some of them very important in themselves and as keys to much else) that are simple enough and controllable enough to be programed even now so that clear communication with the learner can be kept.

From experience with these the programer can go on to more perilous ventures.

The chief problems here are linguistic. They require a wide rather than a narrow concern with language: with the intricacies of comprehension, with the interplay of cognitive and *other than cognitive* components in meanings; indeed, with an extensive field of inquiry lying between literary analysis, psychology, epistemology and linguistics in its more limited contemporary sense. Its typical question [9] is, How does *this* way of saying whatever-it-may-be differ from *that* and how may such differences be made *more fully operative* in the student? Exploration in this field has suffered from its almost total neglect by what were until recently the more fashionable schools of linguistics and language study, whose leaders have been exclusively concerned with other matters. Their neglect has at times been tainted by contumely, due probably to their phobic denials of the relevance of meaning to linguistics—a position from which they have recently and rather suddenly decamped. It is to a further exploration of this field—through experimental studies of the samenesses and differences in the effects of variant phrasing—that we must look for the help the programer will require. Given such exploration, to put limits on what may be programed is premature.

A far more subtle and abstruse objection turns on a supposed ultimate opposition—as hard to formulate as to refute—between men and machines. Men can develop selves, machines cannot: that is the thesis. We develop selves largely by ˢʷputting ourselvesˢʷ (selves, of course, in another sense) in the place of others. Machines, it is averred, cannot do this. Two points may be suggested in reply: First, it is not clear why their human creators should not in time contrive to tell machines how to ˢʷput themselvesˢʷ in the place of others. What account of this ?placing? [10] could be offered would be relevant. Second, we may suspect that this view [11] has not as yet displayed enough of its own real grounds to let us judge it.

The grounds here hinted at are grounds in ˢʷfeelingˢʷ, to use a largely inadequate but still sufficiently recognizable label.[12] It may well be because computers will be unable, probably for a long while, to do justice to more than the *plain sense* of messages (itself a queer abstractive selection) that so many people discount and/or shudder at computer instruction. That computers can be programed to interpret intonations, etc., in any near future will not seem *very* likely to those who appreciate the intricacies and the ambiguities of the means by which people convey their attitudes. And only for a rather special audience does it need saying that an ⁊educated⁊ mind is at least as much a system of attitudes as a system of cognitive information and theory. It should be left to computer technologists to say what proportion of their confraternity may belong to that special audience.

This much at least may be ventured: Those subjects that are most free from attitudinal complexities—those in which the bare typewritten, factual sentence is wholly adequate to what is relevant in the utterance—are best suited to present-day, or near future, computer technique. This points to mathematics, the factual sciences and to languages (if confined strictly to the handling of such plain sense, to factual propositions and to conventional formulas) as the subjects through which the development of computer instruction can as yet be best forwarded. There is, incidentally, fair evidence that first-grade and even pre-school children can learn simple typing. And there are very good theoretical grounds[13] for thinking that suitably designed instruction in typewriting can be an excellent way of beginning the learning of Reading, especially, perhaps, for backward and underprivileged pupils. The computer can accept type, of course; it has a vastly harder task with speech. Further experimentation with entrance to reading via the typewriter would seem to be urgent.

Reading, it is recognized, is the key problem of instruction. It is crucial because it is the learner's introduction to the use of a systematic notation for a naturally acquired activity. *Reading* here means not the mere matching of marks and sounds but intelligent reading for meaning. Contrary to the presuppositions of much elementary teaching, this great step into use of notation is far more easily and securely taken with strictly factual statements *suitably sequenced* (this is fundamental) than with "Jump, Jerry, jump! O what fun!" and the like. By suitable Design (to capitalize the key-term in this connection) the step of seeing how a notation works (writing, print, figures, diagrams, schematic depictions) can be immensely simplified, in comparison with any of the more widely current prescriptions for beginning Reading.

1. Begin by using *sentences* composed with a minimum number of highly distinguishable letters. Seven—*a hi mn st*— have proved a satisfactory set.

2. Add further letters one at a time and only as those in use become *securely operative*.

3. Use unambiguous sentences stating facts that can be visually and immediately *verified* by the learner. Non-distractive depictions showing clearly what the sentences are saying are the most convenient means.

4. Keep the syntax of the sentences *constant* throughout the early stages.

5. Use opposition (*e.g., here ↔ there; this ↔ that*) in arranging the sequences through which the learner develops his power to see how sentences vary with their meanings.

It will be seen that an introduction to Reading following this prescription lends itself very easily to computer handling. That it has been field-tested, with film-strip and film, and revised repeatedly is relevant. That it shocks many conventional teachers may not be. It may be added that a singular absence of spelling troubles later is a marked characteristic of those who enter Reading through this sequence (along with more important scholastic success). The skill in spelling thus developed is marked enough to refute those who assert that the spelling of English is in itself a serious barrier to learning to read well. Of course, it can be, when his introduction to Reading is chaotic and meaningless to the learner.

The heart of this design, which is no dream but a tested reality, is *intelligibility*. The nature of the task the learner is being invited to attempt must be made as fully apparent as may be. Beginners in Reading commonly fail because they do not discover how the thing works or what they should look for. A mode of presentation designed to help them to see for themselves what is happening and to check for themselves why they make mistakes, what went wrong and how to make it go right is—for deep reasons—preferable to any arrangement which relies on mere repetition, corrective drills and external reinforcement. The reinforcement which design (in the great sense) uses is internal; it is the learner's own rewarding sense of his growing power and insight. Design indeed is engaged not only with the structure of the presentation. It is engaged with the structuring of the activities of the investigating mind of the learner. It can order these by arranging the oppositions engaged and displayed in its sequences (as *here* is in opposition to *there*) so that *they* show the learner what he has to take in. When these indications are confirmed and rewarded by success, a peculiar thing happens. The learner has divined three things, for the most part without distinguishing them: how the game goes, what he has to do and how the teaching mind is playing it. The differences between this and the lucky guess merely okayed by authority's word are what the true *designer* must keep his eye on.

If we like, we can relabel these three things the structure of the world, the structure of inquiry, and the structure of instruction. These will not be the learner's labels, but they may bring out for us better than other images: stimulus and response, impression and reproduction, and the like—how the exploration of things differs from other ways of being taught about them. This triple concern puts the learner into a cooperative and creative contact with what is being studied, with his own endeavors and with the would-be helpful presentation offered to him. While trying to form his own ideas, he is also attempting to penetrate the veil and to participate in the thinking of others.

It is indeed a scandal that we lump together various and too often antagonistic processes under such a master term as "learning." There are, of course, plenty of variant conceptions actively promoting divergent views of this prodigious undertaking. Not all human beings, doubtless, can learn well through inquiry. Probably, for those who can, to make them learn in other ways is a grave disservice to them and the world. What they learn will then be only superficially "the same things."

For some time instruction via computers will, of course, be confined to the segments of the world that are growing richer while the rest becomes poorer. This rest is doomed to suffer an increasingly disabling shortage of competent teachers combined with an excess of pupils. But here perhaps, rather than through expenditures on Vietnam, can be found the fit pioneering role of the advanced societies. The computer is beyond the economic means and the technological know-how of the developing countries. Nonetheless, computer-borne, computer-recorded and computer-controlled instruction can produce programs of high general efficiency [14] to be distributed by films, TV, texts, hand-operated phonographs, etc., at costs practicable even for impoverished regions. One or two well-designed computer-aided inquiries into an introduction to English (and the Reading of it) could produce programs for relatively costless distribution. These could redeem many gallant but fruitless efforts being made all over the planet to acquire the keys to participation in world self-realization. And these same programs could, while the problems of the further flights of the computer age are being worked out, be the remedy—if distributed through such relatively inexpensive channels—for the contemporary American capability shortage itself.

This at least we may be sure of. The computer invites, from those who would use it for instruction, a deep consideration of what they are doing, well worth more than the machines. Herein is a fountain of hope. Much about the computer's promise is not less than Shelleyan. In *Prometheus Unbound* (III, iii, 14) there is a Cave, which may well be both Homer's Cave of the Nymphs (*Odyssey*, Book XIII) and Plato's from *Republic* (Book VII), conjoined and reconceived to be fit haunt for a regenerated world.

In this Cave

a fountain
Leaps in the midst with an awakening sound.

"Awakening." The programer, willy-nilly, is in the role of one of Plato's guardians, somehow lifted to the sunlight, awakened and then sent back down into the Cave to serve its inmates and "get used again to seeing in the dark."

It may be wise to append to this account of a designer of instruction, a sentence from a mind far removed from Plato's. Alexandre Dumas in *The Count of Monte Cristo* is describing a man approaching, as he hopes, another sort of treasure: "He then began to climb down into the cave with a smile of doubt on his lips, murmuring that ultimate word of human wisdom, 'Perhaps.' " [15]

Computer-Conveyed Instruction

(1)   *Recent advances:* Few changes so momentous have been as swift. Developments in the switching of these devices into the service of education are outstripping report and appraisal. A wide variety of accounts, comments and projects will be found, for example, in *The Computer in American Education,* Don D. Bushnell and Dwight W. Allen, Editors (New York, John Wiley & Sons, 1967) with an extensive bibliography.

(2)   *unacknowledged legislation of the world:* my emendation. Shelley wrote: "Poets are the unacknowledged legislators of the world." On the grounds for this change see "The Future of Poetry."

(3)   *James Thomson:* from "The City of Dreadful Night."

(4)   *"hate of hate":* Tennyson on Shelley in "The Poet."

(5)   Quoted by G. A. Lauwerys, *The Journal of the Royal Society of Arts,* August, 1966.

(6)   *symbolic similarities and differences:* It is interesting that Leibniz, who was the first to describe a binary arithmetic such as is used in computers, should have been spurred on by resemblances he found in the Chinese *I Ching: The Book of Changes.* See Needham, *op. cit.,* Vol. II, pp. 340–345, for "this extraordinary story."

(7)   *a teacher in action on view:* Film, above all others, is the medium that can best expose for criticism the irrelevancy and distractingness of some teaching behavior. Often it is the very traits which at first impact may seem most

arresting and compelling that become most distasteful, as the facial and vocal excesses and extravagancies grow familiar. The high fidelity of the bigger-than-life close-up has tempted more than a few designers of instructional films to forget what they should be doing.

(8) *Principle of Complementarity:* This immensely important topic—publicized recently by Marshall McLuhan—is discussed at length in my "Toward a More Synoptic View" in *Speculative Instruments* (Harvest Book, HB 128, Harcourt, Brace & World). This, which was originally a contribution to the Eighth Conference on Cybernetics held by the Josiah Macy Jr. Foundation, March, 1951, attempts to put a *generalized* Complementarity Principle connecting (and freeing) all the Faculties (of the mind or of a University) into the required more general setting.

(9) *Its typical question:* Here again is a question to which astonishingly little systematic inquiry has been directed. To some degree Charles Morris in *Signs, Languages, and Behavior* points that way, but his proposed schema is insufficiently tentative, much too neatly cut and dried. My own exploration, indebted in a measure to his as his had been to some speculations in *The Meaning of Meaning,* can be found in "Toward a Theory of Comprehending," *Speculative Instruments.* That set of suggestions is by far the most enterprising speculative intrument I have been concerned to design.

(10) *account of this 'placing':* Such frankly metaphoric phrasing is obviously inadequate. It is a stop-gap or a pointer to some more adequate account. Here again the neglect by conventional linguistics to recognize the centrality of the need for means of comparing the speaker's and the hearer's [nb]points of view[nb] has been remarkable. See "Some Glances at Current Linguistics."

(11)   *this view:* propounded by J. Bronowski, *The Identity of Man* (New York, Doubleday, 1965).

(12)   *sufficiently recognizable label:* The set of distinctions suggested in *Practical Criticism* (1929), pp. 173–181, which have been widely used, were, as I see it, entirely superseded by the far more applicable and clarifying means for comparing offered in *Speculative Instruments*. See Note (9) above. That a crude set of distinctions should command attention and a more refined as well as more convenient set be ignored may seem surprising.

(13)   *good theoretical grounds:* Briefly, operating a typewriter *can* offer the learner, in ideal order and conjunction, action, vision and challenge of meaning. It *can* spectacularly link up manipulative routines with the appearance of typescript as outcome; *and with* perception of the agreement or disagreement of this outcome with required meanings. All this *if the design of the learning sequences is judicious,* not otherwise.

(14)   *programs of high general efficiency:* It should be noted that literacy programs and second-language learning programs for English should, for *linguistic* as well as other reasons, be such as to have no dependence upon the peculiarities of the native languages of recipients. The assumption to the contrary is one of the chief impediments to efficient action. Unfortunately it is so deeply implanted in many of the most influential consultants in these matters that it may long continue to be an embarrassment— as was, say, attachment to phlebotomy as correct treatment in the advance of medicine.

(15)   Edmond Dantes is a very different man from any Guardian, but he too has learned how to see in the dark.

4

Some Glances at Current
Linguistics

*At this point it is reasonable to ask what current linguistics has
to offer as guides in this immense and frighteningly urgent
undertaking. And how far are its authorities interested in, aware
of and ready for the tasks with which they will be called on to
help?*

*Characteristic positions in recent British linguistics are first
outlined and criticized—especially as to the views on the teaching of languages and on inter-language understanding there put
forward. The essay then turns to the movements in Theory of
Language that have been making most stir of late in America
and asks how it is that so much devoted work has so little of
practical use to offer toward world needs and so little concern
for what else might be tried.*

Can a study suffer from an Ishmael complex? Yes, if it has special difficulties in establishing its own independence in its peculiar field and methodology. For a while it may go on in a lonely,
hoity-toity way, full of airs and ires, issuing denunciations, injunctions, and excommunications, venting its hostility toward
whatever it supposes to have stood in the way of its advance. In
time however, as it becomes more secure (and more divided), this
aggressiveness abates.

For some decades linguistics has been the leading "example" of such behavior—much to the concern of that analogue to the U.N., the would-be United Studies. For how we should think about language matters very deeply in nearly all of them. If there is a study ready to settle this for us and intent upon doing so, we should indeed take note. And if this study claims to be alone in charge of saying *how language works,* more is needed. For premature confidence as to *that,* blindly followed in the schools, could do damage hard to repair. Inter-Study trespasses have often done so in less crucial areas and on a far smaller scale.

These two books * are representative of present-day British linguistics. Both stem mainly from J. R. Firth and Daniel Jones. Both are well informed on other schools of linguistics, including past and present American movements, which are themselves only recently coming to take unpolemical account of their rival developments. Both make interesting and detached attempts to relate their own theory and model to those deriving from Leonard Bloomfield, Zellig Harris, Kenneth Pike, and others. Mr. Robins's book, moreover, thoroughly earns its title. It can give the general reader who would like to know what has been and is being done a good over-all view and within a reasonable time. And there is enough detail and exemplification to let him see how it is done and this at all levels of analysis: phonological, grammatical, semantic. What will strike him most will be the amount of concern over which *theoretical models* should be used in description. In comparison, the new insight being gained into language may seem disappointing. Current linguistics regards itself as a *young* science. It is painfully conscious of duties that its new status as a science may entail. It is also sensitive lest it be supposed to be any the less for that among the humanities. And yet a reader coming to linguistics from literary criticism or

* R. H. Robins, *General Linguistics: An Introductory Survey* (Bloomington, University of Indiana Press, 1965). M. A. K. Halliday, Angus McIntosh and Peter Strevens, *The Linguistic Sciences and Language Teaching* (Bloomington, University of Indiana Press, 1964).

philosophy who notes what stern, self-denying ordinances the linguist lays upon himself as a scientist will wonder about the price. Are not its rigors, its ideals of power, economy, simplicity in explanation, its refusals to use in its formulations so much that its practitioners know safely enough in other capacities, are not these postures precluding it from being as helpful as it might be to itself and to other studies? Very probably, however, a strong reaction to this defensive isolationism has begun.

What emerges from both books is how the pendulum of linguistic theory has swung between devotion to *form* and devotion to *meaning* and how these oscillations have speeded up. What was awesomely dominant a little while back can now seem only old-fashioned. For example, only two decades ago any reference to meaning in a linguistic description was widely treated as "mentalistic" incompetence. Today, all but the most devout adepts admit that language, being a notation for samenesses and differences among situations, is inescapably dependent on meaning. Both books insist that replacement of theories and models will "continue for many years to come." And, of course, what is learned about languages will go on increasing, however often or however much the descriptive apparatus may be changed. This cumulative improvement makes the scientific part of linguistics sharply different from, say, poetry, or party doctrine, or fashions in hair-dos, philosophy or education—other activities in which oscillations may also be observed.

The twofold title of *The Linguistic Sciences and Language Teaching* may lead some readers to look there for this contrast. And they will find it. The authors are authorities in linguistics. That is where their treasure is. While they stay within linguistics what they have to say is often valuable, sometimes trenchant, and occasionally seminal. When they turn to language teaching the atmosphere changes. What they write seems frequently perfunctory, as though somebody had asked them to explain and they were wondering what they could find to say. Apart from commonplaces, the discussion is oddly remote from real prob-

lems. They do indeed remark: "We feel that somehow comprehension should enter into the criteria of literacy," but it is
evident throughout that their interest in the anatomy and
physiology of comprehension, in concept-formation and in cognitive or other psychology, is disablingly lacking. Something
hides from them the relevancy to the language-learner of what
language is for. In places they assert their amateur status: "The
linguist can say what is a good description of a language, and
can produce such a description. But he cannot say how the language should be taught. That is a matter for teachers and those
who train the teachers." This sounds modest and reasonable too
—until you realize how badly those teachers and their trainers
need help and how much more help they can be given than is
offered here.

What is needed is something with which a more mature linguistics—of which Roman Jakobson is an illuminating exponent
—can equip teachers: a recognition of the key role of *opposition*
in language use. As Saussure indicated, and Jakobson and Halle
have formulated more fully in *Fundamentals of Language,*
language holds together through requirements and exclusions: in other terms, through forms seeking closure and incom-
patibles seeking for place. Every speech-sound, every word, every
sentence, does what it does through not being others which
would replace it in another situation. *If here,* not *there;* if *this,*
not *that;* if *now,* not *then;* if present, neither future nor past,
and so on. The name for this need to choose between alternates
which must be changed as circumstances require is *opposition,*
and it is this concept which makes possible a *direct* teaching
of how language works, by giving the learners properly arranged
opportunities to *see* for themselves how it does its manifold
jobs. Grammar has pretended to teach this by telling its pupils
about language. That never worked. Most of the revolt against
grammar among teachers has come simply from their recognition
that this sort of thing does not succeed. It does not enhance
either passive or active command of meaning. It distracts. Here

the swinging of the pendulum in teaching fashion becomes evident. After swinging blindly away from all concern with grammar, the profession is now swinging back—to teaching a newer grammar. In America this is chiefly some simplification of Chomsky's doctrines. Textbooks applying the latest things (of five years ago) compete for the market. But the misdirection of effort remains uncorrected. It was *not* the badness of the grammar descriptions which caused the failure, but a simpler and deeper mistake: learning how to *describe* a language is not at all the same thing as learning how to *use* it with power and discernment. In point of fact, current efforts by English teachers to use "transformational grammar" far too often result in glib manipulation of nomenclature—just as of old—and play with "tree diagrams" without bringing any improved understanding of what sentences do or how they do it.

The root reason is the difference between an intellectual apparatus designed to serve linguistic description, on the one hand, and a planned serial ordering of oppositions in sentences and situations on the other. The child's *introduction* to reading and writing is all important. It can and should be the key to all the rest: the model of, the clue to, how a notation represents. Give him this and he can go forward clear-sightedly. As reading becomes more established and ambitious in the mind, opposition, though still the essential principle governing meaning, ceases to need *explicit* exhibition. But without introduction to it the child remains all at sea as to what he is expected to look for and to do, reduced to guessing at his teacher's wishes. The designer of this introduction should use his reflective knowledge of the language to contrive sequences of situations through which the learner can be invited to observe *in detail* (no description is needed and most descriptions distract) how changes in what is uttered vary systematically with what is meant. He will arrange these invitations so that they induce *undistracted* growth of discernment and assimilation in the learner. This can best be done by using *opposition,* the mainspring of comparison, lin-

guistic and other, to engage the learner in seeing for himself
the differences, for example between:

> *His hat is in his hands*

and

> *Her hat is on her head.*

To see such things clearly is really to find out how language
works. But to do so effectively, the contrasting *situations* which
give these sentences their meaning must be clearly presented
to the learner—in actions or in depictions cleaned from all *distraction,* from all that is not strictly relevant to what the sentences are saying. (What is distractive is commonly what teachers
have learned from publishers to call "attractive.") Moreover,
these invitations to observe how language works through comparing changes in sentences with changes in situations must be
so arranged that what has been learned is *used* in the learning
of what is new. And there are other such principles that have
been vigorously preached and demonstrated for thirty years
or more. They have been developed for the most part in the
design of elementary film and TV language teaching and of programed instruction, for which such sequencing is even more
important than for the classroom teacher. Our authors of *The
Linguistic Sciences and Language Teaching* complain sadly that
"there exist very few statements of principles for the guidance
of others" as to sequencing. But the need is not for *many* statements but for clear and relevant ones. These have existed for
some time but the authors have not been successful in finding
them, perhaps because of a philosophic impediment to the
thought of thought, which much of recent linguistics has in-
herited.

Two important consequences concern views on *observation* and
meaning. On observation we are offered a self-destructively limited view, due to according an inappropriate sense to *observe.*
They assert that "concepts cannot be observed, but only postu-
lated through the observation of particular events in particular

languages" (p. 154). How then do they suppose these observations of particular events to have been achieved? Every recognition, every identification, every differentiation among particulars takes place through observation of concepts: capabilities of apprehension. Every sentence in this book works only through writer and reader alike being able to *observe concepts* and their relations to one another: observing, for example, that two words are the same or that two senses are different or that two views are irreconcilable. And this in two of the main senses of *observe:* "notice" and "obey," as in "Observe the NO SMOKING sign." The authors, of course, know all this perfectly well. All their talk of "formal items" and of "abstraction" entails it. But they have at this point followed a fashion in giving to the word *concept* an irrelevant, in place of the required, meaning.

This is no quibble about a use of terms. It is a diagnosis. Here is a grave misconceiving of conceiving, an intellectual infection, which, where it is suffered, prevents linguistics from giving any but trivial advice to teachers since it cuts the needed connection between sentences and what they may be saying. When this spreads it does much damage to education—replacing thought in the classroom by parroting or by prudent conventional prattle.

To come now to meaning. It is as unnecessary to set up a conflict between form and meaning as to stage a fight between muscles and bone or between concepts and language. Language uses an incredibly elaborate system of cooperative relations among its parts at all levels in order to deal as best it can with the infinite variety of situations speakers and hearers may find themselves in. Every utterance has both a form and a meaning. The form has been developed to handle the meaning and the meaning must be explored *both* through the language and through examination of the situation the utterer is attempting to deal with. Both the utterance and the situation are the outcomes of systematic selections from among alternates. For the speaker, the form is his endeavor to accord in his language activity with the situation (as he sees it). For his hearers the meaning (as they in turn see it) arises from their endeavors to take account of and respond to the selections which have generated the form. Normally form and meaning vary together systematically, but naturally much goes wrong all the time, though strangely less, in some types of situation, than one would in theory expect.

Our authors evince somewhat divided minds in their remarks about meaning. (It is perhaps harder for three minds to avoid this old mind-trap than for one.) They quote Firth on Linguistics as the study of "how we use language to live," a sensible formulation but hardly reconcilable with some of the other positions adopted. They go on to report him as emphasizing that "meaning was a property of all the types of patterning found in language; one could not describe language without describing meaning." (Is this: "All these types of patterning mean; in describing language we should try to say how"?) They then proceed to denounce a selection of inferior attempts to describe meanings—not as inferior but for attempting to do it. (These attacks repeat with British examples a standard pattern of denunciation in recent U.S. linguistics.) Meaning *as what x means* and meaning as *how x means* are insufficiently distinguished throughout these pages: "A description must account for the internal patterns of language, and this can only be achieved if the criteria are drawn from within and not from outside language. At the same time all statements about language are statements of meaning, and the task of the linguist is to work out, from observations of language in action, theories of how language works which will enable him best to make such statements" (p. 151). But how is *language in action* to be observed unless we are ready to take into one view "the internal patterns of language" *and* much that is certainly "outside language"? More attention to how "the criteria" *are,* of necessity and in fact, "drawn"—*both* from "outside" and from "within" language—would start another revolution in linguistics.

This opposition of "within language" and "outside language"

invites reflection. Take the somewhat important and typical contrast between *he* and *she,* for example. How far would you get with that if your criteria had to be drawn "from within" and not "from outside" language? You might get a big set of collocations (other words likely to be found in the same units of discourse). Boys' names as against girls' names, *his* as against *her, trousers* (once upon a time) as against *skirt, pipe* as against *compact,* etc. To pursue such collocations statistically with computers and large-scale, grant-consuming samples is, so these linguists aver, more reliable than to consider what *he* and *she* do for us in living. "The formal criterion of collocation is taken as crucial because it is more objective, accurate, and susceptible to observation than the contextual criterion of referential or conceptual similarity" (p. 34). It is sad that linguistics should go on trying so hard to deprive itself of benefit from the analysis of situations—on which its avowed procedures do in fact themselves depend.

There are other strange omissions or refusals. Much praise (and space) is lavished on the work done by French researchers in 1951. *"Le Français Fondamental* and the research work that led up to it are great pioneering efforts" in vocabulary selection, they state. But no mention is made of the British and American labors to which the French effort was a response. "The obvious criterion for choosing one word and rejecting another seemed to be frequency of occurrence," they write, as though this question had not been very fully thrashed out long before the French started. *English Word Lists,* Fries and Traver (1940), could have shown them in a few minutes how profoundly C. K. Ogden's *Basic English* changed the contents of Beginning English Word Lists along with the principles of selection. "Words are not useful because they are frequent but frequent because they are useful," was Ogden's position. But to understand the importance of this change of angle, you have to *think* about "how language works" and about what happens when, as so often, it doesn't. Excommunications are poor policy in scholarship. Basic English brought about a revolution in the design of elementary instruction in languages. A number of informed eyebrows will be raised at the way this is here ignored.

More serious than omissions are misdirections. Languages with sufficiently different resources impose on their users importantly different frameworks of possible meanings. On this our authors seem to be in the grip of a quite non-scientific linguistic egalitarianism. They spend more than a little of their space insisting, with rebuke for other views, that "any language is as good as any other language." Look again and you find this declaration is qualified by "essentially" (!) and that it is to be understood "in the sense that every language is equally well adapted to the uses to which the community puts it" (p. 99). Maybe, but how do they know that? Have they an inventory of all the uses to which every community puts its language? Similarly (and here again they are echoing the injunctions of American linguists) dialects are equally good. Is this science or just sympathy for the underprivileged? One is almost surprised that they do not carry on and extend this anti-snob principle to ideolects (the individual's language resources) and so put an end to the case for education.

"This misapprehension that some languages are intrinsically better than others" they are very severe on. "It is wholly false and can do a great deal of harm." I do not know what "intrinsically" can do for them as an escape word. But certainly languages can be compared with regard to what they can say and do. For some the performances possible within them are immeasurably greater than for others in the variety and extent and delicacy of the connections and distinctions they can compass. Less capable languages have not developed the necessary means. The authors are highly dogmatic on this matter, a sign perhaps that theory rather than actuality is guiding them. "All languages," they say, "are capable of incorporating the lexical additions they require" (p. 100). "Capable," h'm; "require," ha! Their reference is to computers.

Quite apart from this rash abstract confidence about some 3,000 unknown grammars, addition of new vocabulary is in actuality by no means the comfortable matter here suggested. This is in fact a burning question, an atom bomb bonfire question. And our authors' opinions here are fine examples of academic irresponsibility. Hardly any of the key-terms of political thought in the West have as yet been assimilated into Chinese without stultifying distortions. No mutual comprehension in the most vital matters is as yet linguistically possible. And, reciprocally, the central moral terms, the names of the virtues in the Chinese tradition, are no more easily reproducible in English than, say, *sophrosyne*. And for good reason. The situations these great key-terms have to handle and to order and to maintain—their duties in the Western and the Chinese traditions as helping their users to live—are too different. Their concepts of "what to do," as Confucius put it, are too deeply and organically (as with a blood type) connected with their norms of living. The gulfs between the traditions are too wide to be bridged merely by additions to vocabulary. To think they can be is to neglect values and much else in the anatomy of meanings. And alas, as Socrates showed Euthyphro,[1] it is values that men fight *for*—less communicable than what they fight *with*. The future would look a lot brighter if the concepts a culture lives by could be grafted into another language as easily as the technicalities of the missile, and if men could more readily conceive that purposes they are opposed by may be as worthy as their own. But for that there are needed kinds of instruction *in understanding* which official linguistics as yet does not offer, an understanding which the aims at present preferred may easily obstruct.

With this as departure point we may turn to the reconstructions in American linguistics which have sprung chiefly from the discontent of Noam Chomsky in the middle fifties. He became dissatisfied with the aims and the assumptions which had

been accepted by most of the active practitioners of formal
linguistic analysis through the last few decades. Into the detail
of Chomsky's demonstrations of their inadequacies, his innovations, his redesignings of his own new proposals . . . this is no
place to go. Few modern grammarians are highly intelligible
writers, and summaries rarely do more than serve as mnemonics.
They send you back to what is being summarized.

To be as brief as I can: Chomsky's projected revolution asked
grammarians to attempt much more than even a most minute,
meticulous and scrupulous anatomizing, stocktaking and survey
of the structures of languages at all levels. He wanted them to
add something that might formally explain how language
works, how the inter-verbal relations it works through are to
be specified.[2] In the course of conveying and exemplifying this
request he has repeatedly surprised his readers by the rigor of
his treatment and his disregard of the obligation to be comprehensible. Chomsky often writes chiefly for Chomsky and even
to his followers he can offer very hard going. Perhaps because
of these severities his influence has become widespread. A
reaction this, perhaps, to the dreary monotony of inquiries which
have been devoting time and energy to trying to find quasi-
mechanical routines for answering linguistic questions.

Shadows of coming events—here the rise of the computer—
stretch far. Chomsky is at pains to snort[3] at the suggestion
that preparation for possible computer use could have had anything to do with the recent history of U.S. Linguistics. The
public, however, can only guess at the directives followed by
grant-awarding panels. "The advance of knowledge" (though
"what about?" is still a live question) has probably been well
served by this redirection of attention. Whatever ensues, the
agitation has reanimated the theory of linguistics. More than
that, Chomsky's dedication, his demurrers, disentanglings and
retractions have given him a standing nobody in his or a following generation has yet won. He has shaken things up, and re-
formulated the traditional task, though whether he has yet

brought it nearer to being helpful with anything that urgently needs doing is a question in which his supporters show surprisingly little interest. He has, however, and—increasingly in his later work, most of all in his *Cartesian Linguistics*—vigorously reminded the analysts that these inquiries have had a long line (some 2,500 years long in the Western tradition) of highly able inquirers from whose work there is still as much as ever to be learned. All this and more may be counted among this doughty thinker's contributions to current linguistics.

After earlier formulations of his proposals for a generative linguistics Chomsky seems to have settled (tentatively, no doubt) for a broad contrast between *surface* and *deep* linguistic structure. As motion of a point generates a line, as a set of postulates generates their consequences, so something as yet to be formulated generates the possibilities of a language and excludes what is not among these possibilities. From the examinable surface structure, through innumerable comparisons, generative linguistics explores toward this something. It gives a central position to grammatical structure; in part perhaps because the cooperations of words in sentences have been more systematically studied and for longer, and lend themselves more easily to corroboration from the general agreement of language users than either the analogous cooperations and preclusions among the sounds of a language (Phonology), or the cooperations and preclusions among its meanings (Semantics).

As far as this exploration has as yet gone, the Phonology may be likened to the minute texture of a perceptually observable superficies, of a skin, of which comparative microscopic analysis has provided a thorough and, up to a point, adequate account; the Grammar likened to a mechanically limited range of combinations, a muscle-tendon-joint account of the positions and motions an average individual has in his repertoire; and the Semantics to the purposes he may pursue through such a set of mechanisms. This image roughly represents the relative accessibility of the three fields to the layman. He cannot know much about the cells in his skin without special training and apparatus. He can easily observe and unmethodically describe a very great deal about possibilities and impossibilities of his body movement. And he, along with all of us, has an immense though varying and unorganized supply of insight into what he, from occasion to occasion, may be trying to do—*including what you and I are herewith attempting.* It will be noted that *formal* description (with notation for it) is highly developed—though much debated—for Phonology, is rapidly growing for Grammar, and is virtually non-existent for Semantics.

Thought on the relations between the three fields is, not surprisingly, confused. It seeks to do something which would seem to require much help from an organized Semantics. And such help is not available. Thus attempts at *formal* accounts of the interdependencies of the linguistic levels and so on must be recognized as inevitably unsatisfactory. It is interesting to compare, here, the high (ideal) abstractness of a fountainhead deliverance on this subject by Chomsky with the plain matter-of-factness of a more or less popular presentation:

The generative grammar of a language should, ideally, contain a central *syntactic component* and two *interpretive components, a phonological component* and a *semantic component.* The syntactic component generates strings of minimal syntactically functioning elements (following Bolinger, 1948, let us call them *formatives*) and specifies the categories, functions and structural interrelations of the formatives and systems of formatives. The phonological component converts a string of formatives of specified syntactic structure into a phonetic representation. The semantic component, correspondingly, assigns a semantic interpretation to an abstract structure generated by the syntactic component. Thus each of the two interpretative components maps a syntactically generated structure onto a "concrete" interpretation, in one case phonetic, and in the other, semantic. The grammar as a whole can thus be regarded, ultimately, as a device for pairing phonetically represented signals with semantic interpretations, this pairing being mediated through a system of abstract structures generated by the syntactic component. Thus the syntactic component must provide for each sentence (actually, for each interpretation of each sentence) a semantically interpretable *deep structure* and a phonetically interpretable *surface structure,* and, in the event that these are distinct, a statement of the relation between these two structures. . . . Roughly speaking, it seems that this much structure is common to all theories of generative grammar, or is at least compatible with them. Beyond this loose and minimal specification, important differences emerge.[4]

We note the force of "ideally" and "ultimately" here, and that this is a "loose and minimal specification" and "roughly speaking." We perhaps start imagining what a rigorous and comprehensive specification, precisely speaking, will read like. We note further that it is a *meta-semantic* [5] attempt to assign an over-all structure to cooperations between *accounts* of language offered under the headings Phonology, Grammar, Semantics.

Compare now a simplified account of *deep* and *surface* structure written as prelude to reporting "a clutch of recent experiments" (made at the Center for Cognitive Studies, Harvard) "that display, with a clarity utterly convincing to the converted, the psychological validity of this highly abstract notion."

A word of explanation is perhaps in order. Chomsky's distinction is that the *surface* or constituent structure of a sentence is closely related to its phonological representation (the "sounds" of speech) and is derived by transformational rules from an inferred, unmarked *deep* structure to which semantic interpretations can be assigned. Deep structure is not apparent in the superficial characteristics of a sentence, but must be supplied by the linguistic intuitions of the speaker or listener himself. The already-classic example of this distinction is provided by the pair of sentences *John is easy to please* and *Jack is eager to please,* both of which have the same surface structure of the form ((John) ((is easy) (to please))). Speakers of English recognize however that while *John* is the logical object of his sentence, *Jack* is the logical subject of his; *easy* is a sentence modifier, but *eager* modifies the noun alone. These differences are considered to repose within the deep structure of the two sentences, and are representable only in terms of transformational rules.[6]

This report explains that there has been a shift from work based on Chomsky's earlier proposals. "The linguistic theory has been changed to emphasize instead two 'levels' of language— a superficial level that represents its acoustic (or its written) form and a deep level that represents the meanings that it carries, the interpretations of the speaker or listener."

More differences are discernible between these two accounts than present resources for verbal description of them can perhaps display. In the original, grammar ᵣcan . . . be regarded, ulti- mately, as a deviceʳ—a three-component ᵣsystem of abstract struc- tures generated by the syntactic componentʳ. So regarded, is it a device devised by the grammarian or by ˢʷNatureˢʷ? It may be useful to note the dictionary entry for *device*—"That formed by design; a scheme, a stratagem"; and for *devise*—between the obsolete "divide, distribute" and the obsolete "to divine, guess," we have "to form in the mind by *new* combinations of ideas, etc." (My italics.) For the psychologist, on the other hand, the distinction between *deep* and *surface* structure is less between two types of *abstract structure dependent upon the syntactic component* (for each interpretation of a sentence—one interpret- able semantically, the other phonetically) than between struc- tures of sentences as apprehended by the subjects of his experi- ments. In brief, the subjects are dealing immediately with situ- ations; the linguist with the design of a formula. Taken as the psychologist takes it, however, distinctions between deep and surface structures are no more unfamiliar than the distinction between *how the words are put together and what they are say- ing.* Chomsky's formulation is, of course, new. Probably no *grammarian* before him, reflecting on types of linguistic struc- ture, has laid out the matter so. But distinctions hardly different from those used by the *psychologist,* at work with tokens of these types, have often been pointed out and discussed in other terms —notably as a separation of *logical* from *grammatical* form. To quote from a controversy of thirty years ago:

Consider, for example, the treatment of logical form—an important matter since what we are saying at any moment depends upon it. In a recent authoritative textbook, Miss L. S. Stebbing's *A Modern Introduction to Logic,* page 51, we find:

"In a proposition we can distinguish between the *constituents* and *the form*. This distinction is easy to see but difficult to define. The simplest method is to start by considering some examples of propositions which either have the same form or the same constituents. Consider the set of propositions:

(1) Mussolini is ambitious.

(2) Baldwin is mortal.

(3) Voltaire is witty.

(4) Leo XIII is old.

It is obvious that these four propositions are all of the same form."

For the purpose of a calculus such a treatment is perhaps sufficient. But on a closer analysis—such as must be undertaken in any attempt to explain the meanings of these adjectives—it very soon becomes clear that the *forms* as well as the constituents of these propositions are very different. We have only to write out the first partially adequate expansions of them as they come to mind to see this. Thus

1. Mussolini is ambitious	may = M. has a desire, and makes attempts, to do great things.
2. Baldwin is mortal	may = B.'s death will come at some time.
3. Voltaire is witty	may = V.'s writings have a special effect on certain of his readers.
4. Leo XIII is old	may = Leo XIII's age is considerably greater than the average age, or Leo XIII has been living through many years.

It is undeniable that after these symbolic expansions—which, though evidently adequate, are at least the kinds of expansions that are required if we are to show the meanings of the adjectives—these four statements appear as relational propositions of quite different forms. Their *prima facie* similarity of form is merely a linguistic, syntactic similarity—a grammatical rather than a logical matter.[7]

Such examples could be multiplied indefinitely. Pursued long enough and sensitively enough (with pencil in hand and a design for checking and corroboration) such rewriting of sentences can develop valuable and revealing exercises in distinguishing meanings. Comparing, for example, *He fears him, He kicks him, He envies (is jealous of) him, He disparages him*, etc., can encourage more than a little experimental exploration of the rivalries between grammatic and semantic components in interpretation. Such work could generate (in another sense than Chomsky's) good training in reading and writing. It would be looking to improvement in discernment not in linguistic theory. And would not assign to syntax the central place that Chomsky recommends. There might, however, be other, *e.g.*, historical reasons, for assigning such a position to grammar. One at least of these may be important.

Grammar has from its beginnings been thought of as two things: the most obvious way into *describing* language and the most obvious way of *teaching* a language. We should not overlook in our reflections upon grammar the influence of its traditional pedagogic status. Grammar used to be taught through rules and tables and classifications, cases and tenses and moods and voices: through a highly confident, authority-charged account—embodied in rote-memorizations of pages in a book—of *rules* as to how the language *must* be read and written. People who have been taught some language so are often unable to imagine any other effective procedure. They become persuaded that it is through such ʾrulesʾ that a language works. Such a legacy, however much discountenanced by students of the acquisition of language, can very well affect, deeply beyond his writing, even the most original, independent and daring of theoretical innovators. Linguistic theory is, as Jakobson has many times reminded us, a matter of much more than language; it is a reflection of all that is relevant to how any use of language does or does not work.

Languages and the theory of them have thus a very peculiar role among subjects. The learning of languages can become little more than an introduction to and a means of control over the study of literatures. Well and good. The theory of languages can become little more than an acrimonious series of disputes over how it should be prosecuted. Ill and bad. But beyond both these opposite outcomes, language study, language skill and language theory in reasonably close mutual control, have a joint task. It is not to present to us, for some future archaeologist's study, some promising (or not) view of how, ultimately, a device might be devised with the aid of which a less complicated and more economical *account* of language might be offered. No. The task is to design, through a collectively corroborative convergence of apprised judgment, steps that will help our successors to deal more usefully and understandingly with linguistic needs.

It is not easy to connect this urgent aim with the embranglements of academic contention. Nonetheless, with one eye on present shortcomings in world communications, and the other eye on what modernized and methodized techniques in all this could immediately do, how are we to be acquiescent? The *minutiae* of theories of linguistic theory seem so incommensurate with global mutual murder. But in actuality they are not unconnected.

It is from this standpoint that we may wish that more of the critical discernment so brilliantly exercised by Chomsky could have been turned to these more pressing linguistic tasks. The less docile among his readers notice with mingled sympathy and impatience, and not least in *Cartesian Linguistics,* too frequent a repetition of unelucidated phrases far too often received by disciples with a too devoted attention to superficial texture; frequently, indeed, as if they were spells.

For example, in the explanation on page 2 of *Cartesian Linguistics* [8] we are referred to Note 2:

By a "generative grammar" I mean a description of the tacit competence of the speaker-hearer that underlies his actual performance in
production and perception (understanding) of speech. A generative
grammar, ideally, specifies a pairing of phonetic and semantic representations over an infinite range; it thus constitutes a hypothesis
as to how the speaker-hearer interprets utterances, abstracting away
from many factors that interweave with tacit competence to determine
actual performance.

Here again "ideally" is at work and grammar is a "description"
which specifies a pairing. What it describes, however, is still
undescribed. *Tacit competence* is a striking phrase, the more
striking as we reflect on its legal backgrounds: *tacit*—not only
silent, but "by operation of law"; *competence*—"rightful belong-
ingness," "legal relevance," "qualification." The importance of
what the phrase may be supposed to be contributing may be
indicated by our being returned by following Notes to this same
Note 2, which is even described (unless I am mistaken in identifying §2, at the foot of page 108, with Note 2) as discussing "the
fundamental insight regarding language (and thought)." As
such, this "fundamental insight regarding language" (even
though "thought" seems to have slipped in as an afterthought)
should be accorded special attention. "Competence" [9] has indeed been incorporated into the formulary of the school and we
might reasonably expect that its use as a key-term would be
fully and minutely examined. (Alas, in general, key-terms have
to wait till a following generation for examination, by which
time interest or fashion has commonly shifted.) Here it is fairly
obvious that *competence* may be used:

(1) As a mere label (theory free), an equivalent to "what the
speaker-hearer can do" or

(2) As a name for that in him which enables him to perform
as he does. The literature seems to this reader to evince an
uneasy wobble between these two. Sometimes there seems an
ambition to confine "competence" to item (1): to follow the
nominalistic line of the twenties (Russell, Logical Positivism,

early Behaviorism). Chomsky repeatedly takes occasion to condemn "dispositions" and "powers": "These constitute a new
'myth' as mysterious and poorly understood as Descartes' 'mental
substance' " (*ibid*, p. 81). And yet, if you reject all use of any
?ability? (call it what you will: capacity, competence, power,
disposition . . .) as a name for something the speaker-hearer
develops or acquires, something which before a certain stage he
does not possess and after that does possess, you are back—are
you not?—with that merely descriptive survey (explanation and
theory free) in discontent with which Chomsky's revolt started.
For what may as well be called ˢʷdispositionsˢʷ are no less than
necessities for any *general* discourse in which words, concepts,
etc., recur. An account of ?competence? which professes to be
exempt from need to explain ?powers? is still using ?powers?
throughout—while denying that it is doing so.

The old hubs of philosophic controversy are not so easily dismissed. It is true that some uses of ʷdispositionʷ carry theories
from which one may wish to dissent. But one may so dissent
without denying that the nature of dispositions, as a variety of
Forms or Ideas, is the problem, whether one is talking about
conduct in language or in tennis or in digestion, and however
little one may be satisfied with any answers as yet attainable.

Meanwhile there are those who claim—as part of their cor-
roborable account of their tacit competence as hearers-speakers—
that they can perceive (understand) that "dispositions" and
"powers" as Ryle and his followers use them and the similar
words that Ushenko discusses and the similar words when used
by Skinner and his adherents, all three sets of them, are, when
they have disparate theories behind them, differently *paired with
their semantic representations,* one from another and each in
turn from these words as used here by Chomsky. But what "the
fundamental insight regarding language (and thought)" should
be doing about such discrepancies or about the further validation
of its own status is yet to be seen.

To be otherwise serious in what is truly as much a heartrending as a laughable situation, a reasonably detached reader can see, can indeed *not help seeing,* that in these matters able and devoted minds spend much of their energies *mis*perceiving (*mis*understanding) one another's positions, as though the distortion of others' views were a necessary condition for the stability and persistence of their own. Probably, the nearer their discourse tries to come to the centers and sources of the opposed positions the worse the distortions become. Instances of such situations are not lacking in simpler fields; any ingenious inquirer could collect them by the bookful. But no other example has more to teach us than this. Here we have at the least three schools (many more, in fact), each in its own way intent upon reforming current investigation of certainly a fundamental problem. With a benign vagueness (or vacuousness) we can call it, if we will, [sw]The relations of language and thought[sw] or [sw]How is communication possible[sw]? If we try to be more precise we gradually discover that it is not one problem, a common problem (as many of the disputants appear most of the time to suppose), but a number of problems, as their remarks about their opponents' limitations of insight or absurdness of aim can show us. In brief, they are covertly contending[10] for the right to dictate the questions that may be asked and to proscribe those that may not.

Each of the main schools is much given to discussing the views of the others and each professes to share much, at least, of a common language with them. Yet each, in the eyes of the views' owners, misrepresents them in this way or that. Of course, into all this all kinds of personal and accidental factors can interweave. Nonetheless, though the chief reasons for these unfortunate doings are rarely mentioned or even hinted at, they are not, perhaps, for a sufficiently detached inquirer, beyond conjecture.

Sufficiently? We step with this word upon truly perilous ground. Every insight, as to superficial or deep structure and as to their connections, every conjecture, every speculation, every guess has to be corroborated. Everyone will perhaps agree to this. But if we ask: How are the competent corroborating witnesses to be selected?—and, methodologically, this is, I suggest, the fundamental, the foundation, question—we are in for trouble; there enter not only all the troubles that beset the meanings of "consensus" and the practical problems of examinations ("how the hearer-speaker interprets utterances," *ibid,* Note 2) but delicate questions as to vicious and virtuous circularities in proof: those are good witnesses who elsewhere have been . . . etc. All perhaps that need be said here is that among the qualifications of competent corroborating witnesses must be listed certain ranges of experience and a certain ability to retrieve data therefrom. Concretely, in this instance, competent witnesses must manage to adjust their guiding cares and recall what they thought when they were (in imagination) Cartesians, what they thought when they were (in imagination) positivist behaviorists and what they thought when they were imaginatively inclined to suppose that a more vigilant acumen in observing the handling of words would do what was required. It may be added that any such imaginative witness must probably be ready to taste with equanimity the disdainful disregard of all the schools.

In spite of these practical and theoretical difficulties, some attempt to sketch some of these not enough adduced reasons may be worth making, if only to confirm, perhaps, other minds now tiring of contentions that become dreary as they fail to clear the air.

Cartesianism—to mean by that Chomsky's selective construct—goes further back in the Western tradition than most current discussions note. It goes back to Plato, to the culminating passage on knowledge near the end of Book VI of the *Republic*. The great model for "generative" theories is to be found in the exposition of the Divided Line, the first and most influential of philosophic diagrams.

Socrates. Of these two, one is ruler over the intelligible, the other (the sun) over the visible. . . . Represent them by a line cut into two unequal parts: the longer part for the intelligible, the shorter

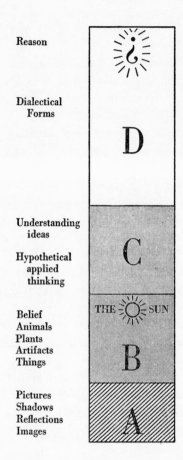

Reason

Dialectical
Forms

Understanding
ideas

Hypothetical
applied
thinking

Belief
Animals
Plants
Artifacts
Things

Pictures
Shadows
Reflections
Images

$$A:B::A+B::C+D::C:D$$

for the visible. Cut each of these parts again in the same proportion.

In the lower part of the lower division we will have shadows, images, pictures, of the *things* which are in its upper part.

In the lower part of the upper division the soul has to take the *things* in the division below as images (tokens, instances), from which it goes on to its conclusions. Though we talk of these tokens we are not thinking of *them,* but of the types they represent. Our questions are about the square itself *as such,* and the line across it from angle to angle, *as such*, not about any one picture we may make of it only. And so, throughout, these very things—which have their shadows and images in water—they take as in their turn only copies, and what they attempt to get at are their forms which are only to be seen by the mind.

Glaucon: True.

Socrates: In this division of the line we do have to do with ideas but with these two limits. First that the soul is forced to use bases or starting-points; it does not go on up to the first rule, for it is unable to escape from and get up higher than these starting-point bases; second, that it uses, as mere pictures or parallels, the very physical things which are themselves pictured and paralleled by the images in the sort lower down still. And in comparison with those, they are said to be very clear and are given a high position.

Glaucon: I see. You are still talking of what comes under geometry and the sister arts.

Socrates: And by the other, higher, division of thought you will see I mean that of which reasoning itself takes hold by the power of dialectic discussion. The things reasoning takes as bases are not taken by it as unquestioned starting-points, but as helps or stepping-stones, as something to give a footing, or as springboards, by which it is made able to go up to that which is no such base which needs to be taken, but is the first principle of everything. And after getting to that, it takes again a grip of the first things dependent on that, and goes down again to the outcome, making no use of any of the things of the senses but only of ideas themselves, moving on through ideas, and ending with ideas.[11]

No one with this in mind would undervalue Chomsky's insistance on the necessity for abstract entities in linguistic description, or his concern for principles from which the particularities of the speaker-hearer's performance derive. The morphemes, the words, the sentences . . . all the units which linguists take as tokens of the types with which they set up form classes: these "reasoning takes as bases," as hypotheses, "as helps or stepping-stones, as something to give a footing, or as springboards, by which it is made able to go on up to that . . ." on which all

depends. It is an antique and a most restorative aspiration, this
ascent to the source, but exposed ever to the old charge that "the
best is the enemy of the good" and to the admonition that the
philosopher has to "get used again to seeing in the dark" [12]
when he returns to his tasks in the Cave.

The history of Plato's diagram and of its explications deserves
far more detached study than it has had; not necessarily as a
means of illuminating, much less of incorporating, the Ultimate,
but as a step toward better mutual understanding. As with other
such mirrors of reflection the views that diverse thinkers have
derived from the Divided Line have been revealingly divided
themselves. They might have been far more revealing if the
thinkers had not so often attached themselves to, and annexed as
their own, interpretations which they then tried to promote and
defend as the only proper or permissible view. I do not know
whether anything in the least comparable to an application of
a Complementarity Principle [13] has ever been tried out in any
such linguistic situation: using different constructions of this
central and supreme speculative instrument with other speculative instruments in varying settings . . . in the hope of some
conjoint, some mutual and collective yield. Again, one must
wonder at, and lament, the fear of experiment that haunts
linguistics.

Chomsky does, indeed, refer from time to time to the Platonism
behind Leibniz and Cudworth, Herbert and Humboldt; but he
leaves it much at the rather dim level of "reminiscence without
pre-existence" and dodges past, so far as I can see, any recognition of the Platonic origins of the Forms. Not that it matters
who discovered or invented them, except in one respect: their
traditional (and natural) connections with theology and with
the soul—as that which can attain to knowledge of the *Forms,*
that which is in*formed* by them, that which, by them, can become
immortal and can even pass out of time into eternity.

A somewhat unfashionable range of views is reflected in the
phrasing of the last sentence; but it is being half-hearted—not

to say "being a trimmer"—to appeal to the tradition unless some sort of speculative concern is evinced as to its invitations. To come to generative theories via Plato himself, rather than via the Platonists in their various degrees, is to be forcibly and continuously reminded how very hard it is to prevent a doctrine that makes the capacity to acquire and handle language *innate* from developing into deeper doctrines which modern linguistics has been resolved to deny or, at least, avoid. What makes *Cartesian Linguistics* interesting as a phase in the war against positivist behaviorism and constituent analysis linguistics is its astute and skillful brinkmanship—the more interesting if unwitting. It comes so near to forming an alliance with the beliefs against which behaviorism was a not at all tacit offensive and toward which Chomsky's newer positions look like being a tacit retreat.

To limn this situation once again: Underlying the superficial structure of these pages is a deep structure (not in Chomsky's sense—and not all of it primarily cognitive in character). Whatever may be the degree of awareness of this in their author and his attached readers, in his detached readers their tacit competence will often enable them to perceive this deep structure with sufficient clarity and some of the links by which from that starry deep the superficial structure depends.

Similarly, underlying positivist behaviorism—but much less tacit or occluded—there is commonly a deep structure (again not primarily cognitive in nature) antagonistic to what it takes generative theory to be. And, so a detached observer surmises, it is from these deep antagonisms more than from any superficial differences in descriptive linguistics that contention is fed. Two rival ambitions are here at strife: to get rid [14] of ?what is not understood?; to improve comprehension of ?it?. The *its* in question, of course, keep changing. Meanwhile, in something of "a plague o' both your houses!" mood, a variegated set of Common Language philosophers, inspired in varying degree by a Cambridge 1910–25 fashion of pretending that "you don't read philosophy, you just do it" and animated by distastes for the claims and constraints alike of the sciences, have looked to their own highly developed verbal and logical acumen to provide them with an occupation, if not a career; with conveniently self-contained studies,[15] problems of the order of crossword puzzles, autonomous insulated subjects, gardens of their own, which they could cultivate aloof from and undisturbed by rumors of linguistic wars.

The cycle sketched in the foregoing paragraphs is deeply familiar to many. The tradition came to them, perhaps, most penetratingly through the Prayer Book:

Issues from the hand of God the simple soul.[16]

And however much in later life they may have been

Curled up behind the Encyclopedia

that first view, that first outfit of speculative instruments, remains for them more inviting, more compelling, more illuminating, at once more natural and more widely satisfying, than any other. It is the view, moreover, embodied in nearly the whole apparatus of reflection, *animating* all the questions it is most interesting and profitable to ask about one's *self*, a view which, unlike most others, gives one a real self to ask about and to ask, not in a technical terminology, but in the everyday and night language through which the poet, the prophet, the priest and the penitent in us all commune.

The traditional view, which is more or less Plato's, grafted onto Hosea-Jeremiah as a stock, is all but constantly active in common speech, all but omnipresent in personal pronouns and sentences which use them. The indwelling soul, as that which knows and wills and feels and acts and suffers, is built into theory of grammar in more ways than any rival constructs can possibly be. No amount of disowning or of good fun made about "pure humunculus theory" gets rid of it. Theoreticians of theory-construction may rebel, "abstracting away from many factors that interweave" *(Cartesian Linguistics,* Note 2), but if what has to be explained is common speech then the soul has to be taken account of. A generative theory of language (of those languages at the least in which Western Man's view of himself is incarnate) cannot do without a knower. It cannot handle any of the words which can replace *know* in "I —— that my soul liveth" or indeed any but sentences about neutral "its" and "theys." It cannot even say what grammarians should be doing. To be truly generative an account of language must find a supreme place for a knower down in the ultimate profundities of its deep structure.

This is not, of course, a proof of, or even an argument for, the necessity of a soul. These considerations may invite but do not require any such belief. They are a part, however, of the explanation of the resentment shown against common speech (and of some of the toadying to its less respectable manifestations) which has been so marked among positivist-behaviorist theorists of language. The unfair advantages of a theological inside track are indeed provoking. Moreover, and this was more often the major consideration, this 'knower' so snugly ensconced in the very heart of the subject is so pathetically fallible, so groundlessly confident, so often and so evidently mistaken. The privileges and pretensions of introspection are so immense, its punditry so arrogant, its fraudulence sometimes so patent, its equivocations often so bare that Behaviorism was perhaps inevitable.

In all this the interweavings of other factors, other ambitions than the academic should be noted. As the possibilities of the computer, of automation and of data-processing were increasingly recognized, their techniques developed, and their military significance appreciated, wishes for a comparable linguistic engineering became pressing. And not only in the hope of soon attaining practicable machine translation but for other communication problems as well. The amount of recent work in linguistics—especially on theories of grammar and, of late, semantics—which has been supported by the Signal Corps, the

Army, the Air Force, the Navy and the National Science Foundation tells its own story. This question of the source of the wherewithal can be important. Those who supply the necessary funds may reasonably expect to receive in return something which really looks like value for their money. Those who endeavor to produce this not unnaturally assume the appropriate professional manner. Much of their most intent reading has, for many of them, been in a literature composed for these patrons. The importance of the ⁿᵇrightⁿᵇ stance, the right lingo, the right resource is well understood by experts "expert beyond experience" in every field.

Among these resources one in particular is noticeable enough in modern linguistics to deserve comment. As most examiners well know, when a question has been asked and the examinee hasn't an answer, an account (the lengthier and the more elaborate the better) of some conditions any answer must manage to meet can often earn a good mark. It looks at least like a step in the right direction and toward something. Hence, if I mistake not, some of the recent prominence in linguistics of theorizing on theory-construction—theory cubed, at least, and to higher powers sometimes—given as much mathematical style as may be. Math is the Queen now to the patrons as Theology was in monastic days. We may note, however, the obscuration, the doubts below the dazzle of the panache, the occultation of assumptions, the palming of the point . . . with which premature mathematical treatment has often, ever since Plato, troubled thought about language.

Another source of unreality in much contemporary linguistics is timidity in facing up to the problem of ʾthe linguistic community ʾ. This phrase, if we took it literally, would ask us to assume that all the hearers-speakers we are considering as belonging to it are alike in their linguistic behavior in all relevant ways. Any close and alert examination of perhaps any linguistic community can show, from indisputable factual record, so much variation in regard to almost any linguistically interesting fea-

ture of this behavior that the phrase ¹linguistic community¹ takes
on a sardonic air. This is an actuality we have many strong
motives for minimizing; to keep up our *morale* we have to pretend a good deal of our time that mutual understanding is occurring when we really know very well that it isn't; really close
and deep accord in interpretation is unusual and astonishing;
communication so far as it succeeds deceives us as to its failures;
meditation upon the matter can induce a melancholy and a
sense of loneliness; and if we speak or write about it we will incur
charges of morbidity and exaggeration. Nonetheless, a critical
study will show that degrees of efficiency in any but trivial communications are as stated.

It is notable that the sentences grammarians use as specimens
in their expositions are usually such as are little likely to be
misinterpreted. And where they do touch upon ambiguity there
is commonly an eccentricity and artificiality in the examples
which may be symptomatic. The real hazards of language are
conspicuously *not* represented. Samples taken from political,
moral, religious, methodological *and linguistic* discussion would
give a very different impression. Studies of language which avoid
dealing with those features of language which have been most
frustrating to our efforts to inquire into our deepest needs may
justly be described as superficial. And this in the face of innumerable and ever-increasing practical needs to clarify and try
to remedy our multiplying misunderstandings, at a time when
there are clear risks of our cultures falling apart. The most indispensable efforts of education are in fact addressed to lowering
these probabilities of misapprehension. We should not forget how
much of the justification of linguistic studies is to be found in
the improved communication to which—it has been hoped—they
may lead.

Let us look then at how linguistics has been handling its task
of selecting the hearers-speakers whose verbal conduct it aims
to study. Two opposed tendencies may be remarked. On the
one hand there are those who have become interested in differ-

ences and have inquired into the variants of spoken and written utterance and (to a less degree) of comprehension or interpretation in the recipients. These variants, as we all know, arise through many circumstances. There are as many dialects— regional, occupational, social, cultural—as you have the patience to distinguish and the energy to order through your type-specimens and descriptions. Many individuals operate in a number of such dialects: classroom, at home, with the gang and so on. These circumstantial variations, which commonly go along with switches in gesture and port, are often called *registers*. Expressions and responses suited to one occasion are unsuited to another.

Look closer, consider as minutely as you can how individuals differ one from another and not least in how they distinguish between occasions. It is a slogan in contemporary linguistics, endlessly re-echoed, that language is 'creative',[17] that people are incessantly saying things that no one has said before, instead of merely repeating phrases they have heard. Go over some of your acquaintances in imagination and listen to a selection of TV ads (or try a Pinter play), and wonder to what extent that is true of which of them. Here is another respect in which *ideolects* (as linguists name the tacit competences of individual hearers-speakers) differ. Anyone who has been a teacher or a clinician or an administrator knows how deeply hearers-speakers differ not only from one another but day by day and hour by hour from themselves. We need, in fact, to extrapolate the series: *Language, Dialect, Register, Ideolect,* and to supply some name for the momentary competence of an individual within a specific ambiance of circumstances. (Would *Compos* conceivably meet this need? X's *compos* then would theoretically range from that of Shakespeare penning *The Phoenix and the Turtle* down to that of the autistic child achieving his first uses of language.)

Against this background of diversity of competences what do the systematic theorists, exponents of the converse tendency, do? They invent a remarkable construct, highly abstract and only after some reflection identifiable, which they refer to as "a fluent speaker." [18] I do not know who invented this remarkable figure or why he is called "fluent" rather than "preternatural." On page 481 of *Structure of Language,* by J. A. Fodor and J. J. Katz, he is thus described. Note that he is introduced as though he were a real person and not a figment. But clearly he is a concoction on the lines of a frictionless inclined plane or a perfect gas—not to say a perfect gas-bag.

"A fluent speaker's mastery of his language exhibits itself in his ability to produce and understand the sentences of his language, *including indefinitely many that are wholly novel to him* (i.e., his ability to produce and understand *any* sentence of his language)." The italics are theirs. They add in a footnote, "There are exceptions, such as technical words that the speaker does not know, sentences too long for the speaker to scan in his lifetime and so on," which lets us see with what concern for actuality the writers are conceiving their subject. Probably "wholly" in *"wholly novel"* is due just to carelessness, to inattention to the essentials. Anyone faced with a sentence wholly novel to him is in the position of the beginner in a new language who has met none of its words before nor any of the constructions in which they are being used. It is fun to imagine this fluent speaker producing and understanding such sentences so freely. The weasel word here may be "his" in "his language." That could contract the segment of the language he is so skilled in to just those sentences, few or many, that he *can* produce and understand. Notice further the assumption in "produce and understand" that of course this gifted chap can compose anything that he can comprehend. If he can understand Shakespeare he can write like him, can he? A semantic theory that ignores the differences between passive and active competence as well as the problems of degrees of understanding is a revealing exhibit.

I have lingered over this crazy construct, the *fluent speaker,* because it illustrates the abstract unreality of much modern theorizing, and may remind us of the ease with which an artificial set of problems can be substituted for those that are professedly under study. This fluent one, as he is described, corresponds to nothing. In practice, however, his description would probably come down to something like this: "A speaker who can produce and understand (more or less) any sentence which we, the authors, are going to use *as specimens* in our pages."

But this, it will be felt, is hardly adequate as a key construct with reference to which a theory undertakes "to determine what mechanisms a semantic theory employs in reconstructing the speaker's ability to interpret sentences in isolation." [19] This sounds a tall-enough order to deserve a better construct. How can we build one?

The authors' theory takes us first to !"an accurate dictionary"! and thence (via an inadequately designed "mechanical" computer) to ?"rules"?. We shall see that the first of these steps is necessary and helpful, the last misleading and confusing. Let us first consider what a dictionary already is and what it can become. Then we will turn to ?rules? and to ?know?. These are two words with huge roles in recent linguistics and yet in few of the contributions at present influential are they treated as though they veiled any threats of confusion.

Modern dictionaries exemplify at their best the advantages of systematic, controlled comparison carried on by many successive observers as a procedure for arriving at trustworthy corroboration. When not so happy they present in succinct and questionable form examples of failings that more successful work has somehow overcome. In both the reliable entry and the defective, what they offer is an *outcome,* the record of a judgment that has been checked again and again. Of the processes by which the judgment is arrived at from the materials we are commonly told nothing—though a dictionary editor may have opportunities less open to others. *Anyone, however, who uses a dictionary in a critical and deliberative spirit himself in a varying degree proceeds much as have his predecessors who have drafted and/or checked an entry.* He has less work to do but it is work of the same sort. To illustrate: He has, let us say, a sentence in mind not yet finally written. Let us say the above italicized sentence, *Anyone* to *entry*. At certain points in it, say those occupied now by *proceeds* and *predecessors,* he wonders whether he is managing to say, as fully and as safeguardedly as he can, what he has in mind to say. Note that he must consider (1) the unfinalized sentence, (2) the discourse including both what has already been said *and* what he proposes to say later, and (3) a series of concentric fields of relevance [20] of which the word under consideration is the center. Influences from any part of this hierarchical ambiance may at any time intervene in the guiding of the choice of a word. What may be the nature or status of this highly systematic ambiance—so determinative, so unformulated and yet so open to exploration through suitably controlled collective inquiry— is among the great challenges to a linguistics of the near future. Here, at *proceeds,* the following alternative candidates were considered:

> goes through a performance . . .
> goes through processes . . .
> is replicating work . . .
> is repeating work . . .

Some of these were rejected before the dictionary came in; the consultation merely reinforced perceptions already decisive:

performance   too strong a component of public display, etc.; these activities are private.

processes   too open to "mechanical" implications, to suggestions of routine successive operations, etc. These are flexible and responsible *acts.*

With the next two, the dictionary entries alerted objections which had not yet fully awakened:

replicating   the etymology (*re + plicare,* to fold) too ready to revive. Also too close to *reply,* and to *replica* with their suggestions of "response" and of "reproduce."

repeat   too dreary a suggestion of "do it again" as in drill and
                a suggestion of classroom reciting and "repeat after
                me."

The final choice of *proceeds* was again made before the dictionary was consulted. Confirmation was clear and further advantage,
not previously thought of, was added. Let me quote the entry
in *Webster's New Collegiate:*

1. To move, pass, or go forward or onward; to advance. 2. To issue
or come forth as from a source or origin; to come (*from*). 3. To go on
in an orderly or regular manner; to prosecute a design.

All three headings converged and united in support of the choice.
The second member of 3—it could well have been headed 4—
and 2 were the additions. When we look up a word there is
an outcoming as from a source in the consulter and there is *a
design to be furthered.*

So *proceeds* was the right word. We may note that it is right
by a union of a plurality of senses. People so often seem to suppose that a word *in use* should not have more than one sense
that this seems worth noting. On the other hand, so many of
the imitators of William Empson seem to think that *every* sense
a word or morph may carry can validly work at full blast wherever it occurs that an opposing note may be sounded.

A further point, of greater theoretical consequence, should be
raised here. The sentence as first written read: "is himself . . .
proceeding" for "himself . . . proceeds." The switch is not
merely grammatical but semantic too: *proceeds* carries much
more sense of activity than *is proceeding* (with which he might
be on an assembly-line bench; compare *procedures* with *processes*). The more closely we consider any sentence that is saying
anything dependent on what has come before it and/or of any
consequence for what may be to come, the more intimately interwoven [21] are grammatical form and semantic import. It is
only by using exorbitant and inapplicable definitions for ?gram-
mar?, ?grammarian?, ?describe?, and ?setting?—on the lines of that

offered for ?fluent speaker?—that such claims as the following can be made: "Grammars seek to describe the structure of a sentence *in isolation from its possible settings in linguistic discourse (written or verbal) or in nonlinguistic contexts (social or physical).*" [22] Ask how the necessary comparisons can arise or can be carried through without consideration of possible settings or how anyone acquires or employs a language, and the heroic degree of this eviscerative abstraction becomes evident. The mummies that result have no communication. Only that fluent speaker, I fear, could have converse with them. The authors explain: "The justification . . . is simply that the fluent speaker is able to construct and recognize syntactically well-formed sentences without recourse . . ." etc. A theory of the construction of semantic theories which displays as a banner heading:

LINGUISTIC DESCRIPTION MINUS GRAMMAR
EQUALS SEMANTICS

is not reassuring. It hardly leads us to expect penetration. What we find are other fancy constructs, *e.g.,* persons who do not speak English but are equipped with a completely adequate grammar of English. This again may make us wonder how theories with such slight relation to actuality can be helpful.

With *predecessors* some questions rather less frequently relevant in dictionary making came up:

(1) Its relation to *decease.* How lively might be the suggestion that those "who have drafted and/or checked the entry" must be dead or at least retired? This was complicated in this instance for this writer by his having previously played somewhat elaborately with these verbal relations in Section IV, verse 5 of his "Birthday Thoughts": [23]

> Predecessors (take heed)
> Need no more be dead
> Than successors succeed:
> Seed ill-sped.

Analogous problems come up for dictionary makers whenever the comprehension of a set of words may be affected by the engagement of one or more of them in a special context.

(2) Co-occurrence of "proceeds" and "predecessors" in this sentence was encouraged by the reversal in *decess* of *ceeds,* which might mirror the reversal of activity in the maker and the user of a dictionary. The relation of *pro* to *pre* might also come in. Such *poetic* [24] determinants dictionary makers must also be ready, if need be, to observe.

The dictionary *user* is concerned with comparing words as to what they may do (their *work*) in a given sentence or in sentences which are its approximate paraphrases. The dictionary *makers* have a wider task: to compare, distinguish and relate the work of words as they occur in collections of sentences each of which will have some appreciable degree of dependence upon its surrounding discourse and frequently upon the ampler ambiance mentioned earlier. For example, the speaker, the audience, the date . . . will often be important—though this will vary greatly with the discourse (or composition). Coleridge defines a poem as "containing *in itself* the reason why it is so and not otherwise." [25] On the other hand, when Winston Churchill speaks of "empires of the mind" [26] we have to take much more than the rest of the sentence and the rest of the discourse into account in arriving at an interpretation of either of those nouns.

At present the development of dictionary making is entering an extremely interesting phase. The mechanical means of data-collection and data-processing are far enough advanced to make it certain that they can soon more than adequately serve any demands that the lexicographer can reasonably make of them. The shortage is in lexicographers, patrons (and advisers to patrons) interested in what these reasonable demands should be. Some part, no doubt, of the motivation behind modern linguistics— of perhaps all the varieties—has been to help toward more informed and more judicious understanding of what might be done toward better dictionaries (and better use of them) through the aid of these machines. But for the most part other aims have overlaid these.

It is hard to sketch what might now be done without being charged with taking to science fiction. Suffice it to say that the machines already can do enough to allow the editors to record for systematic re-examination, consultation, amendment, corroboration, not only their outcome decisions but the relevant considerations guiding these decisions. Work so carried on could, even at current competence levels—which might well be expected to be raised thereby—soon yield us something approximating to the need for a construct that "fluent speaker" could not meet: *the language,* lexicologically regarded.

It might be well to begin such an undertaking with a fairly small trial-run using a few very highly qualified editors and limiting the vocabulary they would chiefly study to a selection of the words most likely to be most useful in describing relations between meanings. The inquiry would thus start off with an intensive examination of the verbal instruments through which the work of analysis, comparison, coordination and arrangement (as well as the description of this work) would have to be conducted. Among such words two of the more important would be *know* and *rule*—to which we will now turn.

One type-specimen will suffice for a frequent use of these two words in recent linguistics. I take it from our devout Chomskyans:

"Transformational grammars answer the question, What does the speaker *know* about the phonological and syntactic structure of his language which enables him to use and understand any of its sentences, including those he has never previously heard? They do so by providing *rules* which generate the sentences of the speaker's language." [27] (My italics.)

Alack! It must be remarked that there is no such knowledge and that no such rules have been provided. Ponce de Leon seeking the Fountain of Youth was realistically employed, compared with anyone looking for such a speaker. Nor are such transformational grammars any easier to find. They have been hoped for and promised. They are not at work answering any questions, possible or absurd, or providing any such rules. There are those who would say that both the quoted statements are, to put it mildly, exaggerations. But this would be poor interpretation. It is fairer to say simply that they are not in fact statements at all, but programatical antics: boosting and prophecy about something which (it is supposed, probably erroneously) someone may some time supply.

With our authors' mantram here compare Chomsky: "In fact, almost all questions concerning generative capacities of transformational grammars and realistic models for the speaker or hearer who *uses such a grammar,* remain completely open and, in fact, can scarcely be posed, without further clarification of the concepts involved." [28] (My italics.) One step toward such further clarification would be to take seriously the question: "What is *uses such a grammar* here talking about?" Is it about someone who is trying to use some "description of the tacit competence of the speaker-hearer" or about someone exercising that tacit competence itself? The most seductive and most elementary of all confusions (that between a description and what it describes) seems not far off here.

That this is not an accidental slip-of-the-pen (or thought) matter, but something more indicative is supported by: "The goal of a traditional grammar is *to provide its user with the ability* to understand an arbitrary sentence of the language and to form and employ it properly on the appropriate occasion. Thus its goal is (at least) as far reaching as that of a generative grammar, as just described." [29] Here it seems clear that the user being talked about *is* a person who has to be provided with an ability (competence) he did not have before, that traditional grammar claimed to be able to do this (with rules memorized from a grammar book, *the rest of the learner's activity being ignored*); and that a generative grammar would not repudiate an at least partially similar aim.

How strange it is that this latest great attempt to elucidate and redirect the goal of 'grammar' should so stir the suspicion that the desiderated description is being taken as able to play deputy for the very thing it professedly hopes to describe! Traditional grammar, pedagogically, inculcated this confusion. Indeed, it trod, stamped and beat it in. We do not yet widely enough realize how revolutionary a liberation is proposed by an *exploratory* technique for learning. It is perhaps not surprising if even the most enlightened modern grammarians do not altogether escape from the reverberations and obfuscations of the torment-haunted classroom of the good old times. Is it immoderate to compare this professionally supported usurpation by *an account* of the powers of *that of which it would be an account* with even the most extreme instances of this indeed classic mistake? The substitution of the grammar book for competence may—in its millenniary continuances—have been, and *may still be,* as unfortunate for man as even ancient Egypt's confusion of the mummy and its picture-galleries with the actualities they replaced.[30]

That too was an enormous mistake, occasionally producing great art, but how much more, century after century, of miserably misdirected and blind industry and spirit-breaking toil. And that too came from a professionally maintained illusion.

Some Glances at Current Linguistics

(1) *Euthyphro:* see *Why So, Socrates?*, dramatic version by I. A. Richards (Cambridge University Press, 1964), p. 14.

(2) All this is discussed from a supporter's angle by Paul M. Postal, "Limitations of Phrase Structure Grammars" in *Structure of Language: Readings in the Philosophy of Language,* Jerry A. Fodor and Jerrold J. Katz, Editors (New York, Prentice-Hall, 1964), and in "Underlying and Superficial Linguistic Structure," *Harvard Educational Review,* Spring 1964. Full references will be found in these accounts.

(3) *at pains to snort:* See "Current Issues in Linguistic Theory," Mouton, The Hague, 1964, p. 25 (reprinted in *Structure of Language,* p. 61). "The equally strange and factually quite incorrect view that current work in generative grammar is in some way an outgrowth of attempts to use electronic computers for one or another purpose, whereas in fact it should be obvious that its roots are firmly in traditional linguistics." The two, however, are not incompatible. It remains true that very much of this "current work in generative grammar" has been "supported in part by the U.S. Army Signal Corps, The Air Force Office of Scientific Research, and the Office of Naval Research" and/or by grants of similar origin. (See *Structure of Language,* items: 3, 4, 5, 9, 10, 15, 19, 20, 23.) Whether the Armed Forces will get their hoped-for return from this investment may well be doubted.

(4)   Chomsky, *op. cit.,* pp. 9–10 (*Structure of Language,* pp. 51–52).

(5)   *meta-semantic:* All must admit that when language tries to talk about language—in this extremely *general* fashion —problems arise which language, at present, is far from being able to state or to solve.

(6)   *Sixth Annual Report,* 1965–66, The Center for Cognitive Studies, p. 4 and p. 19.

(7)   I. A. Richards, *Basic in Teaching: East and West,* 1935, pp. 9–10.

(8)   *Cartesian Linguistics* (New York, Harper and Row, 1966).

(9)   *Competence:* All the words which will substitute for this on most occasions have similar equivocation. It seems possible, and perhaps likely, that to object to them (as Chomsky does) is to overween—to ask more from our thought and language than it can give us. We may very well doubt if we can do without the meanings which these words attempt to handle for us. They concern our notion of being. In Plato's *Sophist* (247E) the Stranger from Elea suggests a description of the real: "I suggest that anything has real being, that is so constituted as to possess any sort of power either to affect anything else or to be affected, in however small a degree, by the most insignificant agent, though it be only once. I am proposing as a mark to distinguish real things, that they are nothing but power." See Francis Cornford, *Plato's Theory of Knowledge* (New York, The Humanities Press), p. vii and pp. 234–239. He points out that this rendering is itself doubtful, the construction being obscure and difficult.

  Dynamis, the key word, includes, he notes, passive susceptibility as well as active ability. It can thus cover all transactions between ?things? and there is a tendency, as Cornford's discussion shows, for *dynamis* to take over and leave *being* nothing more to do than to be a locus for

dynameis. It is interesting to see something similar occurring today in sub-microscopic physics. For example, "Perhaps, at last, man is probing to that level of understanding where there is no clear distinction between what is
and what happens, where the components of the world
and the interaction of these components are indistinguish-
able ideas." Kenneth W. Ford, *The World of Elementary
Particles* (New York, Blaisdell, 1963).

(10)   *covertly contending:* sometimes, however, openly. It is
       part of Chomsky's merit that he occasionally lifts the latch
       of the cupboard door behind which the skeleton lurks.

(11)   *ending with ideas: Republic,* VI, 511.

(12)   *"get used again to seeing in the dark": Republic,* VII,
       520C.

(13)   *Complementarity Principle:* In "Toward a More Synoptic
       View," *Speculative Instruments,* I have discussed some of
       the reasons why people have been slow to admit, or, rather,
       to *realize* persistently, that their own concepts are intel-
       lectual instruments which inevitably shape and limit the
       inquiries they are engaged in. As a reminder of this con-
       dition and as ᵗspringboardᵗ, a collection of interpretations
       of the Divided Line might serve excellently to prepare for
       a more self-critical reconsideration of the varieties of
       ᵗknowledgeᵗ.

(14)   *get rid:* Compare Skinner's ʳmay be dismissedʳ, see page 13.
       As to improving ᵗcomprehension of what is not under-
       stoodᵗ:

> You cannot see the seer of seeing
> or hear the hearer of hearing
> or think the thinker of thought
> or know the knower.
> He is your self that lives in the hearts of all.
> —Brihadaranyaka-Upanishad

(15) *self-contained studies:* "A certain academic dryness, a deliberate rejection of the literary and dramatic, that is for the most part the style of this philosophy." Introduction to *British Analytical Philosophy*, Bernard Williams and Alan Montefiore, Editors (New York, The Humanities Press, 1966), p. 12.

(16) *the simple soul: Animula*, T. S. Eliot.

(17) *'creative':* Chomsky seems to be wincing a little from this reverberation when he justly remarks: "One would not refer to an act as 'creative' simply on the basis of its novelty and independence of identifiable drives or stimuli." What is much needed here is a clear discussion of novelty in utterances, its kinds and degrees.

(18) *"a fluent speaker":* See "The Structure of a Semantic Theory" in *Structure of Language*.

(19) *in isolation: Structure of Language,* p. 491. The phrase 'in isolation' as here used needs expansion. It may mean ᔆʷwithout any apparently helpful actual settingᔆʷ. The authors have been discussing an anonymous letter containing only a single sentence. With this construct they seem to suppose that they have eliminated influence of setting. But have they? In practice (in a way which is most relevant to theory) an anonymous letter is a powerful setting in itself. It puts the reader to work imagining possible composers, etc., and trying to select from among them. A scrap of paper blown off a dump will do the same to a less degree. There are, as most people well know, systematic resources, available to utterers and receivers alike, which supply conjectural settings when needed and supplement normally sufficient settings as required. And, though these authors argue to the contrary, a communicator's "ability to interpret sentences" is very largely his ability to make judicious choices from among such alternative possible settings. All this reliable common knowl-

edge, which could supply solid ground for an account of
how people do in fact come to understand, more or less,
what others say to them (and of how they in turn manage
to say things to others) is here summarily brushed off for
the sake of that fluent speaker.

(20)   *concentric fields of relevance:* I have discussed this, as far
as I can see into it, in "Dependence of Thought on Its
Milieu" in *Speculative Instruments.* Perhaps the sentences
here most relevant are, "However, the general popular
picture of the mathematical forest—the explanatory proposals competing for the sunshine of experimental support—may long continue. . . . But there is no creed and
no administrative headquarters, no court of last appeal,
no focus of authority for science. In this it resembles its
own current picture of the cosmos much more than any
edifice."

(21)   *intimately interwoven:* Compare Chomsky. "In general,
as syntactic description becomes deeper, what appear to
be semantic questions fall increasingly within its scope."
See "Current Issues," p. 51, in *Structure of Language,* p.
77. Compare with this: LINGUISTIC DESCRIPTION MINUS GRAM-
MAR EQUALS SEMANTICS, p. 483. What has happened here
to phonology as well as to grammar and to semantics?

(22)   Fodor and Katz, *op. cit.,* p. 484.

(23)   *The Screens and Other Poems,* p. 18.

(24)   See Roman Jakobson, "Linguistics and Poetry," in *Style
in Language,* Thomas A. Sebeok, Ed. (Cambridge, M.I.T.),
pp. 353–357, where he lays out his schema of the determinants of language. His *type* specimen of the poetic deter-
minant there is "I like Ike."

(25)   *why it is so and not otherwise: Biographia Literaria.*

(26)   *"empires of the mind":* See "Meanings Anew."

(27)   Fodor and Katz, *op. cit.,* p. 483.

(28)   Final sentence of "On the Notion of a Rule of Grammar."
       This is one of the more liberating of Chomsky's disa-
       vowals—worthy almost of Socrates himself. It sets us hap-
       pily back at where the inquiry should truly be beginning.

(29)   "Current Issues," p. 16. (My italics.)

(30)   *actualities they replaced:* "It was the king's duty to ensure
       prosperity for Egypt. He saw to this both by good govern-
       ment and by the ritual carried out in the temples. As he
       could not personally officiate at these rites throughout
       Egypt, his presence *was assured by* the reliefs on the walls
       of every temple, showing him carrying out the office." (My
       italics.) Jean-Louis de Cenival, *Living Architecture:
       Egyptian* (New York, Grosset and Dunlap, 1964), p. 55.
           This is from a sympathetic account. To a less friendly
       eye, the effigy as a substitute for reality will not do: "But
       if death mocks at the infantile fantasy of absolute power,
       which the human machine promised to actualize, life
       mocks at it even more. The notion of eternal life, with
       neither conception, growth, fruition or decay: an existence
       as fixed, as sterilized, as unchanging as that of the royal
       mummy, is only death in another form." Lewis Mum-
       ford, "The First Megamachine," *Diogenes,* Fall 1966.
       The royal mummy called for the Pyramid to protect
       the auto-icon and for the cave-tomb with its extravaga-
       tions of make-believe. And these did not work even at
       their own pathetic level. Thanks to the tomb robber,
       hardly a Pharaoh remained undespoiled. As *Don Juan* has
       it:

> Let not a monument give you or me hopes
> Since not a pinch of dust remains of Cheops.

There are as solid reasons for thinking that the Grammar book too—however grandly extravagated—will not
work either.

It will be recalled that, for Chomsky, the child, *in some*

sense, somehow constructs the grammar of his language for himself. This powerful metalinguistic expression, *in some sense,* is found handy again here: "How Rameses would have relished this situation. . . . Hydrofoils, air-conditioned ships and people from the far corners of the earth, all coming to pay homage to the vast memorial. In a sense, he does indeed live again." William McQuitty, *Abu Simbel* (New York, Putnam, 1965), p. 162.

5

Meanings Anew

In thinking about anything so central as our meanings we should encourage ourselves to take a variety of views from different distances and angles and to arrange them so that they supplement and clarify one another. This is hardly our usual practice, thinkers being more in the habit of behaving as though if one view is right any other views which "differ from it" must be wrong. No doubt in some fields that customary practice is useful, but not in considering how we should consider; for that is what we will be trying to do here under the heading "Meanings Anew."

This then will be a view—one of many different views, some others of which may be found in remarks or in assumptions made elsewhere in these essays. These are, I conceive, compatible, but no explicit attempt is made here to compare, to relate, to adjust and reconcile them one to another. That they will appear to conflict may be supposed. We would have to know very little about meanings and about how language represents them to expect otherwise. These other views have arisen in various connections, as serving, they hoped, this or that local endeavor. Any view is shaped by its connections though for convenience we often forget this. What follows is less tied to local service and more responsible to wider claims. It aspires to ask for more detachment, less engagement, and tries to remember as it proceeds that, if so, it has the freedom of a sketch.

Any word as it occurs *livingly* in a sentence that is occurring
livingly in a discourse may be questioned in three ways:

A. As to its interplay as a sound with the sounds of other
words.

B. As to its interplay as a syntactic item with other syntactic
items.

C. As to its interplay as a semantic agent with other semantic
agents.

These three systems of interplay settle the role of the word in
serving the sentence as that sentence is serving the situation.[1]

A. This interplay differentiates the word from others and enables it *as sound* to serve B and C. It is an interplay not only
with other words co-occuring with it in the sentence and in the
discourse but with all other words from which *for its work in
the sentence* it needs to be differentiated and to which it needs
to be related. It will do no harm here if we conceive a word's
work in a discourse on the analogy of an individual's work in
an enterprise. The character of the word as sound may be compared to the *appearance* of a worker, its distinguishability from
the appearance of other workers. One's appearance *can* have, as
not only ambassadors know, more than a little relation with the
work he can do.

B. Syntactic interplay too can be approached through an analogy—with such organization of cooperations as is needed on a
ship or in a business. Different word classes and phrase, group,
clause structures have their duties to and requirements from
one another, all ultimately deriving from and sanctioned by the
work to be done through their cooperations. Any sentence (*in a
discourse*) has its assignment. To fulfil this an internal organization of its components is required. Which of the many possible
organizations it adopts for the job in hand is settled by the convergence of a prodigiously, indeed an unimaginably, complex
set of determinants offering patterns formerly used in more or
less parallel situations in the past. These may be called *Context
Pressures* (in the sense of ᴿcontextᴿ defined in Appendix B of

The Meaning of Meaning). Another label for these might be *precedents*. Given a sort of work to be done, *how* that sort of work has previously been done naturally comes in, just as it does in any action, such as putting on a shoe. There is therefore much seemingly mechanical compulsion in syntactic interplay. The individual words participating in a sentence may all be changed while the structure of the team (their mutual dependencies) is the same. Syntactical necessities (such as, say, noun-verb accord as to singular and plural: "He eats" but "They eat") are imposed on a *growing* sentence by context pressure [2] from the enormous body of previous situations so handled. This pressure is represented in precedence routines that manage such demands. *His* language (the competence of his ideolect), for any user of it, is the operative system of precedents he has acquired through his traffic in it with other users. The confirmatory and suppressive effects of that traffic vary greatly from user to user and from hour to hour. Hence different degrees of ability in language use. (It is much to be wished that theorists about language would afford themselves more opportunity for reflective study of early stages in the acquisition not only of first but of second languages by variously situated individuals.)

Syntactically, for most hearers-speakers, a person's language is a system of choices and entailments which he accepts as his only means of pursuing the verbal tasks (and indulgences) offered to him. Usually, in conversation and in impromptu speaking he only fulfils syntactic requirements to a socially tolerable degree often relatively low—as anyone will agree who has listened to tape recordings of his own performances in what he had hoped were accomplished speeches. When, moreover, he has propitious conditions and something sufficiently unusual to say, he is capable of departing wildly from syntactic routine. We should remember, though, that any grammarian is under severe pressure from his profession to assume (and find) as much autonomous necessity in his subject as he can.

C. The corresponding analogy for semantic interplay would

point simply to all the tasks there can be [3] for any enterprise to attempt.

As a semantic agent a word in a sentence is participating in one of those attempts; using its sound, when and as that can help, and its syntax, its powers over and subordination to the other words in the sentence, as these can help. But beyond all that it has its own third world of interplay: with the *situation* within which it is used, with whatsoever perceptions and associations and cognitive schemas are characterizing that situation *and* other situations to which it stands in opposition and in relevant connection; with other words, phrases, clauses, of its own sentence and of other sentences in the discourse; and with words, etc., in other discourses: with all this and much more wheresoever. All these partners in the vast interplay we may conceive as being in various degrees alerted, prepared to have their participation tried out: held in reserve or allowed to step in. What accords or denies them this chance is the failure or success of the momentary phase of the attempt. And often this phase will be little more than a tentative exploration (to see how it might go) of some preliminary to or corrective of an experimental move in what may be only a trial of a tactical device, as helpful or not in a stratagem which itself is only a possibility being tested as to its contribution to a larger strategic scheme in the balance with others while the design and choice of the over-all campaign yet waits on the local outcomes. In brief, all degrees of complexity of any task may be reflected in the semantic interplay implicit in the weighing of a word. Those with any lively awareness of the intricacy of their own verbal choices tend to grow impatient of oversimple accounts.

This task-reflection and task-handling is both helped and hindered by the syntactic interplay. For the phase in hand the operation tries out sentence forms much as it might try out possible handlings of the task; and the sentence form on trial can have strong influence on—sometimes amounting to control over—more than the mere phase in hand. It can open up, and close down, ranges of possibility of handling. We all know—and the formal routines of administrative communications (officialese) show—how shifting from the active into the passive may enable us to dodge a problem. Compare

> *The (?) sabotaged the scheme*
> *The scheme was sabotaged.*

The passive lets us get on with our account or theory without having to face up to the task of saying who did the sabotaging. Yet it may be important at that point to be explicit and to recognize then and there how much the speaker is or is not able to say.

The interferences and facilitations of both *syntactic* and *sound* patterns are brought out very clearly in the writing of verse, especially verse with an exacting meter and rhyme scheme. Your choice of a rhyme (which you may have to abandon as impracticable) determines, while you keep it, narrow classes of words as alone possible at precisely defined further points. This both limits your search for solutions and suggests possibilities which would never otherwise have come up for consideration. In trying them out syntactic resource is suppled up and extended. It has the metrical demands to meet too. The local phase may thus direct the entire poem, if the poem lets it. The struggle in such composition between over-all, intermediate and local design can become very apparent. (This is the most respectable reason for the collecting of first drafts and manuscripts of poems in progress.) What is manifest then is the interplay—semantic, syntactic, phonetic—which is active, if in less evident degree, in all use of language. It is with this in mind that we can now approach the question of efficiency in language.

Traditional assumptions, even though most language users know better, are often distorting—as in the rejection by many "generative grammarians" of all sorts of sentences which an ordinarily resourceful speaker can easily imagine as being highly efficient in the right setting and situation. Specialist training and

preoccupation can develop a marked professional disqualification [4] here, due largely to the hangover from the dominion
of the grammar master, and also to the hunger the grammarian
suffers for some mode of controlling language which will spare
him from going into the truly ?generative? question, Who, in
what situation, is here talking to whom and trying to say what?
Anything, however remote from actualities, rather than ask
THAT. It is this shrinking which develops artificially abstractive
concepts of grammar. It combines with the traditional training
of grammarians.

Historically, syntax developed first; phonologic and semantic
studies (under those names) are latecomers. Even very up-to-date
treatments of linguistic theory as a whole still commonly take
syntax as the prime problem, leaving the sounds and the meanings of sentences to be somehow, as subordinate matters, adjusted, tucked into grammatical formulations. But, in the normal
case, we speak to say something; and what we have in mind to
say shapes what we say, within, normally, an accepted grammatical structuring. *In written prose,* especially in what we are likely
to call formal prose, the structures that grammarians have long
ago described (and canonized) still rule ("as a rule"). We fit
what we have to say into them. But in verse, in poetic utterance,
as in its contrary—random, informal improvisation—other structures very frequently are chosen as being more suitable and efficient, as managing the appropriate requirements and exclusions
as to meaning better than a more explicit handling. In much
speech that is under high pressure, practical conditions, urgen-
cies, needs . . . disallow conventional prose structures ("talking
like an *old* book") and prefer structures better adapted to the
actual aims and situation. They can also, of course, be worse
adapted and fail, as with incomprehensible ejaculations. In
air-ground communications the need for precision, succinct-
ness, clarity and absence of ambiguity has led to the development
of a highly formalized and artificial exchange of locutions. Such
forms are misrepresented if we blanket them as agrammatical, or

as exceptions, breakdowns, relaxations, licenses, departures from grammar. When they work well they are merely other grammatical arrangements better suited, in the situation, to the service of the dictating meaning than the conventional written prose arrangements would be. The point is that if we can conceive the situation fully and accurately enough we will find the justification for the grammatical structure to derive almost always from its service to the semantic aims of the utterance.[5] Some semantic aims are, for safety, convenience and economy in operation, conventionalized. For *them* it is safe, convenient and economical to use conventional routines of expression. Other semantic aims, being different, are better served by other, non-routine grammatical arrangements. In brief, both sound relations and grammatical relations between words are ancillary; they serve utterances in their task of coping as best they can with meanings.

In the normal case, the unit of utterance will be a sentence. The one or more words in it will participate in its work in ways which usually entail the subordination or sacrifice of their other possibilities to its purposes. They are doing their duty to the sentence whose business it is to exact this duty from them. Only so can it profit from them and do its duty thereby, to previous or following sentences, all endeavoring to contribute to a discourse which is aiming somewhere. And the aim is the utterance of a meaning. The subordinate parts are utterances of contributions to that meaning, in the sense that they modify, re-direct, amplify, limit, qualify in manifold ways, that meaning, including how we hope the recipients will take it.

In all this, each part—from the sound elements which cooperate to form the words on up—has a double task: to *combine* with the rest in the over-all undertaking and to *exclude* whatever is not contributory to it. Each part has both to help with the sailing of the ship and to repel boarders. It has composition and opposition in hand.

Composition is the supplying at the right time and place of whatever the developing meaning then and there requires. It is the cooperation with the rest in preparing for what is to come and completing what has preceded. It is more than this, though; it is the exploration of what is to come and of how it should be prepared for, and it is the further examination of what has preceded and of how it may be amended and completed.

Opposition is a necessary complementary to composition: the two entail one another. Bishop Butler safely enough remarked that "Everything is what it is and not another thing." (An utterance G. E. Moore took for his motto.) The remark becomes more illuminating if we remake it into: "Everything is what it is *through* not being any other thing." (To ask whether, and, if so, how and *how far* these two are different in meaning here is a pertinent exercise in reflection.) Any meaning, at least, is what it is through selection. It has the features it has as opposed to others it might have. It is *this* meaning NOT *that;* and any subordinate contributory meaning within it has to be *this* NOT *that* as its service to the more inclusive meaning. Of the most inclusive meanings, those that would seem to presume to profess to tell us in a measure what it all is and what we are (so it has been held in Vedantic, Taoist, and other traditions), all that can be said is, "Neti, neti," *not that, not that;* the positive utterance being beyond our means.

For utterances that are within our means, however, each contributor does what it can to help by keeping out other things which would make the meaning other than that which it is becoming and is to become. In many ways this work of opposition, of excluding possible alternatives, is more open to analytic study than the work of composition, for it is reflected in, and indeed generates, systematic classification by division from more fundamental contrasts: $is \leftrightarrow isn't$, $this \leftrightarrow that$, $here \leftrightarrow there$, $now \leftrightarrow then$ . . . on up. If we compare these last three contrarieties we find little or no priority to accord to any one of them. *This* $\leftrightarrow$ *that* are the purest pointers with the least content to them, the least characterizing committed. *Here* $\leftrightarrow$ *there* spatializes, $now \leftrightarrow then$ temporalizes; and we note a new opposition in *then: then in the future ↔ then in the past.* By the space-time, time-space analogy we find the analogue in *there: there ahead ↔ there behind.* Compare now *ahead, in front, before.* We notice that, as between *ahead ↔ in front, ahead* carries a suggestion of forward motion (full speed ahead) which *in front* can be quite free from. In *there before us,* whether or not it lets in this component of traveling: ˢʷthe past is behind us, the future beforeˢʷ, will depend upon the more inclusive over-all meaning and on what in the circumambient wording, in the setting, or in the situation, is present to *encourage* or *discourage* it.

I have been trying with these elemental examples to illustrate (1) how opposition works and how complex and delicate its tasks are; (2) how much analogy enters both into the threats to the required meaning and into the defenses; and (3), with ʷencourageʷ and ʷdiscourageʷ, how what has been roughly called exclusion above can be a matter of degree and to be considered rather by psychological than by such physical metaphors as *in* or *out.* With positional and directional components this is especially so. With nouns and adjectives concerned in routine communications, a binary, *on ↔ off* opposition is more frequent. Visual items, for example, may be *colored ↔ not colored;* if colored, *uniform ↔ not uniform;* if uniform, *saturated ↔ not saturated;* if saturated, *primary ↔ not primary;* if primary a limited number of alternates—each in opposition to the others—compete: red —orange—yellow—green—blue—indigo—violet.

I have chosen an example here into which ingredients of color-theory have entered. Here we have another type of threat to a required meaning. Most speakers of English have, most of the time, no particular color-theory in mind, but a required meaning may very well need a specific structuring of the opposition field of its key-terms which only a particular theory can secure. Most discussions of such topics as concern us in these pages are in this situation, and most misunderstandings in such fields arise through interventions of theories which make the opposition field for the utterer unlike the opposition field for the recipient. Wider, clearer recognition of the probability of this, more diligent search for the sources of misunderstanding are the only remedies experience suggests. It may be hoped that these will increasingly take the place of the contentions, debates, refutations, rejoinders, the legal-logical collieshangies . . . that are more customary.

At many points above, with ᵖdisposition⁷ ᵖcompetence⁷, ᵖfluent⁷ ᵖknow⁷, ᵖmeanings⁷ ᵖrule⁷, and repeatedly with ᵖgrammar⁷, the way in which a word can be charged with theory, act for and represent indeed a whole view of life, has been remarked. Very often indeed it *must* be so charged if it is to do its duty to its sentence. When this happens, we should, properly, treat it as though it were another word from the same-looking, same-sounding words that may occur without any such charge in other sentences serving other arguments to other ends. We may treat it so and yet at the same time recognize that its peculiar powers in a sentence depend on and derive from the very fact that its meanings in other sentences are so different. The theory being sketched in this essay is designed to help us to expect and to handle this quite unavoidable and indeed indispensable part of ᵖverbal behavior⁷.

As I use this last phrase, many of my probable readers will be noting that ᵂverbal behaviorᵂ, when it turns up in Skinner's pages, in Chomsky's pages, in the verses with that title (see *Notes and Glosses* to Chapter 1) and now here on this page, must ask for different interpretations and that, in varying ways and degrees, the force of the phrase usually comes to it from its other meanings elsewhere. This is the case, on their most effective occurrences, with very many of the more interested and powerful words in the language. It is this which makes talk about "pairing phonetically represented signals with semantic interpretations" (p. 78 above) seem potentially so misleading. And it was this that made Chomsky in that passage put in his very necessary qualification: "(actually, for each interpretation of each sentence)."

This aspect of verbal behavior has enough consequences to deserve a distinctive label. My suggested Specialized Quotation Marks are an attempt toward developing a notation by which writers may call attention to, and readers be alerted in passing, to such semantic situations.

Among the consequences of [i]_____[i] uses, three classes are of special interest:

(1) When a writer shows no awareness of such interventions we know where we are and need read him no further. Two minds—one open, the other closed—to such influences, inhabit very different worlds.

(2) In philosophic exercises when a writer seems to suppose that people with very different positions can and should be using their key-terms alike, then we may expect little but fruitless contention.

(3) When it is powerful opposing cultural factors that intervene, very dangerous sources of conflict can focus in a phrase.

This last situation should be discussed and illustrated and the instances analyzed in some detail. Let me use here an excerpt from an address given at Bowdoin College on James Bowdoin Day, October 9, 1964.

I am to speak on a subject which I was a little rash in choosing —Conduct in Speech. (How does this differ here from Verbal Behavior?) I cannot think of any title which more pressingly invites the speaker to practice what he preaches.

Clearly, speech is a central thing in man. Man is *the* talking animal. Most animals, no doubt, communicate in various ways to some degree, but man is pre-eminently the communicating animal, biologically and individually. He became man in the development of the species by learning to talk. He becomes man, again, as an individual by learning to talk—that crucial phase in his development as a child. So, conduct in speech is not very far removed from conduct in being, conduct in life. How are we to say, to do and to be what is most human, what it is most characteristic of humanity to say, to do and to be? At this point, we come up against the terrifying pun that for-

ever besets the word "humanity." Consider the two meanings for it—
humanity the race and humanity the virtue.

Humanity is the name of our species—the supremely ferocious, mer-
ciless, destructive, all-conquering winner in the biological kill-or-be-
killed struggle. Humanity is the champion in that Nature, "red in
tooth and claw," which man has learned increasingly to dominate.
Humanity is also the name for the central most necessary virtue in
man. Why do I say the most necessary virtue? For the same reason
that what are called ˢʷThe Humanitiesˢʷ have their very central place,
their special role in education.

It has become widely recognized that the dangers of omitting the
humanities from our education are increasing all the time. To keep
their due place for the humanities is necessary, because without indi-
rect or direct influence from the humanities, man can neither become
nor continue to be humane. Let me develop this contrast between
these senses of humanity with an instance.

Some twenty years ago, Winston Churchill was speaking at Harvard
on an occasion very similar to this. He was speaking about Basic
English and world communications.[6] He rather resoundingly (and
very characteristically) declared that "the empires of the future are
empires of the mind." Linger a little with this and consider the *very*
different meanings that people may give to such an utterance. People
of equal intelligence may give it meanings as diverse one from another
as it is possible to imagine. How do you understand it: "The empires
of the future are empires of the mind"?

At one end of the spectrum of interpretation, the infra-red end if
you like, it is a pronouncement that can make us shiver. It can
prophesy dominion for those cleverest at deluding and destroying
their fellow men.

At the other end of the spectrum, the ultra-violet end if you like,
it can promise a supreme liberation—the replacement of force by
reason and understanding, the replacement of compulsion by persua-
sion and free consent. Which way you take it depends upon two words
in the sentence: the word "empire" and the word "mind."

Let us take "empire" first. It is an unpopular word, increasingly an
unpopular word. There are all sorts of regions of the planet where the
less you say about empire the better. It took a Churchill, in a typical
moment, to use the word still with obvious approval and gusto, an

expansive, glorious kind of feeling. What can it do for us, this word? It can sum up the most appalling side of history, that side of history to which historians have until recently paid most attention. All that glory-drunk, power-mad struggle for local or global domination. The thing that for the last fifty years, since about 1914, mankind (at first here and there and then more widely and more deeply) has been learning not to admire, not to praise but to deplore and to condemn.

That is one thing that "empire" can mean. It can mean the old-fashioned empire-building of the history books. But there is another sense that we can set against that: something else that "empire" can mean. It can mean the control, under some measure of justice and law, of otherwise endlessly murdering factions, locked in a breakdown of society which only something that can be called empire can take care of until real self-government becomes possible. At this other end of the empire spectrum is the sort of thing we would like the peace-keeping instruments of the United Nations to be able to do. Of course, as we all know, the trouble is, like the wolf in sheep's clothing, possessiveness disguises itself as protection, and its propaganda dresses up greed to look like charity. So much for "empire" and the widely opposite ways in which that word can enter this sentence: "The empires of the future are empires of the mind."

Now turn to "mind." It's a word that can mean little more than willfulness or bullying. The illustration that occurs to me is from an official biography. I will call it *The Life and Work of Mr. Justice Starelee*. The biographer had become perhaps a little tired of his subject. He had concocted a very fine index to his volume. Mr. Justice Starelee is in this index—look him up and you see "Infant Promise," page 6, "Youthful Genius," page 14, "Early Education," page 27, "Awarded Scholarship," page 53, "Academic Success," page 82, and then after that comes "His Great Mind," page 100. Turn to that and you find it's a quotation from a letter and that Mr. Justice Starelee was saying, "This was outrageous. I had a great mind to give the fellow a good thrashing."

That is the willful use of the "mind"—the self-centered, self-assertive, self-righteous focus. But "mind" can, at the other end of its spectrum, mean the opposite to this self-assertiveness. It can mean the most entire, the most complete, the most all-encompassing consideration. It's a high word, this word "consider." When you truly consider something, you put it, as it were, within the most encompassing, the largest, the widest frame of reference. You use the word as if it were referring to the stars. You take the something in its place in the sidereal universe and see how it looks there. That is what considering can mean. When we use it so, there you have mind at its height. Mind at its highest takes into its account all that it can, all interests, relevancies, everything. That is the sense of "mind" that Socrates was using when he was talking about it in the *Phaedo,* fairly late in his last afternoon. "One day I heard a man reading from a book, by Anaxagoras, he said it was. He was reading that it is mind that arranges and causes all things. This pleased me, it seemed somehow right that mind should be the cause of everything. If so, I thought, mind arranges each thing as it is most fitting for it to be." Socrates gets hold of a copy of Anaxagoras and is most disappointed. Anaxagoras did not do that at all. So Socrates had to try to do it, or something like it, himself. The great thing in this endeavor, whose name is, of course, philosophy, is not to overlook, if you can help it, not to overlook anything that may be truly important, truly relevant, and to be as honest and as imaginative, as encompassing as you can be. That is the noble sense of "mind"; it is at the other end of the spectrum from Mr. Justice Starelee's "great mind."

Back now to "The empires of the future are empires of the mind." Winston Churchill's sentence could mean that henceforward those will have the most power—those individuals, those groups—who are most inclusive or regardful, most balanced, most just, most sane, and whole-minded. And in this sense, the thing to be feared most will be self-deceit, the lie in the soul, or, as Socrates says in the *Phaedo,* "our own shadow." Our own shadow, which falls over what we should be thinking of and makes us unable to study it.

What has all this to do with conduct in speech? Everything. The whole duty of speech is to serve and represent mind as fully as may be. Not to overlook, not to ignore anything that may be relevant. Typically not to overlook the fact that sentences like "The empires of the future are empires of the mind" can mean the very opposite of what any individual may quite calmly take them as obviously meaning. Almost every utterance that seems as though it could be of real consequence is like this. It can be taken in these strangely opposing ways.

To conclude with a thought or two about ambition. Consider what tremendous (and I use the word with every sense of the shudder in it), what tremendous new possibilities are being yearly offered to the exploring mind—things that twenty years ago nobody would have dared for a moment to suppose would have come up in his own lifetime. Things with the most ultimate effect for good and for evil. You are all thinking of the bomb. I am thinking more of certain innovations that are coming in teaching. Mispractices in teaching could do more harm than even the worst bomb. Education really is a more fundamental and dangerous study than physics.

On the other hand, there is the possibility of developing increased control over such ambiguities as I've been illustrating with my "empires of the future" as "empires of the mind." We are within reach of being able to make people understand one another better and that would be the deepest of all revolutions.

In comparison, how puny, how pitiable most of the ambitions recorded in the history books are! What trivial, tiny little pieces of inanity compared with what any able student has offered to him today. What a piece of asininity the career of Hitler was! Why should anyone entertain such ambitions? Who would be a Tamerlane? What fun would it be "to ride in triumph through Persepolis"? What a bore! Reread Marlowe's *Doctor Faustus* and see how petty, how despicable the reach of Faustus' imagination was. Faustus, that great scholar, has no inkling of the real aims of any of the studies he surveys. It's a dreadful little mind whose antics we are invited to watch in Dr. Faustus.

I will end with this consideration: Ours is an age beyond all others in which people may be worthily ambitious.

To come back now to the general problem of Meanings, now that this outline of the workings of a word, a sentence, a paragraph, a discourse . . . has been sketched. Among ambitions to which "young imaginaries in Knowledge" may be moved, the most vaulting, and maybe o'er-leaping, is certainly the aspiration to improve our mental and moral communications through closer study of their defects. Language is their major channel and 'meanings' (under one name or another) are what they have to handle. And yet almost any sentence which seems to be attempting to say anything worth saying about them has a way of fading into thin air if we try to seize and examine it. Nonetheless even this disappointing conduct may be instructive.

For example, fundamental in this sketch is the proposition that *Language is an instrument for the pursuit and control of meanings.* Meanings are hard to talk of in part because to talk of them at all we have to find some selection from them which will serve to describe themselves; we are having to fashion sentences, paragraphs, discourse, which may serve as a vehicle for beings which though they are not verbal and can reject any offered verbal vehicles on occasion can for the most part in many fields only find themselves and come to completion through the use of vehicles of one order or another. Any sentence such as the last, which is attempting to describe meanings and consciously exemplifying the insecurities and uncertainties of its task, can hardly help recognizing how at every turn offstage murmurs of "Neti, neti" are a shaping influence in its composition. It was this, perhaps, which put the word "pursuit" into our fundamental proposition: a reference to hunting which may remind us that what we mean is something we can always be mistaken about. The peevish "I wish you would say what you mean" and the proud "I say what I mean and mean what I say!" are ignoring an essential fact of the matter.

Another important recognition is that the danger of speaking misleadingly of meanings increases with each new or old technical term we employ, if the technical term is, as it usually is in this subject, a condensation from a theory: as with ʳsaturationʳ and ʳprimaryʳ in the example on page 121. (An ˢʷexampleˢʷ in the sense which is exemplified in ˢʷmake an example ofˢʷ someone—make him into a warning to others.)

What these excuses and alarums are doing here is preparing for a gloss on ʳan instrument for the pursuit and control of meaningsʳ as used in the opening sentence of the paragraph above. ᵩInstrumentᵩ, ᵩpursuitᵩ, and ᵩcontrolᵩ perhaps need little more treatment than may be taken from a dictionary. But ᵩmeaningᵩ is not so manageable. About all that a dictionary offers is "what is meant."

What seems to be shown is that while useful, acceptable and relevant senses for [w]instrument[w], [w]pursuit[w], and [w]control[w] are available, [w]meaning[w] (perhaps because it is our handle to itself) is still in need of a resourceful clarificatory entry. Such an entry would not, of course, *tell* us how we [nb]should[nb] use the word here. It couldn't do that, but it could help us to make out how it can best serve with [sw]instrument[sw], [sw]pursuit[sw] and [sw]control[sw] the purposes governing our proposed formulation: *Language is an instrument for the pursuit and control of meanings.* The hope is that our practical knowledge of (our [sw]know-how with[sw]) the other words in this formulation can become enough to show us what we should be talking about *here* with [w]meanings[w], on which [sw]know-how[sw] is caught more often than not off balance. It should be that which will satisfy the requirements and exclusions set up by the rest of the proposition. Our question thus can be: "What should [w]meanings[w] here be doing if this formulation is to be (as it seems to be) evident and true?" And our directives can be: "Find a task for [w]meanings[w] which should make the formulation so" and, "Give an account of [w]meanings[w] able to explain why the word should be a source of so much trouble."

It will be noticed that [w]should[w] is here taking over major responsibilities. [sw]Should[sw] is too important a component of all meanings to be left out of any inquiry into ?meanings?. As it enters here, it is a variable amalgam of prudence, probability and ethics: Compare: "You *should* say 'He does' not 'He do.' " "The murderer *should* be taking up his gun about now." "You *should* admit your doubts if you feel them." In general the participation of *should* in this discussion should be salutary: modest, tentative, doubt-provoking and allaying.

It may be admitted that this way of approaching the problem deliberately brings together to the crucial point all the hardest ingredients in it: what ?requirement? here should be and what ?satisfaction?; what the criteria should be for ?evident? and

²true²; and what ²should² should be saying for us on each of its appearances. This approach, in fact, runs directly counter to strong preferences for dealing, where we can, with difficulties piecemeal, for finding formulations which isolate points for separate treatment whenever possible. Its excuse is that, in this matter of a *wise choice* [7] of a [sw]meaning[sw] for [sw]meaning[sw] here in this formulation, the ways in which we take ²requirement², ²satisfy², ²evident², ²true² and ²should² as well as the words in the formulation are jointly and cooperatively relevant. Their meanings here should be an explicative display of this relevance.

Is it not strange and interesting that a proposition, "Language is an instrument for the pursuit and control of meanings" which, if we read it and reflect upon it with a view to checking it against all we know of language, instruments, pursuit, control and meanings, will seem to be obviously in accord with that knowledge, can yet turn, if we start asking certain sorts of questions, into what easily seems an empty quest? And that [w]meaning[w], a word which we use so often and in so many ways with such unperturbed security, can so readily be made to seem an intelligential will-o'-the-wisp?

Let us now ask what it is that the meanings employed in and referred to by our formulation have to do.

(1) They have to mediate for the individual in his thinking, feeling, willing, desiring, loving, fearing, suffering, enjoying . . . between all his cognitive, affective and volitional activities and that actuality with which these activities are concerned. They are what we [sw]think of[sw] and what we [sw]*think with*[sw] when we think —whether we think of our own right-hand thumbnail, an honest man or a centaur; they are what we feel when we admire a dancer or dread an interview; what we want when we covet a yacht or a moment or two of peace and quiet for undisturbed reflection. In each case we find when we think more carefully and self-critically that—though we talk otherwise—it is not actuality that we [nb]directly[nb] think of, feel or want, but no more

than a representative of actuality, something which may or may not faithfully correspond with actuality, as we learn in the outcome through our disappointment or surprise: further meanings which emerge to teach us better. ?Actuality? itself, which we can only think, talk of or feel or seek by way of meanings, is further off. We deal with it through meanings. Our meanings, it is true, are themselves part of actuality, as we are, but our traffic with the rest of it is only through meanings. Actuality is that with which we so deal and probably we should not try to say much more than this about it.

(2) Meanings have also to mediate between individuals, be their common world [8] to them, their common representatives of actuality. They are *not*, as we are thinking of them here, private events, concoctions of an individual, conceivings produced in independence by his central nervous system or his mind. His nervous system and his mind are dependencies along with other meanings. Meanings are public, in any way that any beings can be public. All our most acceptable examples of public objects: a President, the Post Office, a bus line or a stove are meanings, forms through which individuals, however separate in other ways, may act and react upon one another, inherit, build, maintain, and develop their common world.

(3) Meanings have further to be capable of truth and falsity; be true if actuality supports them, false if it does not. If actuality supports them too continuously and completely, we are apt just to mistake them for it, taking a thumbnail to be neither more nor less than what we may think it is. The biologist, the chemist beyond him, the physicist farther beyond and the philosopher farther still have other accounts to offer. But even the truest, the most endlessly verified meanings are not actuality. Meanings are falsifiable; actuality is not. Meanings are what we think *of*, feel, will and the rest, as well as what we think with. They are that portion of actuality through which we deal with the rest, and as actual themselves they share in actuality's incomprehensibility. And yet, to repeat, all our think-

ing, feeling, willing . . . is a traffic with actuality *via* meanings, *via* meanings resulting from our joint and several labors of opposition and composition. Those apt to mistake meanings for the actualities they represent should consider the different views we develop [9] of one another, *e.g.,* a lover's view of his lass and hers of him, as compared with others' opinions of either; a nation's image of itself, as compared with other nations' views. Other people, most of all those we think we know best, are for most of us the most fateful fabrics of meanings we enjoy— solider than our own selves, which are also, as we think *of* them, fabrics of meaning, central, highly determinative and doubtful. But not even our own selves, as thought *of,* can be identified with any further actuality. No vision is that *of* which it is. No meanings are that which they would represent.

(4) Meanings have to serve not only as instruments with which we attempt to explore, invite, accept, defend ourselves from and adjust ourselves to actuality, but even more as instruments by which we attempt to order meanings themselves. They are, in fact, usually so busy reorganizing one another under the impulsion of events that they have little energy left over for concern with either language or themselves. Thought and feeling and will are radically, biologically, evolutionary-wise *revisional.* Theory of them, theory of meanings is so too. As it finds itself so, it comes to take its arrangements, even those which most satisfy its requirements, as essentially tentative: a thought that comes home comfortingly at the end of four such paragraphs as these.

The next question to ask of meanings, the tissues of which all our worlds are formed, is as to their relationship to the notations—here principally linguistic—through which we attempt to distinguish, to order and to control them.

The familiar instance of a notation is writing. But it is worthwhile reflecting that notation relationships occur within many different partner systems and that the writing-speech relationship is not wholly representative of them. In a more general sense, whenever one course of events leaves a record in another course of events by which it can be by some means in some degree represented, we may call this a notation relationship. The configurations of the groove in a gramophone disc, a barograph tracing, tracks of a fox and a hare . . . the unknown continuant conditions in the brain which enable an episode to be recalled, the dispositions which allow acquired skill and knowledge to be available anew, are instances. Obviously each of these is different in important respects from the others. From the groove we can get back the music; from the tracing, data toward a description; from the tracks, a hypothesis; from the continuants, a memory; from the disposition, the return of a power. From writing what we hope for is the reconstruction of a meaning. In each case the record gives us ways of reconsidering the originative course of events.

In this sense, what we hear of our own voices as we talk may be called a notation of our speech, so may whatever we feel of our motions of articulation. These three commonly serve one another. Try silently reciting a favorite passage before and after taking your tongue firmly between your teeth. You can learn to overcome the effect but at first you will notice a difference. If for any reason, we have difficulty in speech, trying to speak, listening to the sounds we make, and attending to what our mouth movements feel like, all these contribute jointly to our performance. Add to them our trains of imagery of what the sounds *should* sound like, of what the motions (as felt) *should* feel like . . . and we see that in picking up merely the pronunciation of a few new phrases of an unfamiliar tongue, we are exercising a highly complex cooperative activity in which a number of concurrent streams of endeavor, running in different but intercommunicating channels, are in *feed-forward* (see *Speculative Instruments,* "Towards a More Synoptic View") and feed-back circuits together, reciprocally prompting and critically controlling one another's performance.

It is permissible to conjecture that no learning occurs without some such arrangement as this: whereby, to use the simplest model, two streams in different channels (ear and eye, or perception and image, for example) are jointly concerned to interpret a sequence of events. Each, in competition with the other, feeds forward whatever its information affords to help the other, and then, in turn, puts itself into the best posture to receive and evaluate the feedback. Each thus becomes not only the competitive inciter to the other but the controller and reviser. Such collaboration requires, of course, that there be adequate means of translation available somehow. The eye is handling color and shape; the ear, tone and duration. Yet they cooperate, superlatively, in conversation. Somehow or other they understand one another excellently, or we could not live. After all, we locate sounds through reflex eye swivelings controlled by differences of phase in the two ears. It may help us in trying to imagine how we handle meanings to remind ourselves of the resourcefulness of the cooperative senses through which we come to have any sensory meanings at all to handle.[10]

Meanings and language are essentially in a notational relationship. It has been suggested above that the partnerships of multiple diverse channels in merely echoic behavior (as in just learning how to pronounce a new word in a foreign tongue) are intricate enough to stretch the imagination. We must not expect that the partnerships developed in the notational relationships between language and meanings will be any simpler. Recall the sketch of linguistic workings offered above. At innumerable points in its three rings (phonologic, grammatic, semantic), opportunities arise both for support to and interference from participants within the growing language-meanings structure. (Language over meaning, *i.e.*, language/meaning it is, for the most part, in the speaker; meaning/language, for the most part, in the recipient.) Seeking its own development, the fabric of meanings may attempt to charge what comes to it as language with grammatic and semantic duties the words refuse to carry. Meanwhile the words' own affiliations and oppositions may be trying to provoke, perhaps, drastic changes among the meanings. This unruly contention between the steeds as to where the chariot is to go is as characteristic of these language-meanings, meanings-language relationships as it was of Plato's original pair.[11] Meanings and verbal schemas are both incessantly launching feed-forward explorations, both as to what load the verbal vehicle can carry and as to what developments the meanings can accept. And the feedback from these, to the writer who is reconciling *How to say it?* with *What should I be saying?* is what shows him how indispensable these notational relationships have been to the development of mind. In brief, meanings serve as notation for phrasing as much as phrasing (on the deadly usual view) serves to record meanings.

Any self-attentive person can witness to all this. What has seemed to have been said earlier can come almost continuously under revision from what the rest of the sentence and the sequent sentences are saying. Feed-forward—feed-back circuits confirm or amend what the discourse ahead is again to amend or confirm. Add in imagery, *not* as some sort of decoration or epiphenomenon, but as a critical and often subversive commentary, checking, through its own notational relationship, the validity of the meanings being developed and of the verbal expression they are receiving. Add in, further, the openings that etymological and metaphorical resources so assiduously supply for divergent developments or for obstructive resistance. At times (as every author, together with his readers, should agree) it seems a continual miracle that sentences attempting to say anything at all *new* can go on making sense.

The inhibiting character of these speculations has been put first; the encouraging note should follow. Perhaps some comparisons between walking and talking can supply it. Normally we no more ask how we talk than we ask how we walk. Both walking and talking are, in a considerable though as yet unassignable measure, *learned activities,* in which most of what has been learned has become, normally, automated. We have *learned how.*

In our brilliant early years we learn to adjust our steps to the ground we are traversing much as we learn how to fit our utterances to the situations with which they have to deal. Only rarely do we become consciously cognizant of distinct features of the continuous field of intake from which our equilibrium as walkers depends. But if we are carrying a full glass, supporting somebody, descending a steep-enough declivity, or have strained a back muscle, the discriminative and selective character of the activity becomes highly apparent. And in our most casual, automated walking, the same though unnoticed mutual dependence of each part of our movement upon other parts is keeping us from a fall.

In more than a few ways walking can be taken as a type-specimen of what notational relationships may do for us. In every moment when we are walking, our balance, as our weight goes onto one foot, is being computed by the nervous system, notation-wise, in terms not only of whatever the transference of our weight to the other foot will require (and must exclude), but of whatever unevennesses in footing we may be meeting, whatever we may be reaching for, whatever we may be swinging in our hands as we carry it, whatever may be the tilt of our head and whatever changes in tempo and/or direction our distance-receptor signals may be warning us to prepare for. And all this is being done in terms of notations from feed-forward—feed-back cycles requiring fine accuracy of timing and coordination, in parallel serial loops, and using labyrinth reports together with muscle-joint-tendon outcomes signaled from all over the body. All this, and Heaven knows how much else—as the cragsman, the river logger or the boxer is in the best position to realize—our walking takes without worry in its stride.

This comparison of talking with walking is not "an analogy only." The two are instances of a general principle. All true activity has this organic character, this mutual though hierarchical dependence of part upon part and of outcome upon whole. Only through this can the activity meet the needs it has to serve.

And no activity—least of all speech—can be usefully described without regard for its use to the organism, what it does to help it to continue living. For this inescapable reason, the recurrently fashionable efforts of linguistic theorists to treat language as "a self-sufficient universe" in isolation from "the world that language attempts to talk about" are self-destructive. These dream-motived efforts are abortive attempts to make matters simpler than they can be. Language, like bodily movement, is a way of dealing with that same world. All reflective attempts to describe how language works are inseparably dependent upon recognition of the varieties of the work language undertakes, fails in or achieves.

In walking there is nothing quite like the gross difference between the production of a stream of speech sounds and the conduct of a course of meanings, unless it be the rhythmic swing over from bearing the immediate responsibility for the support of the body to supplying what is needed, on release, as check. Each leg system alternates between these. In talking, a somewhat analogous alternation sometimes appears. In one phase the sentence has the stage, uttering what has just been and is being thought while meanings wait around to see how well they are being treated and stand by to make any needed corrections; in the next, meanings are being generated and arranged, getting ready to let words record them. But often the connections are closer, more finely intermeshed: the arrival of a word and of a meaning may be indistinguishably welcome, or a proffered word because of an accompanying meaning is instantaneously dismissed.

Reasons in plenty lead us to expect the greatest variability in all this, both between individuals and within the same individual in one hour of one morning. Some of these reasons are on the frontiers of 'inspiration'; others border on fatigue; the topic, its familiarity, its own coherence, the depth of treatment being attempted . . . the audience, the noise level . . . there is no end to factors that may come in. What, however, is essential

to the notational relationship is the way in which the two or
more streams of activity can alternately and all but simultaneously pivot upon one another. A sentence can hold meanings
steady while other meanings work to revise or support them:
alternately, meanings are held firm (but by what who knows?)
while sentence after sentence tries itself out against and by them.
In imagining these encounters we are reminded again that
linguistic form is three-ringed (sound, syntax, sense) and that
it may be carried by full speech, sub-vocal talking, imagery of
various sorts and by writing. And writing itself may be either
visual words or the motions of penciling and typing. (There is
good reason for expecting that many who fail to learn to read
via a pencil could learn via the typewriter, if the invitations to
them to experiment were rightly sequenced.) There is ground for
supposing that many differences in compositional competence
may not be unconnected with the fullness or sketchiness, the
permanence or fleetingness (pen, pencil or voice) of the utterance with which meanings have to "come to terms" to use a
tough concept in a grim matter. We all know people who speak
well enough but are helpless pen in hand—and others who are
ready-enough writers, but quite unable to talk consecutively,
except perhaps on the telephone. In this last case, it could be
that past fear of feedback from the interlocutor's facial expression is sometimes the source of the inhibition.

The complexity of linguistic form has been stressed above.
Much speculative neurology has been concerned with ways in
which perceptual motor activity can simplify itself, can develop
stable-state routines which can represent (act for, serve as immediately available models for) recurrent *types* of situations
requiring appropriate action. No doubt the activity in talking is
vastly more intricate than that in walking, but it is a reasonable
conjecture that the same possibilities for self-simplification are
used in both. We seem indeed to know a good deal via introspection about good *and bad* ways of making recurrent problems
of meaning as easy for us as we can. How intricate they still will

be is obvious enough to imagination whenever it *is intent to apprehend* what linguistic workings must be if they are to do what they must: each item being a node in a spreading multi-fold network, a member of almost endless overlapping sets of alternates and in yet other ways exigently selective. Only through all this can it serve. And we should not suppose that the fields of meanings it serves can be simpler. But in fact we do very obstinately so suppose. When *we are not intent to apprehend what must be* we behave as though managing meanings was as simple as billiards and had much the same beguiling obvious-ness about it. Most minds feel a strong reluctance to face up to the intricacies of their meanings any more than seems strictly necessary. We pretend, for example, that billiards is simple. The physicist (or the expert in a different way, feeling the effects of the weather on the cloth) can tell another story.

In general we make whatever we can as simple as we can. "What we want," cries a character in H. G. Wells' *The New Machiavelli,* "is thick thinking: thinking that will stand up by itself!" This was in opposition to the hero's slogan, "Love and fine thinking." We most of us use thick thinking, as thick thinking as we can, whenever there seems a chance that it will do. Unhappily most of the time it won't do, though it may take us a while to find out that it is betraying us. Bacon's experi-enced pen well records that "As in the courts and services of princes and states it is a much easier matter to give satisfaction than to do the business." [12] Our meanings are ever most insinu-ating courtiers. We discover through the outcome that plausibility really is these instrumentalities' second name.

Among the tasks in which we should not use any thicker thinking than need be are attempts to say what they are. The most tantalizing and baffling part of a theory of meanings has always been the discussion of their status. Certainly, they cannot be identified with the realities—the things, events, facts, possi-bilities—they would represent to us. They cannot because they can be falsified; they often, and can be shown to, misrepresent.

And, as certainly, they are not identical with any *particular* conceivings, fancies, images, depictions, notions . . . that people thinking *with* and *of* meanings have as they think with and of them. These *particular* conceivings, etc., just *won't do* what meanings have to do. These conceivings, etc., are events in individual minds. The ^sw^meanings^sw^ we are here concerned with are no such thinkings; they are what such thinkings are ^nb^of^nb^ and/or work ^nb^with^nb^. The thinkings are particular and private; the meanings are general and public.

This ^?^of^?^ and this ^?^with^?^ here carry, of course, very dubious and puzzling meanings—matched if not outdone by the ^?^representing^?^ duty which meanings aspire to fulfil—for the things, events, facts, possibilities . . . on which their verification or falsification depends.

Thus we have:

1	2	3	4	5
conceivings, etc.	^?^of^?^ ^?^with^?^	^?^ ^?^MEANINGS^?^ ^?^	^?^representing^?^	things, etc.

To make this thicket the more tangled and obscure (it can be compared with Dante's at the opening of the *Inferno* and with Plato's in *Republic,* 432D, when something like a track of Justice is found) we have to add that the first and last columns are quite usually described as ^sw^meanings^sw^ and that ^?^of^?^, ^?^with^?^ and ^?^representing^?^ are often made ^sw^the relation of meaning^sw^. Moreover, swarms of theories, hypotheses, explanations, etc., frequent the thicket, offering accounts of how images, etc., depict (are pictures of) fact immediately, and of how knowings are, in a manner, becomings of what they know. The impulse *to simplify somehow* is here at its strongest. Though only an audacious person would profess to be as happy here as Br'er Rabbit, it is perfectly true to say that, whether we know it or not, in this briar patch we are "born and bred."

The separation of ^sw^meanings^sw^ from ^sw^psychological happenings[sw] on the left and from [sw]states of affairs[sw] on the right will doubtless seem unnecessary and repellent. Its ground has been indicated above; meanings have to mediate in two ways: (1) between action and the situations action is attempting to meet; and (2) between participants in communication. For both duties meanings must have the status of *generals* (or universals) not that of *particulars*.

(1) Action can be accorded to situation only through recurrences of general characters (see *The Meaning of Meaning*, Appendix B).

(2) Two or more communicators (or the same thinker at different times) must have sufficiently the *same* meaning present to them.

This is, of course, recognized to be the most resistant as it is the most central and recurrent problem in philosophy. Whatever may be said here will inevitably occasion every sort of misinterpretation, although the chief aim of any account of meanings may well be to lower the probability of these. The last paragraph, for example, might seem to risk a reader's confusing sameness in what is cognized with sameness in the cognizings.[13] That confusion would destroy the tenuous, precarious understanding here hoped for. An account of meanings must somehow explain how understandings as well as misunderstandings are possible.

To do so it has to recognize that meanings must be *general*. This recognition, if taken as seriously as it deserves, frees us from some unfruitful doubts—from exaggerations of our isolation among them. It is an enheartening doctrine.

But it is well to remind ourselves that this "way of ideas," Plato's solution of the problem of sameness, has traditionally its dangers: temptations to elevate to overweening status what are but conjectures. Socrates (*Republic,* 506E) declined further flight as "an undertaking higher than the impulse that keeps me up today" and this essay on meanings must refrain too. The meanings we aspire to are servants of purposes that clearly transcend ours. Chief among their services may be to explore, illuminate, clarify and even amend these purposes, an exceedingly exalted role.

Such a view of meanings naturally invites us to conceive of them as being analogous to a language, a universal language through which we communicate with reality. It is an invitation which not a few—Herbert, Jonathan Edwards, Wordsworth among them—have accepted. This too, as oracles and prophesyings in all ages have shown us, has its dangers. A theory of meanings can best guard us from them by reminding us of the force of the conditions through which it is prone to err.

Meanings Anew

(1)   *situation:* The prominence given to this word in this paragraph reflects not only the considerations behind the
stress on ʳsign situationsʳ in *The Meaning of Meaning*
but prolonged concern with both the teaching of the
beginnings of second languages and learning to read.
The design of instruction in both these ⁿᵇsituationsⁿᵇ
peculiarly requires and permits close study of the structure of the tasks being presented. These tasks can only
be conceived and compared in terms of the situations in
which they arise and from which they are derived.

For maximal effectiveness the series of sentence-situation (SEN/SIT) parallels offered to the learner must be
kept as simple and as evident as possible. The designer
must therefore examine the structural relations between
the situations he uses as carefully as he does those between his sentences. It is in the course of doing so that
he becomes most fully aware of the linkage between
actuality and language. As he opposes one SEN/SIT with
another, he has to see to it that the respect in which they
are opposed is minimally confusable, for the learner, with
other respects which might come into the question. The
designer's main instrument for exploring this is language.
And language (as he knows or should know) is capable of
confusing such investigations in a high degree. See Chapter 4, "Some Glances in Current Linguistics." So he will
do well to use whatever further instruments for exploration he can. Two of these are *action* and *depiction:* the
use of enactments and of iconic representations or images.

If he can check and support his *verbal* (symbolic) discernment of the situation with these two other modes of representation, he can work far more safely. And he soon comes to see that what he needs for himself—a cooperative, mutually corroborative cross-checking by the three channels—is just what his pupil needs for secure learning that will build self-critical self-reliance. As Jerome S. Bruner has lately and rightly been insisting, these three, the enactment or performance, the iconic, or picturing, and the symbolic or verbal, are "three parallel systems for processing information and for representing it—one through manipulation and action, one through perceptual organization and imagery and one through symbolic apparatus." (See *Toward a Theory of Instruction,* Cambridge, Harvard University Press, 1966.) These three are not "stages": they may be "emphases in development"; through all our lives they should be cooperative resources helping toward comprehension. It is such considerations which show how idle and artificial are attempts "to describe the structure of a sentence *in isolation from its possible settings in linguistic discourse (written or verbal) or in non-linguistic contexts (social or physical)*" such as are remarked upon in Chapter 4. For a typical series of SEN/SIT sequences illustrating the recommendations to which analysis and experimentation lead, the reader may consult *English through Pictures,* Books 1 and 2, and *First Steps in Reading English,* I. A. Richards and Christine Gibson (New York, Washington Square Press, 1961).

(2) *context pressure:* The distinction between ?contexts?, as here used, and ?settings? is useful. May I use again a passage from the Preface of my *Interpretation in Teaching.* "(1) A word, like any other sign, gets whatever meaning it has through belonging to a recurrent group of events, which may be called its *context.* Thus a word's context, *in this sense,* is a certain recurrent pattern of *past*

groups of events, and to say that a word's meaning depends upon its context would be to point to the process by which it has acquired its meaning. (2) In another, though a connected sense, a word's context is *the words which surround it in the utterance* and the other *contemporaneous* signs which govern its interpretation.

"Both senses of context need to be kept in mind if we are to consider carefully how interpretations succeed or fail. For clarity we may distinguish the second sort of context by calling it the *setting*. It is evident that a change in the setting may change the context (in the first sense) in which a word is taken. We never, in fact, interpret single signs in isolation. (The etymological hint given by *inter* is very relevant here.) We always take a sign as being *in some setting,* actual or implied, as part of an interconnected sign-field (normally, with verbal signs, a sentence and an occasion). Thus, insufficient attention to the accompanying sign-field . . . which controls the context . . . is a frequent cause of mistaken understanding. But equally, no care, however great, in observing the setting will secure good interpretation if past experience has not provided the required originative context." As Bruner has recently put it, "Unless certain basic skills are mastered, later, more elaborated ones become increasingly out of reach." This unhappily is true of all mental endeavor at all levels. To continue from my Preface: "The interactions of what I am calling the contexts and settings are as intricate and incessant as life itself. . . . Sign-fields by recurring, generate contexts . . . and which contexts are operative (how the signs are read) is determined later by the new settings." (1937)

(3) *all the tasks there can be:* The selection of these tasks by the speaker, the sorts of attempts he makes upon them, his perceptions of their success or failure . . . all this is as much a matter of *context pressure* as his selection of a

pronunciation, an intonation (A), for example, or of a
grammatical pattern (B). But the context pressures in
semantic choice and strategy (C) are (or should be) far
more various, subtle and mutually accommodating than
with (A) and (B). There is always a danger in linguistics—
it is an occupational hazard—that we will try to conceive
the ʳunimaginably complex set of determinantsʳ which
may be operant in (C) on the model of those relatively
simpler sets appropriate to (A) and (B).

(4) *professional disqualification:* Thus, typically, *John demands Harry* and *John believes love* are ruled out on
transformational grounds (Paul M. Postal, "Underlying
and Superficial Linguistic Structure," *Harvard Educational Review,* Spring 1964, p. 256). Yet any competent
dramatist could write a dialogue in which these sentences
would effectively say exactly what the developing situation requires. These * (starred) unacceptables cheer up the
ordinary reader's perusal of this literature. They often
seem to derive from the linguist's not having taken
enough to heart his own declaration: "Most important,
however, is the fact that a full linguistic description must
contain a *semantic component* whose task is to assign
each sentence a *meaning*" *(ibid,* p. 259). No doubt this
"most important" truth is not saying here quite what we
may think it should. Most of these utterances are private
code messages exchanged by the devout. But at least it
contrasts pleasantly with the denunciations of meaning as
linguistically irrelevant that used to enliven analogous
pages.

(5) *service to the semantic aims of the utterance:* In practice
a description of these aims and a full and close enough
description of the situation calling it forth often turn
into two sides of the same coin. It is this that makes the

current self-denying ordinances of generative grammar so frustrating. "Just as linguistic theory as such does not specify the relation of semantic markers to the non-linguistic world, so also it cannot deal with the relations between a speaker's experiences, verbal or otherwise, and the utterances he produces" (Postal, *op. cit.*, p. 264). A queer nemesis appears here: the Behaviorists denied themselves introspection; Chomsky attacked Skinner's attempt to describe verbal behavior on that basis as "hopelessly premature" (*Language,* Jan.-March, 1959). Now, echoing that famous review, his followers are fashionably denying themselves almost as much as ever Skinner did. Meanwhile to those ready to use every helpful source of information all these preclusions already seem ill-grounded and comically out of date.

(6)   *Basic English and world communications:* Churchill's and Roosevelt's pronouncements in favor of Basic English (September 1943) had the effect of making it be generally supposed that responsibilities for the support and development of Basic English were in good-enough hands. George Bernard Shaw, for example, redrafted his will, writing next spring, "Basic English is a natural growth which has been investigated and civilized by the Orthological Institute on the initiative of Mr. C. K. Ogden, whose years of tedious toil deserve a peerage and a princely pension." (London *Times,* March 30, 1944.)

At about this time (February 20, 1944) T. S. Eliot wrote to me of my *Basic English and Its Uses:* "It seemed to me a very good job and extremely persuasive. Running through it I seem to find a strain of indignation, the causes of which are obscure to the common reader here, but which tie presumably in with imbecile attacks by American critics. The case you have made out seems to me, on a first reading, quite unassailable. My own doubts about Basic are not on this level; they are more like the objections to aeroplanes in "Rasselas": if you put such a tool in the hands of human beings, what unexpected devilish use will they put it to?——What one positively clamours for, after reading your primer, is a more extended book on the right and wrong ways of using it in the teaching of English (especially to English-speaking pupils)." This more extended treatment is attempted in the work in progress, *Learning Every Man's English,* by C. M. Gibson and I. A. Richards.

(7) *wise choice:* These complexities, and the choice of such a phrase as "wise choice" here, in place of remarks about ?fact-finding?, reflect the status, in the hierarchies of consequence, of what we are inquiring into. Meanings—whatever else we may find to say about them—are man's means of conserving and extending his unique powers as the most resourceful species known. His powers derive from his complexity in sensory-effector resource and its attendant flexibility. If we investigate his highest instruments (?meanings? for which language serves as an instrument) with apparatus comparable to those he developed to study arithmetic, macroscopic physics, descriptive botany, logic . . . we wreck our subject matter, destroy our preparation. Such mis-applications of inappropriate techniques (though at present barely avoidable) disqualify the inquiries in which we attempt to use them.

(8) *their common world:* A further discussion of the positions here indicated may be found in my *Coleridge on Imagination,* Chapter Seven, "The Wind Harp."

(9) *views we develop:* Compare "Complementary Complementarities" in *The Screens and Other Poems* (Harcourt, Brace & World, 1960).

(10) *any sensory meanings at all to handle:*

One eye sees—what to one point is shown,
A figure almost flat, depthless, and dull.
Our two eyes join their fields, the sieves unite,
Their lines of sight converge: a rounded, full,
And living image on the Screen is thrown.

Our two ears do the same: what one could hear
By the other's limits finds itself unbound,
The two together in their differing phase
Locate our sound; but not alone through sound:
Reflex eye-searchings orient the ear.

Thus do the senses—no more led to strive,
Named for an omen—make the World of Sense
The model for the Mind; nor less for State.
Its fateful summary of experience:
Consentaneity alone will thrive.

From "The Screens"

(11) *Plato's original pair:* Phaedrus, 68.

(12) *do the business: Valerius Terminus.*

(13) *sameness in the cognizings:* There are important questions
as to when and how far (if at all) differences in cognizings
in different minds need prevent them from cognizing *sufficiently* the same meanings. Comparisons between cultures—African, American, British, Canadian, Chinese—
necessarily raise these questions; the answers may very
likely be decisive for hopes of a unitary human advance.

6

The Future of Poetry

The variety of views as to how meanings should be considered mentioned at the beginning of "Meanings Anew" is illustrated in the differences to be found between that essay and this one on the future of poetry.[1] So are, I hope, the advantages that mutual support of complementary channels may offer. The separation of the channels here is not great: far less than that between eye and ear; hardly more than that by which what each eye sees helps out what the other takes in. Both essays amplify, it will be found (in different registers), positions summarily indicated in the "Prologue" and in "Some Glances at Current Linguistics." Each develops aspects of the working of language only very sketchily outlined in the other.

Traditionally, and rightly, the prophet trembles. On him lies a double duty: that of actually swaying the future by his words; and that of being a *true* prophet—not a false one. The penalty for being a false prophet, we may recall, is to be stoned to death. If we will consult Deuteronomy 13, we will find that "if there arise among you a prophet or a dreamer of dreams and he give thee a signal and a wonder" and if then his public—as directed by the Deuteronomist [2]—doesn't like the prophet's message, even though his signs and wonders come to pass, "that prophet or that dreamer of dreams, shall be put to death. . . . So shalt thou put away the evil from the midst of thee."

These are grim and dour opening remarks, you will, maybe, be thinking. They reflect my sense of responsibility in delivering an Armstrong Lecture here in Toronto—in a city I first visited and came to regard in 1926—and in a University rightly famed for its studies of poetry and of poets. My reference to prophets is a reminder of early connections between poetry and prophecy, true and false. It asks whether these can ever really lapse: whether, if we conceive both prophecy and poetry aright, they are separable. I am speaking, of course, not of the evident announced intention of a poem, but of the implications, the impulsions, in its phrasing. All this is an indication of the central importance of poetry and of the dangers to which it is exposed.

The chief of these dangers is, of course, that a phrase like "the central importance of poetry" gets, no doubt, a somewhat various reception in all our bosoms. Various. Try it again: "the central importance of poetry." What do you feel about that? However we may vary in detail, I would guess that we can all feel the claim to be hardly more than a courtesy, a bit of correct academic ritual; innocent, maybe; innocuous, but nugatory. That would be a danger: should not enough people care enough to resent poetry's exacting and perennial claims.

Let us see, for a few moments, how great these claims are. W. B. Yeats [3] wrote of Shelley's *Defence of Poetry:* "The profoundest essay on the foundation of poetry in English." The culminating and closing sentence of that *Defence* is, you recall: "Poets are the unacknowledged legislators of the world." It is with a view to heightening, not by any means reducing, this claim that I would propose an emendation—as a quick way of making a crucial point. I would like to read, not *"Poets* are the unacknowledged legisla*tors,"* but "Po*ems* are the unacknowledged legisla*tion* of the world." That would take the weight off the poor, brief, human, limited poet and put it on the august, enduring, superhuman artifice of eternity the poet can be the means of bringing into existence. That would hand the legislative function over to a Being much better fitted to bear it. An influence that is to help us with how we should and should not *choose* needs all the authority it can be given.

Incidentally, I find a source of amusement in some of the ways in which Shelley's climactic claim gets treated by the best qualified. Take René Wellek, for example. I revere René Wellek, and often have wondered how anyone can have read all that he has read or remember all that he remembers. But, with Yeats's "the profoundest essay on the foundation of poetry" doubtless present to his mind, he can pronounce, expressly of Shelley's "unacknowledged legislators," as follows: "It must be obvious today that this kind of defense of poetry defeats its own purposes." [4] To serve Yeats—and others from Browning to Hardy and on—as Shelley's *Defence* has done, is, surely, much more "its own purpose" than to be grist to whatever academic mills.

By transferring these dangerously high claims from the *poet* to *poetry,* we gain great advantages. We clear the poet from intolerable curiosities. If one-tenth of the attention which has been given to portraying poets—since Dr. Johnson, that harbinger of modernity, launched the lives of the poets on publishers' programs—had been given to making poetry more accessible, the world (I venture to suggest) would be much better off and poetry have a different order of audience.

Actually, until and unless a poet (I am talking of the *man,* not his *work*) meets a student with extraordinary capacities of understanding, he is better off unstudied. Happy was Isaiah, who had no biographer! Unhappy, Jeremiah, about whom we know too much. Amos again: what a noble figure! Poor Hosea, the type-specimen victim of the Nosy Parker! If only the attention had been linguistic not novelistic; it appears that there's no reason whatever to think Hosea and his wife, Gomer, were not an entirely happy, faithful pair. You here in Victoria University have been extraordinarily graced with students of poets who have succeeded—by and through severe scholarship—in exalting the poets they have inquired into. For example, Northrop Frye with Blake, Kathleen Coburn with Coleridge. But not all poets can stand—I fear—the amount of looking into which, in the end, suits a Blake or a Coleridge. And—here is my point—there is no clear implication (often none at all) from the poet to that in his poetry which matters.

Now here I have been taught to expect symptoms of dissent.

I have noticed sometimes, when putting forward this view—to whit, the work (when it is really something) is greater than its author—some touches of *umbrage*. I have been corrected quite sharply over this. There are persons who don't like to be regarded as possibly less than their works. I surmise that there may be type-differences here. Some people feel very modest toward, much surprised by, their work; others seem to feel that what really makes it great is the fact that it is theirs!

To press the point home, let me here insert a prophecy as to the future of the poet. A prophecy is usually two things over which a struggle occurs in the breast of the prophet. (1) What would he like to see happen? (2) What does he really think or fear will take place?

So now: (1) What I would like to see happen is a disappearance of all poets: a return to the anonymity of the Homeric poets or of the ballad composers. A wise and powerful state would establish machinery making it easy to publish poetry but impossible to be identified as its author! That would save the composer of the poetry much—though, no doubt, there might be poets who would somehow regret such salvation. On the other hand, think of the expenses of spirit they would be spared. If no one knew who they were, why! how happy they ought to be! Nothing I can imagine would do more for poetry than the evanishment of all poets.

But what about (2): What do I, as a prophet, really think will happen? What has changed can change again. Until relatively recent times, a Poet was no object of interest or curiosity, let alone of admiration or enthusiastic regard, to any. To other poets, he was a good or bad workman in a common craft. To possible patrons, he was not very different from a tailor they might employ—certainly not anyone to feel uplifted about. Then suddenly—I don't pretend to guess why—it began: a treatment of poets by spokesmen, and livelihoods for the spokesmen not forthcoming, I believe, in former days. The leading poets became NEWS—for people many of whom could never be induced to read them. I do not somehow see this trend being soon reversed.

But let me return to my main theme: the point that there is no clear and open implication from the poet to his work—or from his work to the poet. This takes us to rather deeper considerations than I have touched on yet. It leads to the question: "What sort of thing is a poem?" Ask yourselves, for a moment, this question: "What sort of thing is a poem?" with as searching an insistence as you can. "What sort of thing is a poem?"

I don't mean: "Which would be a typical specimen poem?" We could *all* name at least one.

I don't mean: "What sorts of things should I say in praise of a good poem?" We could all produce some adjectives; for example, it is *poetic*.

I don't mean: "What, do we suppose, happens in a poet to make him write a poem (of all things!)." We are not here concerned with psychopathology—or, for that matter, with mental health or theory of the normal.

No. Take this question "What sort of thing is a poem?" just as you might take "What sort of thing is a pin, a table, a TV receiver, a moon-observation satellite, a cell, an eye, a brain?"—or, going down below the pin, "What sort of thing is a molecule, an atom, an electron and so on?" Put this way, the question "What sort of thing is a poem?" yields to reflection an interesting outcome, an outcome not found with any of the things in the list I have just run over.

I have put "What is a poem?" in this sharp contrast with "What is a pin, a table . . . a moon-observation satellite, a cell, an eye, a brain" . . . and so on? for two reasons: (1) To remind us that poems are among the most complex products (if that is a wise word to use here) of the most complex organisms known; and (2) to remark that the phrase "this poem" has a duality not shown by any of the things in my list of artificial and natural objects.

This duality it shares with all the words which denote parts of a poem, *e.g., verse, sentence, line, phrase, word.* Also with the *person* in whom the poem originated and all the persons in whom it may, as it were, be reincarnated as they read it.

Contrast the two components of this duality which is the poem. On the one hand, evidently, we have one of the most identifiable, problem-free entities imaginable: the black marks on white paper that are printed and may be bought, the physical, visual poem—a configuration of letters on a page. As this, it is almost, if not quite, as clear and reliable as a fingerprint; it is a public object of the highest status.

But, alas, this public object, with such high public credentials, is not what any reader, any critic even, any historian of cultures, any philosopher of civilizations is interested in. Only bibliopoles and compositors care for the page. What the rest are interested in is something else, a something else most intimately connected with the visual printed page, but quite other: something that isn't a physical object with at all the same status as the printed page—something which is an outcome, an agitation, an activity, an endeavor . . . a phantasm, a fiction, a vision . . . a *what-not* arising in readers who read, as we say, the poem. And these readers care for the page only insofar as it supports this something else.

The trouble about this something else is that—in contrast to the black marks on the white page—it is among the least identifiable, the least honest-to-goodness-this-is-it entities that can be sought. Its credentials—however it appears, and its appearances are endlessly variable—are, whenever they are critically examined, most shaky.

I realize what a subversive thing this almost comical contrast between the perfectly identifiable *page* and the dimly-if-at-all identifiable *something else* can become. If the poem, as opposed to its vehicle, is really as elusive as I am suggesting, then this contrast would seem to cut at the very roots of much current educational endeavor; it should pull the chairs from under innumerable professors and leave reviewers little or nothing to stand on. There are tremendous investments of energy, routine, and prestige threatened here, and massive resistances are to be expected. Whatever the outcome, let us not be too much uplifted or downcast. Sir Douglas Haig—who in Flanders in World War I had surely plenty of opportunity for judging—used to remark, "No news is ever so good or so bad as it seems!" And, in this instance, we may add, this news is by no means so new.

Let me try out a diagram now, as an aid in talking about this twofold, this dual thing we name a poem. This is the engineer's diagram used in discussing the Mathematical Theory of Communication.[5] It may seem to offer us two names which we may try to use for the two components of the dual poem: Message and Signal.

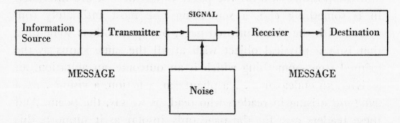

On the left is a source of Messages from which some Message is selected and handed to the Transmitter, which turns it into a Signal, sends it through a Channel to a Receiver, which turns it back into a Message, which is then handed to a Destination on the right.

Nice and neat, isn't it? I am offering it to you in part to take occasion to suggest why we ought to be very wary in taking over these two terms from telephony and so on, and with them the great words *information, encoding,* and *decoding,* with which the engineer does such magical things.

I've a further reason. A development from this diagram is the handiest way I know of thinking over the duality of the poem, and it is on how this duality is taken or handled—handled by writers and readers, *handled, rather than thought about:* we all handle it; few people think about it—that the future of poetry, as it seems to me, will depend.

Back now to the engineer. His concern is with how Message at Destination compares with Message as taken from Source and how much he can send over a given channel and so on.

How much *WHAT?*

Here the mathematician introduces his word *information.* As he uses it, it is his word not ours. This is important. *Information,* for him, does not mean what other users of *information* variously mean by it [6] (any more than, say, the word *literature* in "the literature of dental decay" or "the literature of sewage disposal" means the same thing as the word means in "English Literature" in a Catalog of Courses).

The mathematician is explicit and insistent about this. He warns us, and his best popularizers warn us, again and again: "The semantic aspects of communication are irrelevant to the engineering problem" (Shannon and Weaver, p. 3); "information must not be confused with meaning" (p. 99). For his purposes, he points out, "it is first necessary to represent the various elements involved as mathematical entities." Accordingly, he defines ^{sw}information^{sw} as ^{r}a measure of one's freedom of choice in selecting messages^{r}; it is for him ^{r}the logarithm of the number of available choices^{r}.

You see why he insists that information, for him, isn't what we ordinarily mean by it. And yet—sad to say—the warnings don't work, as anyone much concerned with linguistics and semantics could have been sure they wouldn't. As communication theory gets away from the mathematician and into the critical essay and the classroom, ᵂinformationᵂ is more and more being used as if it meant what ʔmeaningʔ can mean, and the result—as I hope to show you—is dangerous confusion. A fine and convenient example, this, of Message at Destination not being in due accord with Message at Source.

Let's look. And to aid in this, let me introduce a more elaborate diagram.

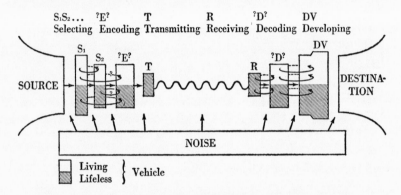

S₁S₂... ʔEʔ   T   R   ʔDʔ   DV
Selecting Encoding Transmitting Receiving Decoding Developing

What is this Selecting? What is this Encoding? What is this Transmitting—in the case of, say, a poem or in the case we have in train, here and now, of a speaker addressing an audience?

Parts of the whole affair are clearer than others. Obviously I now have two channels: (1) an oral-acoustic-aural channel—my voice, your hearing, and (2) a visual channel through which this diagram reaches you. In part it can speak for itself; in part I must speak to it.

I add boxes for *selecting* (S₁, S₂), and *encoding* (ʔEʔ) before *transmitting* (T) to make it over from a picture sufficient for the engineer's purposes to one more adequate, a little, to the purposes of a lecturer, or a critic, or a teacher—a teacher of beginners in a second language, say, or of beginning readers. Also more adequate, a little, I hope, to thought about the future of poetry.

Corresponding to S and E are added on your, the receiver's, side two more boxes: D (decoding) and DV (developing). DV because it stands too for Deo Volente—God Willing! In the story, you recall, the rector sent his brother parson a postcard saying: "Good! I'll be with you Thursday, (DV); and on Friday, in any case." There is a lot of DV about the arrival of messages, intact, at Destinations.

But now, what about the Destination? And what about the Source?

Are you the Destination? I should hope not. Do you *feel like* a Destination? What's going forward in you, I hopefully suggest, has its front somewhere between D and DV. And you are wondering what about it. How you understand me will depend upon what I go on to say but more still on what you find (now or later) to say to yourself (or to others) about it all.

This is what the great theorist of sign-situations, Charles Sanders Peirce, meant by his doctrine that every sign needs other succeeding signs as its interpretants—and so on and so on. If so, the Destination is a long way off. Harlow Shapley has said it might be as much as six thousand million years ahead.

I would be sorry if anyone here felt like a Destination. That would only mean he was continuously putting my remarks into his mental wastepaper basket—to put it politely. Accordingly, I open up the Destination box toward the future

And what about the Source? Am I the Source by any chance? Not to my knowledge. Not in any ordinary, everyday sense. No. The only way in which I could be the Source would entail an extreme transcendental, Vedantist, mystical position in which All becomes One. That is in place in some kinds of poetry, but not here, where we are dealing with some sort of embryo of a science—a science of meanings.

I say I am not the Source for many reasons: partly, because what I find to say seems to be handed to me. Not necessarily now—sentence by sentence—but at various times in the past when I wrote down these notes I am using; and, before that, when notions I have remembered to use here *first* happened to me. "First," I say. But there is no first in these things. Any ingredient in an utterance is shaped by former utterances— much as any cell in our bodies has its function through division and differentiation from our own earliest cells, and they in turn inherit their possibilities from yet earlier cells.[7] Mind and body alike go back and back and back.

By this we will be reminded of *The Prelude* (which has, maybe, more in its title than we ordinarily suppose. A prelude— is it?—not alone to other poems of Wordsworth's, but to a future for humanity for which certain developments in poetry would be a necessary condition). The lines in *The Prelude* I refer to, the lines this part of my argument derives *through,* are in Book II, lines 200 onwards.

Addressing Coleridge specifically as "one/More deeply read in thy own thoughts," [8] the poem goes on:

> Hard task to analyse a soul, in which
> Not only general habits and desires,
> But each most obvious and particular thought,
> Not in a mystical and idle sense,
> But in the words of reason deeply weigh'd
> Hath no beginning.

Accordingly, let us open out this box, the Source, as with that Destination box.

In our new diagram S_1, S_2 . . . represent Selecting activities: the selection, not merely of what shall be (in various senses and varying degrees) *in* the poem, but of what shall be allowed to arise for consideration as to possible inclusion. It is probably wise to make no assumptions as to how consciously, or with what sort of consciousness, or under what sorts of pressures, these activities proceed. Probably vast individual differences among composers, as among poems, must be recognized. Here, above all, it is well to remember Coleridge's prayer, nominally addressed to

Thelwal (December 17, 1796): "Do not let us introduce an act of Uniformity against Poets" (I would add, or against poems, or against the interpretations thereof).

These S_1, S_2 . . . are marked in the diagram in ways which I hope will indicate how much mutual, cyclic interdependence there is among them. Each possible item, as it comes up for consideration, automatically increases or decreases the chances of incalculably many other items being considered. As it progressively establishes itself, its excluding influence becomes the stronger, and so does its *pull* as regards further choices. We should bear in mind, however, that excluded items need by no means be inert. What is being kept out of a poem may well have a role in it as important as Satan's.

Selecting, Encoding, Transmitting . . . for most of the engineer's processes, one box will take care of them all. He is busy, typically, with how to get a typewritten sheet—that, as it were, falls out of Nature to him—typed out again correctly in a satellite on the moon. What is on the typewritten sheet matters not a jot to him, in his capacity as engineer; it can be nonsense syllables, provided only that they are identifiable nonsense syllables! But for a concern with poetry, all this must look very different. Selection, for that, is everything—a dauntingly, inexhaustibly complex responsibility—whenever satisfactorily, then mysteriously, if not miraculously, discharged. Even though we may suppose we see why one phrase—in its context of duty—is better than another, and can happily find ways to suggest why this is so, there will always be, if we can keep our ears open to them, other explanations—maybe of a different sort altogether. As a sample of the sort of thing I have here in mind, may I append the following conversation, though it concerns a poem written through me?

LOTZ: I would like to ask Mr. Richards two questions, if I may, concerning the title of his poem. Is it to be regarded as a metric text as the rest of the poem, or as a sample of prose? And why is the

quality of the title so much better as it stands than if we reverse the
two phrases and read "April in Harvard Yard/Harvard Yard in April"?

RICHARDS: Well, now, let me see whether I can remember about these
things—they meant something. (Laughter.) Following Jakobson's elec-
trifying contrast between a rapt soul and the crypt analyst, in which
of my capacities—as rapt soul or crypt analyst—am I to reply? It seems
to me I must use a little history here. I think I called it, after the poem
was written, something very flat-footed indeed: "Harvard Yard in
Spring." That wasn't anything more than a label and then something
made me feel that more ought to be done, and against a lot of
critical resistance by people who had got attached to "Harvard Yard
in Spring" (that always happens; any emendation, I think, always
meets resistance from people who at all approve of the first form),
I tried this. But the question of which phrase should come first, I
think, is crucial. It seems to me unquestionably in the right order
now, but reverse it and you begin to analyze and here's where the
crypt analyst raps the rapt soul. The crypt analyst comes forward and
invents, I'm quite sure, as much as he finds. "Harvard Yard in April"—
well, Harvard Yard is a queer block of speech. It is an awkward name
—"Harvard Yard." I am perhaps haunted by the number of people
I have met in different parts of the world who pronounced Harvard
in other ways. There is some tension around that. I have very good
friends who ought to know much better and who have visited the place
yet go on saying, "How are things at Harvard?" (Laughter.) Harvard
Yard—how monotonous! When it recurs it is much more monotonous.
It has a finality because of its having been initial. There is a great
contrast, it seems to me, between HARVARD YARD and APRIL. "Harvard
Yard in April" is just a temporal and locating phrase, no more. But
when we reverse it it seems to me that April, in slight personification,
has changed its function. It is no longer mere location. It's what *she*'s
up to, and April has become a she instead of a month. What she's up
to in Harvard Yard has something to do with the nostalgia of the
persona, the mask for the speaker. Well, that's the best I can do.

JAKOBSON: What is repulsive in the suggested inversion "April in
Harvard Yard/Harvard Yard in April"? The title of Richards' poem
displays a clearcut metrical integrity: it begins and ends with a word
stress and consists of two hexasyllabic parts, each with an initial and
two further stresses. All six stressed syllables of the title are separated

from each other, in four instances by a single unstressed syllable and in one case by two. The whole is both opened and closed by the same leading phrase "Harvard Yard." An inverted order of the two sentences would abolish their rhythmic continuity by a clash of two stressed syllables ". . . Yard/Harvard . . .": such an inversion would abolish the symmetry between the stressed onset and end of the title and its penult stress would discord with the final stress in all subsequent lines of the poem. The figurative, metonymic tinge of the sequence "April in Harvard Yard" is particularly palpable when preceded by the nonfigurative, literal meaning of the reverse construction "Harvard Yard in April." [9]

Now what about this Encoding and Decoding business? And, with it, what about the contrast between Message and Signal?

Encoding

After S_1, S_2 . . . in the diagram comes 'E', bracketed in interrogation marks. This is, indeed, one of the most dubious points in the whole account: one of the two points at which we will be wisest to walk most warily. We are exposed to a somewhat typical and exceedingly grim semantic mind-trap: the term *code*.

We have two major senses of ᵂCODEᵂ which often cooperate but need not. One is illustrated in ˢᵂcode of lawsˢᵂ, ˢᵂcode of conductˢᵂ. The other is illustrated in ˢᵂthe Morse codeˢᵂ. Their cooperation appears, commonly and characteristically, in ˢᵂthe highway codeˢᵂ. In the first sense, a code is ˢᵂa collection of regulations or agreements, or observances, explicitly formulated or notˢᵂ; it is a more or less systematic set of *if-thens,* covering such and such a field of behavior. In the second and narrower sense, a code is a ˢᵂformula of transformation between one set of signs and another, or between a set of signs and a set of performancesˢᵂ. For example, the Morse code equates letters and words with configurations of dots, dashes and spaces; and the highway code equates the signals that a driver should give with his subsequent actions. In a wider or deeper sense, however, ^{sw}the highway code^{sw} can cover not only these but the general conduct, courtesies, etc., obligatory upon good drivers.

In the engineer's theory of communication, it is customary to say that messages selected from the Source are *encoded* for Transmission; that is, they are converted into a signal suited to the channel. Here the second sense of code seems in place. The message (which may be a sequence of spoken or written words, or music, or a photograph, or a game) is transformed into something which can be carried by a channel to a Receiver, which will then by a reverse transformation recover the message from the signal. Whether the transformation is performed mechanically, as in a telephone, or by operators, as in old-style telegraphy, is no matter.

Consider now the poet 'finding words', as we say, for a poem which is in course of composition. Here we have a very different transaction. There is no identifiable and describable !message! prior to the occurrences of words in the selective S_1, S_2 . . . process. Nor as yet are the words finally selected which are to be handed to the vocal organs, or to the hand or typewriting routines, for transformation into the signal. Nor is there any formula of transformation between the yet-to-be words and their yet-to-be meanings. No encoding, in the second, narrower sense is occurring.

On the other hand, in the first sense of code, there is no question that a language forms a code. Every word and phrase in it has very elaborate observances to keep—under penalty of becoming inoperative. At best, only rough accounts of these observances can be obtainable for any language. Such accounts are what linguists work toward—immeasurably more remote from them than the physicist is from his similar goals. The system of interrelations is not fixed. Language grows. Words, etc., change their senses and much more. Poets and others can bend them to new service. Some of the more obvious interrelations of words, their

substitutabilities, their variations, are recorded in the dictionaries and the synonym compilations. And so on . . .

This belonging under a code is a very different thing from being assigned by a formula of transformation to one-one, meaning-
word, word-meaning couples (ʳpairingsʳ, as Chomsky calls them,
p. 84 above) as in a symbol-signal code (*e.g.*, as speech is represented in writing) or in a sign-performance code (a driver's signals). Confusion of the varied senses of code, I hope I can show,
can encourage and protect dangerous misconceptions.

Feed Forward [10] and Feedback

But first, let us consider further the interdependencies of ʔEʔ
with S_1, S_2 . . . and with T, the Transmitting: here either the
aural-articular activity of speech or the optical-motor activity of
writing or drawing.

Although the time-arrow is from left to right, there are innumerable eddyings in the process which finally give T what it will
utter. If the sounds of the words offered to T are too awkward,[11] or otherwise inacceptable, that can kick back and
require their replacement. Similarly, if what is forming in ʔEʔ
(which I will now read as Embodiment, in place of Encoding)
cannot complete itself, locally or in full, by what is offered by
S_2, E can enforce recourse to S_1—the far wider, wilder field of
possible choices, from which S_2 was a short-list selection. Every-
body knows how a word which is just right from one point of
view may have a fatal drawback from another; and how this
trouble can be cured by finding another word or phrase, by
changing some other word, maybe, in the passage, or by a more
extensive reorganization, or by a radical restart. The whole
process by which possible parts accept, exclude, modify, mold one
another to form a whole, which is only forefelt until it is found,
operates both through *feed forward* and *feedback* (*i.e.*, outcome
reports as to the success or failure of tentatives in attaining ends

which have been fed forward). Throughout the writing of poetry, coming events cast their shadows before; they cannot come until they are prepared for and yet, as with the chromosome theory[12] of *Psalm* 139:15, how, "when as yet there were none of them," could the coming events determine what the preparation should be?

At present, and for a long while yet, I suggest, we have just to admit that they do. We are likely to understand how chromosomes work long before we can give any comparable account of how a poem achieves its unity or closure.

Reception

As Transmission occurs, that which has been living activity (of unimaginable complexity) dies—to become merely physics: undulations in air, configurations in a surface. After an interval, as an ear or an eye responds to these, the reincarnation begins. It is open, as the candid and reflective well know, to enormous hazards. What is surprising is that it ever is as good as sometimes it seems to be. As good? How are we to take that? As having $^{?}$*more or less the same potentialities*$^{?}$—not necessarily actualities—it had before its death into the signal.

We can keep ^{w}signal^{w} here, provided we are clear that it is the physical transaction in the channel and not any words that we are talking of. We can even keep ^{w}message^{w}, provided it is the words-*with*-meaning that are thus put into contrast and connection with the signal. The dangerous use is that which would connect meaning to wording as message to signal, for this would obscure the key question: How does a word in a given setting—or field of duty—get its meaning?

$^{?}$More or less the same potentialities$^{?}$: here is the other point at which caution will be most appropriate. What are we here talking about? Not the accidental adventures of a verbal organism among the inconceivably diverse, and in general lamentably undernourished, ill-equipped, and (according to public posters) –teen % deranged mental population it may met. No. The proportion of its readers in a given year in whom the poem returns to something near (more or less) its potential (in view of the rest of the language active in them) is, as literary history can confirm, no sort of guarantee or assurance of anything. "For whom is a poet writing?" is a very badly formulated question. We should ask instead: To what sort of *'condition of the language'* does the poem address itself? Even this, however, is far too narrowly conceived.

Let us suppose, to clarify this situation, that ill-advised methods of teaching Reading—under, perhaps, the pressure of threatened decline into illiteracy and barbarism coupled with a competitive need to produce large numbers of technologists—should have produced a public no longer interested in or capable of reading poetry. The supposition is, no doubt, ridiculous. Nonetheless, it illustrates the argument. With such a general decline in reading ability—suppose it severe enough—would the best poetry of the best periods of the language lose its value? It would loose its *accessibility,* of course.

On the other hand, entertain a fancy as extravagant. That, thanks to scholastic labors and the rise in the standards of living, increase in leisure and opportunity and so on, the poetic potentialities of the available operative language were to *rise*— would poetry that our best judges most esteem nowadays come to seem commonplace?

Both suppositions have, I think, some use as *screens* or filters bringing out interesting speculative possibilities as to fluctuations in reputations and fashions of appraisal, especially if we consider, not general, but relatively specific risings and fallings of poetic potential. (Examples here, not hard to offer, would, in my experience, be more likely to confuse and complicate than to clarify—being themselves so variously interpretable.) The over-all point, however, is that a poem is responsible to the *resources of the language* as regards its task—not to any public (except a public in command of these resources). The inde-

pendence of language from poet or from reader (or critic) is remarkable. No one can *wish* anything into, or *wish* anything out
of, a composition—though we authors and critics may differ indeed upon what it admits or excludes. In the end, however, it
decides for or against us.

From Receiver (eye, ear . . .) onwards, a process of conjecture and check (feed forward and feedback) similar, except in
sequence, to the composition leads ideally to an organism
having potentialities comparable to those belonging to what was
transmitted. The poem, we say, has then been *read* (as opposed
to being *misread*). There will, in an account of this process, be
the same temptation to insert a Decoding activity 'D', and the
same objection will hold that between the signal taken in by
the Receiver and *meaningful* words, no transformation formula
holds. The formula holds only between sounds heard (or words
seen) and auditory articulatory activity (spoken words) in the
recipient. And again there is the same danger of mistaking the
transformation from signal to word for the passage by which
words develop their meaning.

Development (or interpretation) sometimes brings out the
feed-forward–feed-back cycles very clearly. A tangle, a blemish, or
a blank in a later phase sends us back to re-examine the text,
which may have been misread, or may actually be corrupt. (I
remember my bewilderment as a child when I first met a poem
by William Morris with the title "A Good Night in Prison."

> Feet tethered
> Hand fettered
> Fast to the stone
> The grim walls
> Square-lettered
> With prison'd men's groan.

A Good Night in Prison? The printer had omitted a K before
the middle word.) And again, years later, when a Master hap-

pened to recite *The Defence of Guenevere* to his 5th Form
(are there such schoolmasters still?):

> at Christmas time
> This happened: When the heralds sung his name:
> 'Son of King Ban of Benwick,' seemed to chime
> Along with all the bells that rang that day
> O'er the white roofs, with little chains of rime.

So I heard. But what Morris had written was:

> O'er the white roofs with little change of rime.

Which seemed, when I read it, to complain of a monotony
Queen Guenevere would be unlikely to be feeling.

There are many ways in which Reception can go wrong.
Hasty assumptions as to metre (feed forward) may block our
perception of a poem's movement, until we wipe them out and
start again. A whole circus of technical and critical preconcep-
tions (see *Practical Criticism*, VIII, pp. 16–17) can intervene to
prevent *just* reading—their analogues can embarrass and frus-
trate composition.

All these can be compendiously described as NOISE. Noise, the
diagram maintains, can afflict the whole undertaking all the way
from the earliest Selection to the latest phrases of Development.

There remains one feature of this diagram to discuss. S_1, S_2
. . . , 'E', 'D', DV are two-story boxes. This is an attempt to
reflect the duality of a word and of a poem as a union of *sig-
nifiant* and *signifié* (in Saussure's terms), a union in which the
body, while it is alive, is not to be conceived apart from that
which informs it, that which it embodies, and conversely.

It is, I suggest, wise to make this very powerful metaphor
explicit to the point when we may ask: Is it not also more than
a metaphor here? Has it not a justifiable literal sense *as well?*
(The opposition: metaphoric-literal is *often* not exclusive.) The
motions of the organs of speech, of a writing hand, are living;

the resultant vibrations in the air, the script on the paper, are not—in the straightest most literal sense of the word. They are dead. My two sentences above, under the heading *Reception,* have, however, said this already.

At a time when linguistics is paying more and more heed to the development of speech in the infant (and to its inverse: loss of speech in the aphasic; see Jakobson and Halle, *Fundamentals of Language*), we will do very well to hark back again to *The Prelude* and the sequel to the passage quoted above to note how "the infant Babe" becomes—

> An inmate of this *active* universe . . .
> And powerful in all sentiments of grief,
> Of exultation, fear, and joy, his mind,
> Even as an agent of the one great mind,
> Creates, creator and receiver both,
> Working but in alliance with the works
> Which it beholds.

The linguistic structuralist is so often in danger of confining his attention to the relations of words with other words only that it is salutary to be reminded that the initial charges of the poet's earliest words come to them, normally (I stress the normative meaning of *normal*), from his mother's face: in her tones of voice, in her frowns and smiles,

> there exists
> A virtue which irradiates and exalts
> All objects through all intercourse of sense.
> No outcast he, bewilder'd and depress'd;
> Along his infant veins are interfus'd
> The gravitation and the filial bond
> Of nature, that connect him with the world.
> —Such, verily, is the first
> Poetic spirit of our human life.

Poetic plaiting is threefold: there is the duality we have discussed of the meaningful words and there is "the filial bond" that connects us with "this *active* universe," which, if we will take *interfusion* seriously and considerately enough, weaves that duality. The strength of a passage comes from all three: from the phonologic and morphologic network linking words with words (their rhyme fields, root-branching, and so on); from the semantic network of substitutions, oppositions, implications (and how much more) which by countless routes links every word with every other; and from the mutual control of the contexts [13] (recurrences of utterances in situations) which give all reference and concern to whatever may be uttered. Through these threefold ways language has built up its strange power. If I may quote some sentences I wrote some time ago:

So far from verbal language being a "compromise for a language of intuition" (T. E. Hulme's misleading phrase)—a thin, but better-than-nothing, substitute for real experience—language, well used, is a *completion* and does what the intuitions of sensation by themselves cannot do. Words are the meeting points at which regions of experience which can never combine in sensation or intuition come together. They are the occasion and the means of that growth which is the mind's endless endeavor to order itself. That is why we have language. It is no mere signaling system. It is the instrument of all our distinctively human development, of everything in which we go beyond the other animals.[14]

Structuralists stress for their purposes, for the sake of an operable technique, opposition (mutual preclusiveness) among linguistic elements. For poetics, we need also to note the multiplicity, the limitless variety, of the linkages among phrases, the threefold web of potential inter-inanimations. They are of course dispositional: no one is actually aware of more than a very few of them at any one time. Nonetheless, these verbal potentials [15] —potentials in a sense which looks for help to the mathematicians' and the physicists' senses—are what the poet works with.

No one will deny that there are meanings (to call them that: virtualities, dispositional conspiracies) which are active before they embody themselves. The process of writing a poem—in many instances—consists of cajoling an unembodied something into its incarnation. The formal aspects of poetry—rhyme, metre, etc.,—are largely dodges which have been found to be propitious in slowing down selection and widening the scan. Before it has found itself in its words by finding the words for itself, that *something else* has as little overt character, is as indescribable, as a name that we are failing to recall.

One thing, I suggest, is clear and certain as well as highly familiar: it is tested and verified billions of times a minute in human experience, entirely trustworthy and reliable. And what is this reassuring and comfortable truth? It is that *what is said* depends on *how it is said,* and *how it is said* on *what is said. What we say* and *how we say it* are inseparable—in utterances which are entire.

There are exceptions—in various measure. Briefly: what can be translated in any utterance without change—put into other words, into another language without changes—is a sort of precipitate, a derivative from the entire living fluid utterance. There are sciences, there are technologies which operate almost exclusively with and in such precipitates; they can be translated without trouble: you can make up new terms, if need be, to fill gaps and so on. That is one end of a continuous series—spectrum, shall I call it? At the other end is the sort of poetry for which there is either no precipitate—no factual or propositional or directive derivative—or what there is that could be separated as such is trivial, negligible. In between are many sorts of poetry. Near the center there is the sort exemplified in the lines from *The Prelude* I have quoted, where there is a very important propositional precipitate but where the interpretations—the further signs and further signs and so on—for the parts of the utterance and for their connections with one another are not what they are in the precipitate. The words moderate one another, give and take among themselves in ways mostly beyond the means, as yet, of linguistic analysis.

I am not talking, however, of the future of linguistic analysis, which I imagine as illimitable—but of the future of poetry. The great danger there which a crude use of *encode* and *decode*, *message* and *signal* would bring in would be a recrudescence of the separation between *what is said* and the *how of saying it*.

Back to the engineer for a moment. His *message* is typically a script, a telegram, or a photographic image (for TV, for example). This he transforms to suit his channel into a *signal* he can send. Ideally, he can reverse the transformation process at the Receiver end, *decode* and regain the message. Well and good!

Contrast that, now, with what happens when an utterance is forming here in me and I am trying to speak so that a sufficiently similar utterance may (DV) arise in you.

We are dealing with whole utterances, mind you, not with precipitates.

In whole utterances rhythm, stress, intonation, pausing, the expression of a face, gestures are as important as choice of words, all these things moderating one another, qualifying one another, adjusting one another to the over-all aim. And the over-all aim, we can add, only finds itself through all this. What sort of separation can you make here between message and signal?

You can't make any: the coming into being of the signal is too closely inter-inanimated with the coming into being of the message.

The more minutely and imaginatively we examine the process by which an utterance forms—and, correspondingly, is understood—the more fully we realize how interdependent WHAT and HOW here are. This unity of content and form, of spirit and letter, of intuition and expression, is, of course, a perennial theme of criticism and of poetry itself.

> O body swayed to music, O brightening glance,
> How can we know the dancer from the dance! [16]

The most important thing about poetry, the thing which most makes its future a matter of concern, is that it exemplifies this interdependence, this unity. It strives to be exemplary in this; it is our exemplar—for that kind of mutual and just control of part by part which is health.

So now: if we suddenly leap into the middle of this delicate subtle mutuality (bull-in-the-china-shop fashion) with a bad metaphor and old error mistaken for a bit of scientific discovery and teach that what we do in using language is to make up messages which we then encode in words and transmit with our vocal organs . . . and so for the other side . . . look what happens: we are flung back into what I want to label now (damagingly, destroyingly, I hope) as the VULGAR PACKAGING VIEW.

According to this, here's the poet having a 'poetic experience', poor fellow. (I should put shrieks of derision round every phrase of this account.) Then he wraps it up well in a neat and elegant verbal package—air, damp and rust, mold, moth and fungus proof, guaranteed to keep forever . . . and sells us it so! We unwrap it, if we can, and enjoy the contents. We have the 'poetic experience', believe it or not!

You may suppose I am pulling your leg. But no. This sort of thing, with garnishings, is being served up as the latest word in scientific "Theory of Communication" under cover of talk about *message* and *signal, information, coding* and *encoding.* How is it, I wonder, in Toronto? In my classes at Harvard I have for some time been meeting graduate students—in good standing and pretty certain to climb to important positions in educational administration, designing and directing programs of instruction in reading and so forth—whose handling of "Theory of Communication" jargon amounts to just that.

Of course, it is an old error—this Vulgar Packaging View— but that does not mean that, under new labels and new management, it won't be successful. Indeed, no; in general, it is the oldest errors—newly dressed up—that most often get the market. And—I am sorry as I say it—you can catch both Wordsworth and Shelley, though not Coleridge, I think, preaching the Vulgar Packaging View like a gospel.

We have, of course, to bear in mind how constantly language leads us to *talk* in ways which do not correspond with our *thought*. I will borrow a convenient label from Roman Jakobson and call it the Sunrise-Sunset, or pre-Copernican, or pre-Einsteinian Style. It may be that many people who use Vulgar Packaging expressions really know better—just as people talking of sunsets have not forgotten, and are not denying, that the earth rotates. I am suggesting, though, that very often people not only use Vulgar Packaging Language but *think with,* and are attached to, Vulgar Packaging THOUGHT. And that these people are finding this scientific lingo: of *message, signal,* and so on an intellectual Godsend.

What's chiefly wrong with it? This. It stands squarely in the way of our practical understanding and command of language. It hides from us both how we may learn to speak (and write) better, and how we may learn to comprehend more comprehensively. Managing the variable connections between words and what they mean: what they might mean, can't mean, and should mean—*that*—not as a theoretical study only or chiefly, but as a matter of actual control—that is the technique of poetry. If anyone is led into a way of thinking—a way of proceeding, rather—as though *composing* were a sort of catching a nonverbal butterfly in a verbal butterfly net, as though comprehending were a releasing of the said butterfly from the net, then he is deprived of the very thing that could help him: exercise in comparing the various equivalences of different words and phrases, their interdependencies, in varying situations.

Every word or phrase in a language known to any one person (one utterer-comprehender) is—I have been insisting—potentially linked with all his other words and phrases in an unimaginably multifarious manner. Some words *substitute* for others (in a given situation), some *modify,* some *oppose,* some *exclude* others; some *invite* others, some *repel* . . . it is endless. Roman Jakob-

son, who has done so much to enlighten us on all this, is fond
of recurring to the suggestive example of the NAME that you
have temporarily forgotten. You don't know it—except perhaps
that it begins with C. But of any name that comes up you know
undoubtingly that it is NOT THAT. And equally, if the name were
said, you would know it. Here is this vacuum that is so exactly
choosy as to what could fill it. There are similar exactly choosy
relationships of partial synonymy, modification, implication,
opposition, etc., uniting a language in any mind.

Consider what we know in knowing some part of a language.
We know to some extent which words will *work how* with
which, in the varying vicissitudes in which we meet them and in
which we may try to use them. Every word, through this potential work, this network of possible cooperations, is connected
via other words with all the rest in a *living:* a growing, changing,
decaying lexical structural would-be system. That system has
its claims—as we know—to be *you,* in your case, or *me,* in mine.
I don't myself support these claims, but this much seems certain: the quality of our living—not only of our thinking, but of
our feeling, desiring, willing, and the rest—is most intimately
mixed up with the state of order-disorder within our lexical-
structural would-be system. And Poetry, as I have been saying,
is our exemplar of that would-be system at its most entire—being
most itself.

Perhaps *system* is too abstract a word; suggesting something
doctrinaire. The cure is to remember Shakespeare. He is, it
seems to me, the ink-well, the crystal ball in which we may best
see our visions of poetry's future.

Shakespeare has been—has he not?—the most variously interpreted and interpretable of poets; and, moreover, the most
widely influential. I connect these three: influence, range of interpretations, and the prophetic. This brings me back to my
opening point—the connection of poetry with prophecy. Poetry
offers, with the widest scope, exercise in choices. Prophecy demands, with equally wide scope, the exercise of choice. They are

both concerned—acknowledged or unacknowledged—with legislation: what to feel, to do, to be, or to try to be.

So, now, after these preliminaries, three short remarks on what may and should happen to poetry.

(1) I have dwelt on the dangers of badly applied and misunderstood linguistics. Let me proclaim the hopes that well-applied, well-understood linguistics might warrant.

There really have been astounding advances in linguistics in the last few decades—not only in detailed description, but in principle too. Some of this offers new promise, new power, new hope, and new sanction to poetry. Chiefly, the view that behind a line of verse may stand, not the mere experience of the poet, but the immense reserves, the accumulated potentials, of language, due to the equivalences, the oppositions, reinforcements, resistances and so on of phrase to phrase within it. Though all this, language can really represent, can really speak for human experience as the poet's ¹experiences¹ (the things his biographer shakes his head over, sobs, giggles, or goggles at) can't. It is this same vast interconnectedness among phrases, of course, which is responsible for our understanding one another at all. The meanings we share are the possibilities, the potentials, we can rely on in explaining our words to ourselves in parallel fashion.

(2) My second remark is that *for a good future* poetry *needs a good audience*. Its present audience is, I fear, very small and very poor; indeed, it is highly incompetent. I doubt if it is improving. The root of this, I believe, is bad techniques in the teaching of Reading and in the early stages of language teaching. I believe these can be remedied, and that an audience much more capable of reading well enough to explore and enjoy and appraise poetry could be produced pretty quickly if we really tried. The trouble is—as I see it—the prevalence of methods which appeal to those who think that the ideal pupil, the dream-student, is one with the right surface for the stencil of the mimeograph: one who takes in, to give back unchanged, just what he is told. Mind you, every teacher today will indignantly

disown *this* as his educational philosophy. I am thinking, though, of what teachers *do*.

Somehow I have for the last few decades been deep in this field, and out of Poetics and Literary Criticism. But, you know, it is the same everywhere. When, at different hours of the same day, you may be busy on, say, *Troilus and Cressida* with graduate students and on early pages of a pre-primer for complete beginners to Reading, it is enheartening to perceive that *learning itself*—when it is the outcome of successful exploration—is renewing and refreshing, a self-reinforcement at all levels; and that rote instruction, tamped down by drill, is everywhere the same: a dehumanizing replacement of spontaneity by psittacism, which, being interpreted, is parroting. But it is in the earliest years that obstacles to poetry—to *poiesis*—are most firmly set up.

(3) My third and last remark can be brief. Poetry needs to wake up. It is being neglectful of, irresponsive to, what is happening. In a spring dawn such as never before broke, dazzling with promise and power never offered before, here is poetry—as though it were old and frail—all huddled up and with, I fear, its head under the bedclothes.

The Future of Poetry

(1)   *the future of poetry:* a topic touched on, for understand-able reasons, only in the concluding pages of the essay.

(2)   *the Deuteronomist:* the most formidable author in our tradition.

(3)   Yeats, in *Ideas of Good and Evil,* thought *Prometheus Unbound* ᵣa sacred bookʳ. The closer and more con-tinual anyone's study of it the more one will agree. See my discussion in G. B. Harrison's *Major British Writers,* Vol. II (Harcourt, Brace & World) and in "The Mystical Elements in Shelley," *The Aryan Path,* June-July, 1959.

(4)   *defeats its own purpose:* René Wellek, *A History of Modern Criticism, 1750–1950,* II, *The Romantic Age* (Yale, 1955), p. 125. Such pontification looks like a po-tentially useful diagnostic indication for a disease in scholarship which current conditions in Departments, as in Foundations, seem likely to spread.

(5)   Diagram: from Claude E. Shannon and Warren Weaver, *The Mathematical Theory of Communication* (Urbana, University of Illinois Press, 1949), p. 5.

(6)   *variously mean by it:* For indications of how venturously the mathematicians themselves use the word, see D. M. Mackay, "In Search of Basic Symbols," *Cybernetics,* Transactions of the Eighth Conference, New York, 1952. The risks the mathematicians run are, however, child's play compared with those the general reading public incur as a result.

(7)   *yet earlier cells: Cf.* p. 16 above.

(8)   *"More deeply read in thy own thoughts":* Mental in-
        debtedness—for others' help in such [nb]reading[nb]—is il-
        limitable. Those who are thus indebted to Coleridge may
        feel that Wordworth's debt was greater than he could
        know.

(9)   *Style in Language,* Thomas A. Sebeok, Ed. (Cambridge,
        M.I.T., 1960). The poem in question:

HARVARD YARD IN APRIL: APRIL IN HARVARD YARD

> To and fro
> Across the fretted snow
> Figures, footprints, shadows go.
>
> Their python boughs a-sway
> The fountain elms cascade
> In swinging lattices of shade
> Where this or that or the other thought
> Might perch and rest.
>   And rest they ought
> For poise or reach.
> Not all is timely. See, the beech,
> In frosty elephantine skin
> Still winter-sealed, will not begin
> Though silt the alleys hour on hour
> Débris of the fallen flower,
> And other flowery allure
> Lounge sunlit on the Steps and there
> Degrees of loneliness confer.
>
> Lest, lest . . . away!
> You may
> Be lost by May

(For a commentary, see *Style in Language.*)

(10)   *Feed Forward:* "Take looking for something, hunting,
        searching, for example. We do not *find* anything unless we

know in some sense what we are looking for. Nor do our humblest cousins among the animals. (I'd like, here again, as with *acteevity,* to put vocal tags on *find* and *know.* They are correlative terms here. We may happen on something but we don't *find* it unless we are looking for it. *Finding* is the end-phase—in both main senses of ᵂend ᵂ—to the acteevity of searching. Something is fed forward by co-incidence with which that acteevity reaches its terminus and goal.)

"In my pocket are some pennies and a dime. I am going to find the dime by touch and partly by hearing: by the feel and sound of my finger-nail scraping on the milled edge of the dime. Something is being fed into my search (and into your observation of my search) which will, when the search reaches its END, tell the acteevity that it is successful." See *Speculative Instruments,* "Toward a More Synoptic View."

(11)   *too awkward:*

> Ah, how can fear sit and hear as love hears it
> Grief's heart's cracked grate screech?
> —Swinburne, *Heptalogia*

The most euphonious poet could also be the most cacophonous when he so wished. Those who still sniff at Swinburne may probably not have noticed how often he uses monosyllables as few ever have; *e.g.,* "The Pilgrims" or in "The Last Oracle," *Poems and Ballads II.*

(12)   "Thine eyes did see my substance, yet being unperfect;
And in thy book were all my members written;
Which day by day were fashioned:
When as yet there were none of them."

(13)   *contexts:* in a technical sense. See *The Meaning of Meaning,* Appendix B; *Interpretation in Teaching,* Preface, pp. viii, ix; *Philosophy of Rhetoric* (Oxford University Press, Galaxy Books), pp. 28–42.

(14)   *beyond the other animals: Philosophy of Rhetoric*, pp.
       130–131. See on this Allen Tate, *Reason in Madness* (New
       York, Putnam, 1941), "Literature as Knowledge," p. 55.
       I am indebted to Mr. Tate for drawing my attention to
       the passage. See also, as to mutual control of recurrences
       of sentences in situations: *First Steps in Reading English*
       and *English through Pictures,* I and II.

(15)   *verbal potentials:* It is deeply disturbing that this funda-
       mental concept, though in use since before Plato, hardly
       ever gets useful attention from inquirers into language.

(16)   *dancer from the dance:* from Yeats, "Among School Chil-
       dren." Compare Note 8 to "Some Glances at Current Lin-
       guistics" on Plato's and modern physicists' views of ?being?.

7

Variant Readings and Misreading

In this paper I shall later be attempting to construct a definition of [?]misreading[?], and it is a sound rule—is it not?—to consider on such occasions, as closely as we can and as explicitly, what we want the definition for. Such consideration commonly lightens the strains on the definition and can make it relatively less necessary. I would ask therefore that much of the following be read as an account of [sw]misreading[sw] for which it may prove useful and important to have a definition marking it off clearly from [sw]variant readings[sw]. Inevitably, behind this will be a concern with possible meanings for [?]reading[?]. We will be considering what uses we should be endeavoring to make of this term. It is well to note that among them will be normative *uses. Every definition no doubt sets up a normative field: uses are either conforming to it or not. But among uses of [w]reading[w], [w]interpretation[w], [w]understanding[w] and so on, there will be some that are normative in a further sense: they lay down principles by which instances may be judged as [?]valid[?] or invalid, as [?]correct[?] or mistaken. Some uses escape this: We may say of a reader that he is reading without raising any question whether he is correctly interpreting what he reads.*

I have left the paper as it was written: in the register that there seemed appropriate, or at least customary. The reader may

*well feel, as much from its style as from the specimens of mis-
reading offered, that such academic exercises will not do much to
meet our need.*

It is worth remarking that a paper such as this is inherently
circular. Each sentence is attempting to form itself and relate
itself to the others so as to reduce the probability of its being
misread. Whatever its success, it is itself continuously exposed
to the accidents and disasters of which it is professing to supply
some account. And it is guiding itself—in part wittingly, in part
unwittingly—by the considerations it is hoping little by little
to present.

The occasion for this paper[1] is a conference in which minds
are hoping to meet, minds that have undergone different train-
ings and have thereby developed different patterns of procedure
and tendencies toward technicalization. It will not be unwise
therefore to allow a margin of our time and attention to bound-
ary questions and to devices for the treatment of misconceptions,
which may be expected to abound. Even for so experienced a
company I may spend a sentence to note the peculiar importance, theoretical and practical, of improving (if we can) our
means of discriminating between variant readings and misreading. This distinction is, I take it, a chief operating assumption in most education, and its application is a prime aim of
much discussion: the recognition, on the one hand, of the inevitability and desirability of diverse understandings and, on the
other, their sharp contrast with the mistake, the inadmissible
interpretation. It is not surprising that the distinction should be
somewhat complex and difficult to formulate. What is puzzling
is that a matter of such theoretical status and practical moment
should be, currently, so little discussed. Possibly the neglect may
have a ground in fear. I confess to a feeling of urgency in this.
You develop it if you are in a position to observe[2] the lin-

guistic disabilities of many who are going into the teaching of English and the teaching of reading.

Let me start out from an adaptation of a familiar diagram:

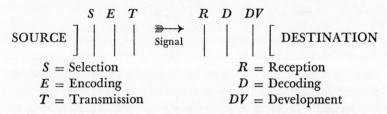

$$S \quad E \quad T \qquad R \quad D \quad DV$$

SOURCE] | | | $\overset{\ggg\longrightarrow}{\text{Signal}}$ | | | [DESTINATION

S = Selection	R = Reception
E = Encoding	D = Decoding
T = Transmission	DV = Development

Let me stress first the cyclic mutual dependence, the complexity of feed forward and feedback between S, E and T.

What is selected is commonly selected in order to be encoded and transmitted. One selection is, indeed, only doubtfully distinguishable from another, except through some encodement. Hence the old question: How do I know what I mean till I see what I say? This encodement need not be what is transmitted. Many people, in writing and in speaking, use, here and there at least, private codings, ellipses, substitutes, schemata, which would be useless to others; they compose in these, translating thence into public language for transmission. Most people recognize the process describable as ˢʷmaking up one's mind to say X rather than Y—without either X or Y being as yet put into words.ˢʷ (We may, of course, differ deeply on what account we would prefer to give of this process.) The point here, however, is that priority of X over Y may be, among other things, determined by encodement problems that have not yet explicitly arisen.

A similar cyclic mutual dependence holds between E and T. The encoding is with a view to transmission: a coming tongue-twister, or a word that we do not know how to pronounce or spell, can kick back to cause extensive revision, obviously, not only in the encoding but in selecting. More interesting are the modes of composition for which especially exacting conditions to be satisfied in encoding and transmission enforce especially rigorous and revisionary activity in selection: for example, meter and rhyme. As *Hudibras* has it

> Rimes the rudders are of verses
> By which, like ships, they steer their courses.

These courses commonly entail much more thorough and varied search for what is available to be encoded than would occur in prose composition. Thus verse form, as we know, may improve the semantic order of what is being versified. Furthermore, in most composition for which the encoding conditions are exacting, the composer is pressed fairly continuously into a dual role. He has to be his own pilot audience, to be destination as well as source, and go through (with modifications that would probably repay study) R, D and DV in critical response to his own transmission. Somewhat similar effects may be induced by the restrictions of translation and by composition within limited vocabularies,[3] as in the design of graded language-learning materials. The importance of this dual role in developing our power to compare what we would say with what we have said is evident.

The reason for noting—even in so summary a fashion—these familiar involvements is that a perhaps important point about our descriptive technique is thereby brought up. It concerns the use—sometimes insufficiently reflective—of the words "encode" and "decode." How much of what sorts of agreement, I wonder, will there be in this audience if I suggest that these words are frequently—for example, as I have just been using them—unfortunate because they are too general, because they name alike processes that may need to be recognized as differing importantly from case to case?

Such an operation as writing down a spoken sentence, or tapping it out in Morse, is different from composing a sonnet, and that again from finding a tactful phrase, and that again from formulating an argument. How much that is useful and not misleading are we saying by calling any of these last ?encodings??

No doubt some reference may be made thereby to the possibility that rules might be found to govern the operation. But in writing something down according to an explicit convention (or in Morsing it), the rules are fully worked out; they are familiar and available to give rulings. In the other cases, in any instance of enterprising and adroit use of language, the rules are conjectural merely and as yet, in fact, barely conjecturable. Meanwhile, however, in more than a little of the talk about coding and decoding that goes on there is present, I fear, a suggestion that Morsing and composing are closely alike. I have listened to "communication theory" being offered to teachers-to-be in such a way that you would suppose that to speak or write well is no more than to emit—in parallel with strings of received notions—the clichés that have the highest probabilities. What is odd is that some who are ready to call themselves ˢʷeducatorsˢʷ have a difficulty in seeing why such a degradation of crude usage theory should be debilitating. An account well suited to the purposes of the communication engineer may be highly misleading as an instrument in teaching writing and reading. I am not doubting that the engineers' formulation has been convenient in phonology, but only whether its extension into higher levels of linguistics may not need the especial attention of critics. I hazard the guess that higher levels can help out lower levels more frequently than lower higher.

All this is a practical objection to much current talk about encoding. There are also serious theoretical difficulties, of which we are all more or less aware, as to the status of the ˡmessageˡ which is said to be encoded. We can, if we like, regard the ˡmessageˡ as a fictive construct not to be identified with any of ˡitsˡ encoded forms, but convenient as a means of referring to certain equivalences or transformation relations and the rules they obey. That may make ʷmessageʷ harmless, if we keep strictly to transformation relations: from ABC we can pass to abc and back again. But, even so, this is a discreditable sort of ghost to have haunting a modern theory, however well its migration from the telegraph office may be understood. And when, as is too likely to happen in even well-conducted discussions, it strays out of transformation theory into attempted explorations of the relations of, say, a Shakespeare sonnet to some specific experience or bit of a biography of the author, which the lines could be supposed to be an encoding of, where are we? Well over the frontier and inside that very ghostland itself whose inmates are precisely privileged to elude our grasp.

I should attempt to divine and meet objections that will be stirring in some at this point. I prefer as an opinion, and hold to it (in these topics) as constantly as I find I can, that the meaning of a line of Shakespeare is, for linguistics, to be conceived (in some way, at present insufficiently defined) in terms of its relations to other utterances, actual or possible, in English. And I am willing to add that an appeal to some hypothetical event in Shakespeare's ¦mind¦, or to equally hypothetical events in any readers' minds, is not—unless recognized for the mere stopgap it is—propitious procedure. (Of course, in a novel or play or sermon I would use such appeals unhesitatingly.) And yet I find in myself, and observe (so it appears to me) in others, that when we do really set aside any such appeal we are, to put it mildly, short of means for making and establishing the very distinction between variant readings and misreading that we are here concerned with.

It is time to come down to an example, the second line of Sonnet 66 which I had innocently supposed would be well-enough understood by a class of graduate students:

> Tir'd with all these, for restful death I cry:
> As to behold desert a beggar born.

What did I get from a budding Master of Arts in Teaching who will, I fear, be teaching English hard [4] for the rest of her working life? This:

> Weary of these sights, for reposeful death I implore:
> As I see desolate one born a beggar.

Feeling, perhaps, a need for something more, she added a comment: "That one could be born a beggar seems to presuppose that there be someone around to beg from." (?Desolate?: not ^{sw}entirely alone^{sw}): No doubt the banishment of beggars from modern streets does make all this more difficult.

Now what can we allege here to confirm our opinion (in which I, for one, am unshakable) that we have here a *misreading,* and not an allowable *variant?*

I do not see how the answers can avoid, at present, a somewhat dogmatic air. We have to seem to be laying down the law with a confidence, schoolmasterly and authoritarian, that deserves to be noted. If our role, for the moment, is not so much to make these declarations as to inquire into our grounds for them, this confidence will, I fancy, strike us as in mysterious and interesting contrast with our difficulty in producing, specifically and explicitly, what will even look like actual and adequate evidence. This observation, I hasten to add, should not in the least make us doubt that our confidence is justified; it is merely the recognition that it is not *easily* justifiable.

In this instance we can be confident, I suggest, that this reader's attempt to take "desert" as here equivalent to "desolate" will not do. We can conjecture—with much less certainty—how she came to think so: probably by equating "desert" with "deserted" and then substituting "desolate." But that is a necessarily precarious guess about an individual's mental process. The solid confidence that the "desert"-"desolate" equivalence will not do is something very different; it is not a guess but an observation, a linguistic perception.

Such perceptions may of course be fallacious: no perceptions, perhaps, are immune from error; but with large classes of these linguistic perceptions risk of error is happily extremely small. Our task in this paper is in part to inquire how risk of error in these perceptions increases and how it may be controlled.

It will be well, though, to note that a linguistic perception may be veridical, and yet the description anyone may offer of what is perceived may be mistaken. The description is an application of theoretical machinery; it is a picture or representation we try to give of certain facts. The facts may be truly observed, even though the account we give of them is defective. It is part of the aim of linguistic studies to improve both literary perception and the techniques of describing what is perceived. I have an uneasy sense that of late they are being more successful in this last.

To return to our example, we had better separate two questions: (1) On what does our perception that ˢʷdesolateˢʷ is a misreading of ?desert? depend? (2) How would we support or defend this opinion if necessary?

(1) In broad outline the answer, of course, is "On our knowledge of English—including the English of Shakespeare's day." And perhaps this very broadness is here a merit: a wide and varied familiarity with how words have been used then and since may serve us better than a more limited, even though more precise, focus on other instances of the use of ʷdesertʷ. We must put into this ˢʷknowledge of Englishˢʷ, knowledge not only of lexical distinctions, overlaps and so on, but of the varied sentiments (to use a stopgap term) that such lines as these have variously uttered.

"As to behold desert a beggar born." I had better risk my own gloss here, hoping that those who will differ may allow it to me as a variant reading.

Having to see and recognize and admit and deeply realize that Merit, the possession of the highest virtue (of which men of good will should be most regardful, being beholden to and in duty bound to aid and comfort its possessor) may in fact be as little esteemed by the passer-by and its subject even be as suspect as one born into the beggar's trade.

I have tried to mix the concrete or literal interpretation: in modern terms "the most gifted child may be most gravely underprivileged" with some of the abstracter, and perhaps optional, metaphoric reaches. How much we personify 'desert', how far we turn what is beheld into a strangely or horribly disguised, perhaps maimed and deformed, presence which, however much we want to avert our eyes, goes on crying out with importunate demands and forces us to be aware of it and take it in: all this, which of it we make focal, which penumbral, which background —these variations I would offer as samples of variant reading. We may dissent [5] from this or that, take the line ourselves another way, and yet not be inclined to condemn even readings very unlike our own as wrong—in the fashion in which we can, I think, unhesitatingly reject "As I see desolate one born a beggar."

(2) A good deal that may occur to us as confirming our reading (whichever variant it may be) we may have to admit on reflection to be not strictly relevant: etymology, for example. If we were trying to show this reader that she had gone wrong, we might draw her attention to the entries in the nearest dictionary, and this might be an effective way of reminding her of things which, in a less precise way, she perhaps knew already. She would probably not know anything of the etymological detail, but this is not the sort of knowledge of which she is in need. What she did not know was how to see which of the various meanings was present in the line she was reading. The dictionary cannot tell her that, although it may be helpfully suggestive.

The Dictionary (to accord it a capital of respect) often seems to be the contemporary representative of Holy Writ. Its invention should, I suppose, be considered an innovation every bit as momentous as those we associate with Galileo or Newton or even, perhaps, with Einstein. The audience this paper is primarily addressed to is rather sophisticated about dictionaries: it knows more about how they are written than the general public. Nevertheless, even great lexicographers may sometimes be observed to adopt devout attitudes toward the institutions they direct. It is perhaps natural, therefore, that today we look to the Dictionary (or to something a Dream Dictionary of the future might embody) for the guidance and even for the vali-

dation we are in search of. What a simplification it would be
were it to turn out that an interpretation is *wrong,* is a *misreading,* when it conflicts with information stored in that super-
dictionary.

The solution cannot really be quite as simple; although, with
qualifications by no means easy to be clear about, something
of the sort is no doubt in part what we seek. One set of such
qualifications must preserve flexibility. Languages change. New
words, new uses of old words, obsolescences, revivals, shifting
fashions in reading, changing types of invitation to readers, en-
larging and dwindling sensitivities to nuance, to the figurative,
to status, to implication, to attitude—limitless variations, not
only in new utterance but in how old utterance may be understood—all these have to be taken care of. That Dream Dictionary
would have to be much more than a mere storage system, a
record of records. It would have to respect creativity while dis-
couraging crudescence. It would somehow have to combine the
uttermost literary discernment with a complete freedom from
prejudice. And yet, at the same time, it would have to protect
the language from those forms of disabling confusion for which
my "desert"-"desolate" may stand. It is clear enough that this
Dream Dictionary is no actual project but a Platonic idea of
the most ineffable order:

> the unimaginable lodge
> For solitary thinkings, such as dodge
> Conception to the very bourne of Heaven
> Then leave the naked brain.

And yet, even as such, it has something to offer toward the
definition of ?misreading? we are attempting to approach.

Can we advance a little by considering further the knowledge
a good reader must have and a bad reader manifestly lacks? The
same misreader, in dealing with the fourth line of Sonnet 66,

> And purest faith unhappily forsworn,

offers us what looks like additional evidence. Here is her paraphrase:

> And the most absolute confidence sadly renounced.

This seems to me to show two related characteristics: (1) isolated word-by-word procedure; and (2) inability to recognize pluralities of potential meanings and to select from among them.

1. *Purest:* having kept, I fancy, little beyond the superlative. (I doubt, from collateral evidence, whether "absolute," for her, had much of what made Shakespeare so fond of it, or was more than emphatic.)

Faith: lacking the control of [sw]completely sincere[sw] (for '?purest'), lapsed from naming a virtue of active engagement to become the passive thing we associate with confidence men. And then,

Unhappily: losing all its august relations—with Fortune, with intellectual activity as, for Aristotle, man's highest happiness—it deteriorates into a mere description of a feeling, [sw]sadly[sw]. Which leaves

Forsworn undefended (to a reader who can render "cry" by "implore"); all connection with "faith" is missed and what remains is only a change of mind.

2. The failure to select goes along with the word-by-word jumping at the first meaning that turns up.[6] There is a randomness about the process in striking contrast with what, to a better reader, will seem the continual invitation to perceive connection and design, tension and outcome, variously balanced throughout the sonnet.

This failure to connect, word with word and line with line, extends to an inability seemingly even to look for an over-all mutual relevance, a control of whole over part, and beyond that to an impercipience of significant relationships between wholes. Such a sonnet as this is no doubt near the top of a scale on which a laundry list would be near the foot. But if on a scribbled laundry list we found ourselves reading "teas" for "ties" we would know that we were in danger of letting the local point of focus cease to be duly guided by the ambient. Perhaps in such mutual influences between focal point and ambient we can find what is needed to unify the concept of an ideal Dictionary into a definition of misreading.

Two difficulties must be recognized first. This discussion, these approaches, are haunted by the concept of *knowing* and by the concept of *comparing*. Each of them is very likely to get itself represented in our definition in too explicit, too conscious and too deliberate a guise. This trouble with *know* is, of course, notorious. To know is both the end and, it would seem, the means of intellectual endeavor, and yet who knows anything about knowledge? Here, in the key role in all exploratory activity is an inexplorable, and this admission becomes the more discomforting the nearer we come (as in considering misreading) to asking about what we may know and how.

A similar and closely related trouble attends *comparing*. If advance in knowledge is through comparing (and I suppose the triumphs of linguistics in recent decades to be among the clearest illustrations of the powers of systematic comparison) where is our theory of the comparing of meanings? This may be the place where a Principle of Instrumental Dependence which seems needed everywhere else breaks down. "The properties of the instruments or apparatus employed enter into, and confine, the scope of the investigation." [7] Does this hold too of our key concepts and procedures? Does it not hold pre-eminently of them? Or are these questions self-destructive?

Is it not very odd, when we consider on how vast a scale outcomes of comparing are recorded in the Dictionary, how little explicit reflection upon comparing has been recorded? Each article presents vocables which, *in some respects* but not in all, may be compared with the head and found the same in meaning. But how scanty, when set beside all these difficult and hazardous comparings and decisions, is the discussion of the respects.[8] And, as I have remarked above, the readings on which the com-

parings and decisions are based are strangely confident—
strangely, in view of the uncertainties that arise as soon as we
try to justify them and the obscurities of any theoretical accounts of how we arrive at the compared meanings. And yet
our practical confidence about meanings ought not to surprise
us. It may on occasion betray us, but we would understand
nothing at all without it; this widespread assurance is the necessary condition for every local doubt.

It should, however, be added, and with some emphasis, that if,
with sentences having more than a minimal routine content, we
ask for a paraphrase, we will be supplied (as with lines of
Sonnet 66) with enough misreadings to make us wonder how
high the price we pay for this necessary confidence may be. For
example,

> To behold merit born a beggar (without merit)
> To see a wretched beggar getting what he deserves.

And these, too, are from students planning to devote their working lives to teaching.

I must now try to put the parts that have been looked over
into some sort of unity, and the uniting idea will be that implied
by the undertaking the Dictionary makes to explain any word
in a language by means of others. A language, this assumes, is
a system such that each part (we need not worry, here, whether
these are necessarily ?words?, or how a ?word? should be defined,
or whether different languages may not differ as to these parts)
has its various duties or tasks under quasi-control by other
parts—a quasi-control reflected in the fact that it can be replaced by them—at the price of some adjustment or awkward-
ness. A word can do, that is, what the rest of the language will
let it. The limitations that the system imposes on any component
much resemble those that a society imposes on its members or
those that an organism imposes on its constituent cells. They
are normally inseparable from (commonly reciprocal to) the

dependencies that every word has (in any sentence) on others. Normally a word works only through the cooperations of other words. These restrictive-permissive, controlling-enabling interrelations, which tie the utterances possible within a language into a system, give us our means of distinguishing between variant readings and misreading. Once again, we must never forget that the system in living languages is nowhere fixed or rigid, though it will, no doubt, be more rigid in certain regions of use than in others. The interrelations correspond to the needs the language has met and is meeting, to the tasks it has attempted and is attempting to perform. As need and task change, the interrelations undergo strain which may be met by adjustment and by growth. Here is where novelty, in phrasing and in interpretation, enters, the opportunity for variant reading and original utterance.

We are not far here from valuative considerations. The analogies I have mentioned with a society and an organism suggest that we may properly be concerned with linguistic *health,* whose connections with "whole" we should keep in mind as well as its forward-looking implication: we would not say anyone was in good health if he were unable to continue so for some while. It may be very deeply doubted whether any great language has ever really been left to its own devices unsubject to effective criticism from those who were, by privilege or by profession or by poetic or social endowment, unusually well able to use it and to judge how it should be used. The language arts, after all, are arts. Perhaps we should not take too seriously those who seem to claim authority from linguistics as a ¹science¹ to tell a rather helpless generation that what is said by enough people thereby becomes what *should* be said. (Are we to think that what is thought by enough people thereby becomes what should be thought?) And yet in this age of the advertiser (¹Everybody's buying it¹) there is occasion for concern. It is not quite enough to leave the matter to the experience of anyone speaking or writing with care, reflection, and intent. In selecting our phrases are we seeking (1) what most people in our situation would most probably say,[9] or (2) what will best do the work in hand? Only in a very exalted linguistic community indeed would 2 be in general the same as 1; it would be a diseased community in which there was widespread doubt which to prefer. Similarly with interpretation. What we should seek is not the sense that is, or would be, most widely accepted, but that which most fully takes into account the situation the utterance is meeting and the integrity of the language. It was with this in view that I inserted in my diagram DV (development) after D (decoding). There should be—although it may slow reading down—a cyclic mutual dependence between R, D and DV, as with S, E and T. In spite of Plato's jokes in the *Phaedrus* the chief service that writing and reading can do us is to help us to reflect: to reflect, *Deo volente,* to some purpose. Counting hands in interpretation cannot do that. Misreadings may, as scholarship frequently discovers, be universal through long periods.

Most speech and writing, and most interpretation, is not, I have urged above, as conscious as the word ?seek? above may suggest. Commonly a series of possible phrases or interpretations offer themselves (more or less schematically), and our choice is not ordinarily guided by highly explicit considerations. It is this that makes a crude usage doctrine dangerous; it can present *the thing to say* in a fashion which blurs the vital distinction between *what I should say here* and *what is said*. And this is not only for the form but for the content of the utterance, as ad-men and opinion promoters have noted.

To sum up, a sound account of interpretation must build into itself a duty to be critical. A linguistics that is properly aware of the processes through which language grows in the individual and of the effects that his attitudes to language can have upon its health in him must be concerned with pedagogy and with

what sorts of assumptions are spread in the school. Poor pedagogy in the thinking of linguistic authorities is in its own way
quite as alarming as bad linguistic doctrine in the classroom.

After all this my definition of ²misreading² will still have to
lean on much more than has been said if it is not itself to be
most variously misread. In this it corresponds to the statesman
whose responsibilities as guardian expose him to misrepresenta-
tion. He does well not to formulate his policies in ways that give
handle to his opponents. My definition too will be well advised
not to do more, seemingly, than advance a modest request: "For
the purposes outlined above and on the appropriate occasions,
may *misreading* mean the taking of a sentence in such a way that
the equivalence relations of one or more of its parts to the rest
of the language lapse and thereby, if such taking were to continue, harm would be done to the language—due regard being
given, in applying this criterion, to the necessity for change in
language activity with change in the situations to be met, and,
in general, to the health of the language."

Variant Readings and Misreading

(1)   *The occasion for this paper:* The members of the conference were linguists, psychologists and literary critics—
in about equal proportions. The last felt some surprise,
and perhaps consternation, to hear themselves described
by the others as those who seemed to have understood the
most. Interdisciplinary Conference, Bloomington, Indiana,
reported in *Style in Language,* Ed., Thomas A. Sebeok
(Cambridge, M.I.T.).

(2)   *in a position to observe:* teaching at the Graduate School
of Education, Harvard.

(3)   *composition within limited vocabularies:* a therapeutic
resource likely to have great developments. See the last
essay (Chapter 10). Discussed also in the work in progress,
Learning Every Man's English, by C. M. Gibson and I. A.
Richards.

(4)   *be teaching English hard:* The incompetence with English
of far too many of these teachers-to-be could be illustrated
at any length. It is a grim thought that better-qualified
candidates are not available and that little enough can
be done at this stage to improve their handling of language.

(5)   *we may dissent:* I confess to some skepticism about this
type of analysis or explanation. Within my lifetime—I
seem almost able to recall a specific beginning—a practice
of expressing whatever a line or passage could possibly
yield under squeezing has grown up. At first the practitioners were few and some of them (Laura Riding and

William Empson, for example) early became renowned
for powerful grasp; but competition jacks up standards.
There are fashions in reading as well as in writing. Perhaps questions of relevance are now due for more searching discussion. It seems unlikely that run-of-the-mine
students today should really be able to find so much more
in Shakespeare than earlier readers. Have they learned
how to cultivate their garden more intensively or is some
of it just an old-new conjuring trick?

(6)   *the first meaning that turns up:* I connect this faulty
        behavior in reading with the grave defects of much cur-
        rent instruction in reading. Word calling of isolated words
        and the vacuousness, the lack of significant content of the
        characteristic texts, have their consequences. It is to the
        very beginning of the teaching of reading that we must
        go for a remedy.

(7)   *the properties of the instruments . . . investigation:* from
        "Toward a More Synoptic View" in *Speculative Instru-
        ments.*

(8)   *the discussion of the respects:* see "Toward a Theory of
        Comprehension" in *Speculative Instruments.*

(9)   *would most probably say:* On this great theme and on the
        harm that usage doctrines do, see *Interpretation in Teach-
        ing,* Chapters 15, 16.

8

Mencius Through the Looking-Glass

*Classroom mistakes are often enough due to cultural diver-
gences to make them directly relevant to international mis-
comprehensions. There may be something to be gained by considering them together. In both, what may at first sight seem
perversity, mere stupidity or malice, may, when more adequately
examined, be found to have its explorable etiology and to be
open to treatment. The gravest wrenchings of meaning frequently come from intelligence operating on insufficient or
distorted evidence, or from self-protective efforts prompted by
an alien situation.*

*This essay is intended to serve as a reminder that immense
and threatening divisions in mankind can spring from differences
between* virtues *as well as from envies and greeds. When the
virtues on each part are largely inapprehensible by the other,
the danger is heightened by Man's natural fear of what he does
not understand, and his inclination to suppose it not worth
understanding. To attack is easier than to study. There are also,
in this case of China and the West, intense and complex cultural
vanities on both sides to be taken into account: vanities largely
inexplicable the one to the other. The discussion of some "Sources
of Conflict" which follows this essay would have been more
inadequate than it is without some attempt to convey something
of the sources of the strength of the Chinese position for living.*

*Would that voices in China could be doing something of the
sort for the Western Barbarians' merits!*

The odd title of this essay comes from T. S. Eliot. When I was
working in Peking at *Mencius on the Mind* about 1930, he
wrote to me (referring probably to his own early Sanscrit studies)
that reading in a remote text is like trying to be on both sides
of a mirror at once. A vivid and a suitably bewildering image.
To ask how exact it may be would be to raise the prime question "What is understanding?" anew. I have not made it easier
by adding in Alice. Lewis Carroll had his twists, as we know.
If we want to *understand* adventures in Looking-Glass land, we
have somehow to guess what the principles of the distortion are.
They are not obvious. So the doctrines of Mencius, their adventures in my mind as I write and in yours as you read, might
seem strange, indeed, to Mencius were he watching them. They
have to be because of the changes in the media. It is not our
fault nor his. The distortions come from the photography, the
telescopy . . . the operations, far more mysterious than radar,
through which alone we find anything in him to see. Compare:

> Mencius said, "Men talk loosely because their words are unlikely
> to be put to the test. Everyone wants to be a teacher; that is one of
> life's problems." (Dobson, 7.10)

> Mencius said, "Men's being ready with their tongues arises simply
> from their not having been reproved. The evil of men is that they
> want to be teachers of others." (Legge, 4A 23)

Reports on two radar screens. What in their signals could account for the differences? How easily we see the 19th- and 20th-
century settings of the translators here! How delightful the contrast is! And what, through it all, may Mencius' own meaning
have been?

Mr. Dobson's charming, readable, current-English version
comes out of more than half a working lifetime on the detail

of Archaic Chinese.[1] Yet it is not, he points out, intended to supplant "the definitive translation" of James Legge, published in 1893.[2] Instead, it is to convey something of the pleasure "from Mencius as a work of literature" to a wider audience than students of Archaic Chinese. And it should succeed in this as well as in forwarding the aims of scholarship. But look again and ask what these aims are. This sample illustrates only minor divergences; in general the rule is: the more important the utterance, the greater the discrepancies between translations.

The mirror image *has* its point. What we see there most readily are our own concerned or contented faces or, as here, urbane or condemning. That is what a looking-glass is for, and who will say it is not a very useful thing? But, if it is Mencius we want to meet, we need other devices: among them, a display of diverse translations from different translators in different periods to protect us against oversimplifying our conception of the task. To enjoy Mr. Dobson's version fully we need to have Legge's (or Couvreur's) open on the table too to help us in recognizing its felicities and theirs. And also the Chinese characters, with an analysis of their components and a literal rendering. And a recording of a traditional reading to hold constantly before us the contrast between a succinct and resonant utterance and the relatively relaxed ramble of vocables readable English sentences employ. The original was composed to be known by heart and cited with authority.

Even with such helps—and in part because of them—we are not very likely to be able to say, exactly and clearly, what Mencius thought. Insofar as *his* thought was dependent on his age and tradition and our thought is dependent upon ours, we cannot be very faithful to it, however hard we try. Making up for ourselves as good an account as we can of the society and tradition Mencius lived in, soaking ourselves in his reading and writing—the way of scholarship—may be our best resource; but it cannot be expected to turn us into Mencius. It is much more likely to turn Mencius into us! Mencius was not a modern

scholar, trained in the fabulous discipline of contemporary research, balanced and sobered by an awareness of the hopes and
despairs of how many ages.

Knowing even *all about* the thought of Mencius would not
be the same thing as *having* it. It wouldn't even be a good
preparation for that. And, to have it in some measure and if
possible make a reader *have it* is my aim here. I will delay only
a few pages before beginning this essentially magical, dramatic
or poetic attempt.

Mencius was a teacher, not an expositor. He was *not* giving
a lecture on Mencius. At important points, he did talk about
his teaching, but that was to make it stronger. His audience was
to be helped and improved. He was not presenting a view to
be discussed and criticized. When from time to time he gives
out one of his great secrets of the conduct of life in an anecdote
or a formula, the thing to do is to remember it, treasure it up
and live with it for a time, and see what it does to you thereafter.

Mencius gets these secrets himself by a process he hints to us.
It is up to us to guess what it was. It certainly was not in the least
like anything the main Western philosophic tradition would
recognize as philosophic method. It is a question indeed if the
ˢʷthoughtˢʷ of Mencius is ˢʷthoughtˢʷ at all in any accepted
Western interpretations of that word.

That might sound derogatory. We are apt to give ˢʷthoughtˢʷ
a higher rank and dignity than ˢʷfeelingˢʷ. The point is that for
Mencius no such division has been made. For Mencius, the intellectual and the moral are not separate. The suggestion that
there was some important distinction to be made between intellectual knowledge in general and right living would probably
have made no recognizable sense at all to him.

For Mencius—and this seems to be true, with some doubtful
exceptions, of all early Chinese philosophers possibly until Sung
times—the mind was not so split. There was no *separate* problem
of truth or problem of knowledge. There was no epistemology,

no theory of ideas, no logic—in the modes of these things which belong to the intellectual main stream of Western thinking. There was no such thinking in Mencius or for Mencius. In a sense, the intellect was never invented by the Chinese, and it may be doubted whether, outside the sciences, it has been imported and transplanted by them. One of the interests of Chinese ˢʷthoughtˢʷ is that it lets us ask ourselves sharply whether the intellect has been on the whole a useful invention to man. It is well for those who believe in it to say so, in an age in which it has been openly and variously attacked (think of Bergson, D. H. Lawrence and Hitler). Chinese studies help us to realize that the intellect (as something separate from the whole man, as an instrument of pure theoretic inquiry, the rational organ) is a cultural invention,³ a Green invention probably. Man is not born with it; he is not, by nature, a rational animal. He becomes one through education into a tradition which gives him a ˢʷreasonˢʷ (in this sense), which installs in him this feature of possible human design, as a given feature may be put into one airplane and not into another.

It is well to remind ourselves too that even such a fundamental feature as ˢʷthe intellectˢʷ may seem to be has upkeep charges. As William Angus Sinclair put it, such a selecting and grouping "is a continuing process which must be sustained if our experience is to continue as it is. . . . If for any reason a man follows a different way of grouping in his attention then the experience he has will be different also. . . . Knowing is not a passive contemplation, but a continuously effort-consuming activity." ⁴ Take this far enough and the probabilities of our comprehending Mencius will look low. It asks us to conceive that our concepts are less stored in containers than kept up as a breed may be.⁵

All this is preparatory. What we have to prepare for is the probability that, as Mencius begins to speak for himself, the words will mainly carry ideas of the Western tradition which Mencius would know nothing of. I have listened to very learned scholars, Chinese and Western, lecturing to me on Mencius. What I mostly learned was which *Western* philosophers had most captured their imaginations. Probably that, in my own case, is all that I will be able to show you.

I ought to give one other example for those not familiar with the condensed and cryptic style in which Mencius spoke—to let them see how easy it is to read different things into his words. One of his key remarks (IV, II, 26) has been translated as follows:

LEGGE All who speak about the natures of things have in fact only their phenomena to reason from, and the value of a phenomenon is in its being natural.

UGALL That which everyone below heaven calls nature is nothing but habit; and habit has its roots in gain.

COUVREUR Everywhere under heaven, when we speak of nature, we have in mind natural effects. The special characteristic of natural effects is that they are self-acting.

Three utterances on three different topics. Word for word it goes like this:

Heaven   below   their   talk   Nature   about   causes   only
Causes   use   profit   as   root.

And now I do my best to disappear, and we will pretend it is Mencius who comes through the mirror and addresses you.[6]

(IV, II, 26) "What I dislike in your wise men is the way they niggle and chip. If those wise ones would do like Yü when he moved the waters, no dislike for wisdom. Yü moving the waters did what was without toil. If the wise ones did what is without toil, their wisdom *would* be great."

(VI, I, 6) A disciple, Kung Tu-tse, said to Mencius: "Kao Tzu says 'Man's nature: without good, without not-good.' "
    "Others say, 'Some natures good, some not good.' "
    "But *you* say, 'Nature good.' "
    "All these wrong? Are they?"

Mencius said, "In the impulses which make it up, our nature may be seen to be good. Thus I call it good. When men do evil, that is not the fault of their *natural* powers."

Sympathetic pity; all men have that.
Shame and avoidance; all men have that.
Respect and reverence; all men have that.
Sense of right and wrong; all men have that.

Sympathetic pity is human-heartedness.	JEN
Shame and avoidance is righteousness.	YI
Respect and reverence is good behavior.	LI
Sense of right and wrong is wisdom.	CHIH

Human-heartedness, righteousness, good behavior and wisdom are not influences infused and molded into us from without. We already have them; only we do not realize this. Therefore I say, 'Seek then get it, let go then lose it.' Men are incalculably different here because unable to make the most of their powers. In a fruitful year, the children are most of them reliable, in a bad year they are most of them violent. This is not because Heaven gives them different powers but because their minds were trapped and drowned. Only that!

Things of the same kind are alike. Why doubt it only of man? Mouths have the same tastes, ears hear sounds the same, eyes see the same beauty in colours: are minds alone without their sameness? What is the mind's sameness? Its name is Order and Right. It is the Sage who first grasped the sameness of the mind. Order and Right are agree-able to our minds as grass-fed animals are agree-able to our mouths.

All men have a mind which pities others. The ancient kings had it, so they had a government which pitied others. With a pitying mind acting through a pitying government, ruling the whole world is like turning something round in the palm.

Why do I say, "All men have minds which pity others?" Even today a man suddenly perceiving a child about to fall into a well has a shuddering qualm of sympathy and pity—*not* in order to strike up a useful acquaintance with the child's parents, *not* to get a great name for sensitivity with the neighbors, and *not* because he just dislikes the sound of the child thudding down into the well.

From such things we see that

> Without pity and sympathy, man is not,
> Without shame and avoidance, man is not,
> Without respect and reverence, man is not,
> Without sense of right and wrong, man is not.

> Pity and sympathy is the active principle of (Jen)
> Human-heartedness.
> Shame and avoidance is the active principle of (Yi)
> Righteousness.
> Respect and reverence is the active principle of (Li)
> Good Behavior.
> Sense of right and wrong is the active principle of (Chih)
> Wisdom.

To man these four principles are as his four limbs. Having them, to say "I cannot" is to rob himself; to say of the Ruler "he cannot" is to injure *him*. Since we all have these four principles, if we know how to develop and fulfill them, it is as a fire that begins to burn, as a fountain that begins to flow. If fulfilled, they are enough to guard the four seas; if not fulfilled, they are not even enough to let us serve our parents.

(IV, II, 18) A disciple said to Mencius, "Confucius praised water saying, 'Water! Water!' What did he so approve of in water?" Mencius said, "Here is a spring; it gushes out, unlessening day and night, fills its courses and flows to the four seas. Such is a source. This, in water, he praised. But, if there is no source, in the rainy months the fields are filled, but while you wait they are dried up. Therefore, when his reputation exceeds the facts, the superior man is ashamed."

(IV, II, 19) "That wherein man differs from the birds and beasts is small and slight; common folk let it go, the superior man keeps it."

These then are for Mencius the four virtues: Human-heartedness, Righteousness, Good Behavior and Wisdom, which together form man's essential nature and from the fulfillment of which his perfection comes. We easily misconceive them and obviously they are untranslatable by simple names in our tradition. The overtones of *Jen,* for example, are quite different from those of the word "Love" to us. *Jen* lacks the erotic, the affectionate and the theological uses which make the word "Love" for us one of the pivotal points of the Western mind. It spans no such hierarchy of meanings, from the most transcendent—for example, Aristotle's "All things are moved by Love" or Dante's inscription over Hell Gate, "What made me was . . . the eternal love," down to Alexander Bain's view that love is the response to soft surfaces at the right temperature or the schoolgirl's "I love candy." On the other hand *Jen* has plenty of widely spreading links and ample reverberations in Chinese. It sounds the same as the word for man. Its character looks as if it meant "What two men have in common" or "What is mutual between men." It is charged with some of the feelings we put into "human," "humane," "humanity"—though we must beware of just putting in *our* ideal of man. That was an invention of our tradition—a Greek invention. As Werner Jaeger strikingly put it, "The greatest work of art they had to create was Man." In this invention, and the invention of the Western type of education outlined in Plato's *Republic,* the education which could produce this type of man, the Greeks approached through the philosophical and the universal, the logos, as that which is common to all minds. And, as these words, universal, logos, idea, form and type suggest, this which is common to all minds—?the mind's sameness?—was for the Greeks something before them for contemplative realization. To quote Jaeger again, "The

Greeks relied wholly on this clear realization of the natural principles governing human life, and the immanent laws by which man exercises his physical and intellectual powers."

That might be a description (an excellent one) of what Mencius is doing. And yet what great differences there are! The Greek interest in "the principles governing human life," which was to culminate in Plato, was theoretical in ways which never developed in Chinese thought. And when Mencius says, "We already have them; only not *realize* this," it is fair to note that the sort of "clear realization of the natural principles" Jaeger is talking about is not at all what Mencius' work led to in China. Greek cultivation became more and more intellectual and led toward *knowledge what;* Chinese cultivation remained primarily moral or social and led toward *knowledge how.*

It is not that the followers of Mencius failed to study "the immanent laws by which man exercises his physical and intellectual powers." The point is, rather, that they worked on them another way and in so doing, by their sort of philosophical or educative art, created (or developed) another type of man. So, the part of the meaning of *Jen* which we might translate by *human* or *manlike* must not be understood simply in terms of what *we* traditionally assume a man should be.

Similar considerations apply to the names of the other virtues. Thus *Yi,* Righteousness, may easily be given a too Hebraic meaning. Its seed or active principle is somewhat negative—shame and distaste. *Li,* Good Behavior, Good Form, decorum, propriety, is concerned with doing the socially right thing in view of one's position, in one's family and in society. And *Chih,* or Wisdom, combines sound judgment not only of what *is so* or *not,* but of what *should be* or *shouldn't be* so.

There is one parallel with Greek morals (as we find them in the *Republic,* say) which may be accidental or unimportant. Mencius and Plato alike list four main Virtues. Plato's four as commonly labeled are: Wisdom, Courage, Temperance and Justice, misleading though these names may be. There is more than a little in common between Mencius' *Li* and Plato's Justice. Both have to do with keeping in one's proper place and knowing what is due to it and especially what is due from it. Wisdom seems a more intellectual thing for Plato, though we must not exaggerate and must remember how Plato made the virtues the indispensable basis, without which the philosophic or dialectic activity could come to no good.

And we must not draw any inferences from the absence of Courage among Mencius' list of virtues here. Elsewhere he has much to say about Courage. He is concerned with military conduct. Plato, you remember, defined Courage as "the knowledge of what is truly to be feared." Mencius had this (VI, I, 10) which comes quite near to Plato:

"I like fish and I like bears' paws. If I cannot have both, I let the fish go, and take the bears' paws. I like life and I like right too. If I cannot have both, I let life go and take the right. I like life indeed, but I like some things more than life, and will not do wrong to keep it. I dislike death indeed, but I dislike other things more, so I do not always avoid danger. All men have what they like more than life, and what they dislike more than death; not only great men but all men. The great men are those who do not lose these things.

"Here is rice and the want of it means death. A beggar will not take it when it is offered with an insult. Yet a rich man will take 10,000 chung, regardless of what is decent or right. What can 10,000 chung add to him? Mansions and concubines? Was it not possible for him to refuse it? This is called losing one's first mind. The great end of learning is the recovery of the lost mind."

Here again we may feel not too far away from Plato:

"We have been talking of how it seems to us at present. We have been looking on the soul as men did on the sea-god Glaucus. What he was might hardly be made out because his arms and legs were broken off and cut and crushed by the waves, and he was coated over with shells and seaplants and stones so that, to look at he might have been any sort of beast in place of what he truly was. So do we see the soul, lowered to this condition by unnumbered evils" [7] (*Republic,* 611D). But around this passage there are plenty of things to warn us that we are in another world from that of Mencius. Nonetheless, it is tempting to go on looking at their resemblances.

The first half of Mencius' life (c.390–c.305) coincided with the last half of Plato's (429–347). Each was as widely informed as any then living in his culture. Yet Mencius knew nothing of Greece and Plato seems hardly to have heard of China. Both were teachers, in terms of their influence on later men among the very greatest. But in what different ways! A remark that should be repeated, and with emphasis, each time any of their interesting correspondencies in life and work is mentioned. Both looked for a king who could put their doctrines into action, and failed to find him. Both were sure that "licentious words, and perverse theories, ought never to have been allowed to begin. Beginning in the mind, they cause harm to the practice of things" (Dobson, 3.3). "But one law our guardians must keep in force, never letting it be overlooked and guarding it with more care than all the rest. This law keeps new ways out of the state which already has its fixed and reasoned order . . . because forms and rhythms are never changed without producing changes in the most important political forms and ways" (*Republic,* 424).

Both had hoped to restore a former perfection and held that this could be achieved by a turning round, a conversion, of the mind. "It is when a man sets his face primarily towards the greater parts that the lesser parts are unable to obtrude. It is this, nothing more, that makes him a great man" (Dobson, 3.4). "The instrument of knowledge has to be turned round, and with it the whole soul, from the things of becoming to the things of being" (*Republic,* 518). Both put something for which "good" seems a good word at the heart of nature. "It is of the essence of man's nature that he do good. That is what I mean by good.

If a man does what is evil he is guilty of the sin of denying his natural endowment" (Dobson, 4.11). "This good, then, every soul looks for, and for this every soul does all that it does, feeling in some way what it is, but troubled and uncertain and unable to see clearly enough" (*Republic*, 505).

In Mencius' four virtues there is a certain unifying bond. Together they are Man's nature. Man is essentially these virtues striving for operation; but he does not know it. Coming to know it is becoming *sincere*.

"All things already complete in us. Reflect and find ourselves sincere; no greater happiness. With effort become mutual and so act; in seeking *jen,* nothing is nearer." (Legge) "All things are complete within ourselves. There is no joy that exceeds that of the discovery, upon self-examination, that we have acted with integrity. And we are never closer to achieving Humanity than when we seek to act, constrained by the principle of reciprocity" (Dobson, 7.24).

Or again: "Do not be what you are not; do not desire what you do not desire; just this only!" (Legge.) Less arrestingly, "Do not do what you should not do; do not wish for what you should not wish—there is nothing more to it than that" (Dobson, 7.24). More literally: "Do not do (be) its-what-not-do, do not desire its-what-not-desire, just this only." (See *Mencius on the Mind,* Appendix 28.) There is another tempting parallel with early Greek thought here: the great utterance of Pindar's Second Pythian Ode: "Become what you are!" in which Werner Jaeger saw the seed of so much of the doctrine of ideas.

What was by Mencius' own account his own greatest merit? One day a disciple spoke to him as follows:

"Dare I ask, master, what you are best at?"

Mencius replied, "I know Words, I excell in cultivating my vast *chi!*"

(*hao jan chih ch'i:* vast flowing passion nature: animal spirits, vitality.)

"Dare I ask, master, what is this vast *chi?*"

Mencius replied: "Hard to say. Most great and adamant is *chi*. When straightforwardly cultivated without being injured, it fills everywhere between heaven and earth. It matches *Yi* (Right) and *Tao* (the Way) without being daunted by them. It comes from the accumulation of *Yi*. It is not something which single right acts may make use of. If our conduct dissatisfies us, then the *chi* is daunted."

The disciple asked again: "What is knowing Words?"

Mencius replied:

"When Words are one-sided, I know where the speaker is blind. When Words are extravagant, I know what pit he has fallen into. When Words are evil, I know where he is lost. When Words are evasive, I know where he is at his wit's end. Such Words growing in the mind are injurious in the government; carried out in government, they are injurious in affairs. A Sage, when another comes, must be in agreement with my Words."

The chief of Mencius' Words was that *Hsing*, human nature, is good.

Necessarily there is much in Mencius still pointing to our future. The designs being uncovered by modern biology and explored through the new models for the working of the brain may make his prime doctrine—*Man by nature is good*—especially relevant. To believe this may seem to some a mere feat of willful optimism. To a culture like ours, built in part upon the conception of original sin, such a belief may seem dangerous, either blind or pit-fallen or lost or at an end of its poor wits. But Mencius was not blind to or unafraid of evil or at his wit's end. The world he lived in had plenty of evil to show. The seasons went astray; princes were cruel and incompetent; war raged throughout his time; floods broke loose; despair was widespread. "The black-haired people," he said, "do not know where to place their hands or feet." All this he deliberately set out to remedy. These evils were for him a gigantic reflection of a frustration in man's mind. Only if the mind could return to its true nature and find itself again could all this be set right. With the mind turned round, setting things right would be no more toil than turning a pebble round in the palm of the hand. For him the cardinal virtues were what can be trusted, and human nature was that in us through which they could be trusted—that which made them trustworthy, namely our true selves.

What is there here for us? Nothing directly perhaps. But such an opportunity as few other Sages offer of considering anew for ourselves what we may put *our* trust in. We have our resources too, on which we too little reflect. And we may learn to know ourselves the better for studying a teacher who has been second only to Confucius in his influence on the mores of the Chinese people, helping in a large measure to sustain the most stable, the longest lasting and one of the most satisfying modes of human living that have been tried.

"What to do! What to do?" said Confucius. "Indeed I do not know what to do with a man who does not ask himself this." We may ask ourselves this—and its companion question, What are we doing?—the better for traveling into an archaic world and imagining another order of morality no less lofty and exacting than any we may be trying to achieve.

Mencius Through the Looking-Glass

(1)   A new translation arranged and annotated for the general reader by W. A. C. H. Dobson (Toronto University Press; London, University of Oxford Press, 1963).

(2)   James Legge, *The Chinese Classics,* Vol. I, Oxford, 1893.

(3)   *a cultural invention:* or a consequence of a social structure? Needham, *op. cit.,* p. 340, remarks that "a theoretical organicism which Leibniz and Whitehead applied to Nature had perhaps originated as a reflection in Nature of Asian bureaucratic society." Asian here means Chinese. He adds, "The gigantic historical paradox remains that although Chinese civilization could not spontaneously produce 'modern' natural science, natural science could not perfect itself without the characteristic philosophy of Chinese civilisation."

(4)   *a continuously effort-consuming activity:* William Angus Sinclair, *The Conditions of Knowing* (Harcourt, Brace & World, 1951), p. 35. Perhaps the "effort" is overstressed here; better perhaps ˢʷenergyˢʷ.

(5)   *kept up as a breed may be:* Order in a language and order in a society may not be too unlike one another for each to serve as parable to the other. Permissions and preclusions in one language may be as unlike those in another as any other customs in two cultures. But different though they may be, within each the same principle may be supposed to hold. And if we would judge between them we would be back with Coleridge before his swan and dove: "Absurd would it be" to pronounce "from any ab-

stract rule common to both . . . or on any ground indeed save that of their own inappropriateness to their own end and being, their want of significance as symbol and physiognomy." Thomas M. Raysor, *Coleridge's Shakespearean Criticism* (Cambridge, Harvard University Press). What Coleridge is laying out here is perhaps the only "abstract rule common to" all animals, languages and societies: that each must be judged in terms of its own organization, not that of any other. So taken, every organism: animal, language, society . . . may be found in this or that respect faulty—*i.e., wanting in significance as symbol and physiognomy,* containing components which do not cooperate as they *should* to their own over-all being and end. Two doctrines as different as those of Mencius and Plato come remarkably close to Coleridge on this. They seem to agree on the great liberating lesson, the root of charity (as, for Plato, of Justice): for each being, its virtues and its defects are due to accordance with or departure from itself. "A word may do what the rest of the language will let it." So with a cell and with a citizen.

(6)   The excerpts that follow are taken from my *Mencius on the Mind: Experiments in Multiple Definition* (Routledge, 1932).

(7)   *Unnumbered evils:* from my simplified version in Near-Basic English, *Plato's Republic* (Cambridge University Press, 1966), p. 187.

9

Sources of Conflict

In what follows I have kept for the most part to what I have myself been able to observe of obstacles to communication between Chinese and Western minds. I have indeed made large use of sections of a long out-of-print essay I wrote in 1934 immediately after my first prolonged encounter with these problems as visiting professor in Tsing Hua and Pei Ta Universities, Peking. What I found to say then, as this concern began to claim highest priority, may well be more veridical than what I might write now. Of what has happened since the first six months of Mao's rule in Peking (April-August, 1950) I have no personal evidence. I doubt, though, whether there will be—even should a chaos ensue—any permanent breach with tradition. The very difficulties that Western opinions are having in their efforts to understand in the least the contemporary changes of course in Chinese policies: the incomprehensibility of the internal and external situations that arise, the equally puzzling fashions in which they are resolved, all this may well be evidence that the thinking which guides Chinese leaders may not be becoming any more comparable to the political thinking that goes on elsewhere. But who knows? My own guess is that the values Mencius represents will recover their ground after every interruption.

What this essay invites the reader to imagine is how explosive a mixture can be composed by two equally proud cultures sus-

*tained by such opposite and mutually incomprehensible grounds
for their pride: oldest against newest—with all that that can
imply. The sad and horrifying thing is that the responsible people in this (Chinese and Americans) are almost equally ignorant
of one another's position while professing to know all about it
—and through their own willful and cultivated fault. Meanwhile
official utterances from both sound, to the other side, like the
crudest, barely intelligible insincerities. Some of the current ex-
acerbations of this tension may soon pass, we will hope, but the
deep incomprehensions will remain, until some remedy such as
is sketched in these pages is effectively carried through. Meanwhile the mistrusts being currently generated will go on building
up a situation for the coming generations that should make the
whole human race tremble.*

It is with sciences as with trees. If it be your purpose to make some
particular use of the tree, you need not concern yourself about the
roots. But if you wish to transfer it into another soil, it is then safer
to employ the roots than the scions. Thus the mode of teaching most
common at present exhibits clearly enough the trunks, as it were, of
the sciences, and those too of handsome growth; but nevertheless,
without the roots, valuable and convenient as they undoubtedly are
to the carpenter, they are useless to the planter. But if you have at
heart the advancement of education, as that which proposes to itself
the general discipline of the mind for its end and aim, be less anxious
concerning the trunks, and let it be your care that the roots should
be extracted entire, even though a small portion of the soil should
adhere to them, so that at all events you may be able, by this means,
both to review your own scientific acquirements, re-measuring as it
were the steps of your knowledge for your own satisfaction, and at the
same time to transplant it into the minds of others, just as it grew in
your own. (BACON, *De Augmentis*, I. vi, c. ii. Translation by S. T.
Coleridge.)

It was I believe this passage that first made me attempt versions [1]
of both the *Iliad* and the *Republic* simple enough, though

faithful, to serve newcomers to English for China, Africa, India,
etc., as well as deprived educables in English-speaking countries.
These books, with the Bible, are certainly the roots of our
moral and political timber. They are a short cut for whoever
from another culture would find out what has given its peculiar
tensions to ours. When I made them I did not realize how firmly
Mao Tse-tung's government would rule against such things.
I could indeed, in Peking in 1950, have some fun trying out
the core of the *Republic* on unsuspecting audiences of students.
They liked it so much that they asked leave to print it in their
magazine as "utterance of the month," and I encouraged them
to go ahead. How healthy their bewilderment when they found
it a forbidden book! As for the *Iliad* I could give a public reading of the central drama. But get people to experiment with it
in classrooms, no. Perhaps as well! And yet nothing could give
them a better lead into many of the things they most need to
know about the West, or give them more help with a "Chinese
Renaissance."

This phrase "The Chinese Renaissance" came into general
use as a description of the pre-World War II literary movement in China; but the parallels to be drawn with our own
Renaissance are few. China was not renewing contact with a
past phase of her tradition, though a few scholars may have set
this as their program; she was being violently and reluctantly
torn from it. Here, for example, is a description of the attitude
taken up toward Confucius, Mencius, and their followers by
the creator of the Chinese Revolution, Dr. Sun Yat-sen (died
1925), whose portrait, before it was successively replaced by
those of Chiang Kai-shek and Mao Tse-tung, looked down on
every schoolroom or university auditorium, and whose influence
then dominated the political ideology of China:

He was not in the habit of picking up the doctrine of any great
author for discussion. Perhaps their great power over him was mainly
negative, in affording a ground for his attack on the existing social
order, although he showed a great respect for these thinkers of his

native land. His work was to overthrow the then existing Government, and he found no support from the philosophers whose views had been adopted to support a regime that he intended to overthrow. To popularize the work of revolution he needed to have an intellectual basis. It is evident that this new intellectual basis of his must go contrariwise to the old. As we know, he was a revolutionist in thought as well as in action. (*The History of the Kuomintang*, by T. C. Woo.)

Two points that appear clearly in this extract must be kept in sight if what is happening is to be understood. The intellectual movement in Modern China has been throughout a consequence of the political movement. The traditional Chinese outlook was to be remade—not because it was felt to be unsatisfactory in *itself*, but because it plainly put China at a disadvantage in the world struggle. In itself, it is probably (to those brought up in it) the most satisfying that has been developed in the world. Its historic stability is almost a proof of this, but to the leaders of the revolution it had already ceased to be satisfying. The second point to which my quotation witnesses is the extraordinary candor with which the pragmatism of the movement is confessed. A Western reader may have a queer sense that the unwritten rules which govern decency in our dealings with philosophical principles are being broken. The intellectual game known as the Pursuit of Truth is being given away. If he feels this he will be tasting one of the fundamental differences between the Chinese and the Western traditions.

Pragmatism, as a doctrine that ideas are tools to be judged by the work they do, we have, of course, in the West, but with us it is a fairly modern doctrine, a result of reflection and a result treated in most European schools of philosophy as a heresy to be refuted. In Chinese philosophy, in its main stream at least, there seems to have been no Problem of Truth as such. Reflection has not exercised itself on the question What do we mean when we say that a statement is true? The place of this problem has been taken by an assumption, so initial as to be unformulated, that what is true is what had better be accepted.[2]

The purposes of Chinese philosophy have been different from ours, and therefore the problems and the forms of argument and the structures of ideas. The methods of comparing, analyzing, defining and uniting notions, which we know in the West as Logic, never gained a permanent footing in the Chinese tradition. They developed instead another kind of subtlety.

Naturally, such a difference as this makes the translation of Western ideas on politics and morals into Chinese terms, and the introduction of Western methods into Chinese political practice, an extraordinarily difficult undertaking. And the difficulty is immensely increased by the linguistic obstacle. Not only are the characters still to a certain degree ideographic but they carry highly coercive etymologic interlinkages. The effect is to make them seem too often to contain or to be themselves what they mean. The Chinese classical language (only acquired fully by those who have been through an elaborate memory-charging education which is already becoming rare) is, through its very aptness for its own purposes, a most embarrassing medium for Western thinking. Often an impossible medium, in fact. The first great translator, Yen Fu, who gave China versions of Huxley's *Evolutionary Ethics,* Spencer's *Sociology,* Mill's *Logic* and *On Liberty,* Jevons' *Elementary Lessons in Logic,* Montesquieu's *The Spirit of Laws,* and Adam Smith's *Wealth of Nations,* used a modified form of Classical Chinese, going back to the earliest language available, because, as he says, "refined theories are better explained in the language current before the Ch'in and Han Dynasties than in the (prevalent literary-classical) language of today, which has a tendency to adapt the meaning to a certain stereotyped phraseology." But this device was, I think, generally regarded, even from the first, as impracticable. One sees, though, why he tried it; he might well have been reading Bacon.

The alternative is to use the colloquial, the new literary language of China, the *pai hua* whose relation to the classical language, *wen li,* is so hard to describe precisely in general terms. Perhaps we can come nearer to understanding the relation by comparing *wen li* to the language of the Authorized Version of the Bible and *pai hua* to our current spoken idiom—always remembering that each word in *wen li* is essentially a character, which cannot be spelled out but must be known, a character whose sound is by itself not a sufficient clue to its meaning, since the same sound will belong to many characters. *Pai hua,* on the other hand, is essentially a spoken language, though it is written also in characters, a large part of which are the same as those used in *wen li.* As a language it has a more explicit structure and a greater facility in borrowing alien forms.

These considerations, and the overwhelming advantage that the colloquial is spoken and read by millions while *wen li* is known *thoroughly* only to thousands, made the creation of a *pai hua* colloquial literature the great effort of the pre-war decades.

So the problem of translation and explanation between some form of English and some form of Chinese divides into two. Its main part concerns transactions between English and the contemporary colloquial; a less but still very important part concerns transactions between the traditional thought of China— preserved in *wen li* but influential throughout the culture—and that Western thinking which aspires to become the intellectual tradition of the world.

One of the most important reforms in Chinese education made by the Kuomintang was the substitution of Dr. Sun Yat-sen's *San Min Chu I* (Three Peoples' Principles) for the Confucian *Four Books* as the dominant source of influence in the schools. Those who are acquainted with the *San Min Chu I* are agreed that the views of Western thought which it contains make it a startling example of the very grave difficulties that are encountered in China's struggle to learn from the West, unless some more satisfactory method of making Western thought available to the Chinese can be devised.

The root difficulty is that the fundamental Chinese attitude to statements is unlike that attitude to statements which in the

West led to the development of an explicit logic and of that critical reflective examination of meanings which had produced modern scholarship. In brief, the difference is this: The modern Western scholar, *ideally* (the intention of these italics should be observed), devotes himself, first, to determining (as neutrally, consciously and explicitly as possible) what the meaning of a passage is, and second, to discussing by an open and verifiable technique whether it is true or false. But traditional Chinese scholarship has spent its immense resources of memory and ingenuity upon *fitting the passage into* an already accepted framework of meanings. This is clearly a perfectly proper aim if we grant the premise that it is the business of scholarship to support an already established moral and/or political system. But the practice is maintained where this premise is absent. The framework need not be a traditional Chinese framework; it may be a Kuomintang program, as we have seen, or some version of Marxism-Leninism, or of Maoism. But whatever it might be, it will in almost all cases be used in the traditional Chinese fashion as something to which other meanings, it may be of Chinese classical writers, are to be *accommodated*. Apart from the physical sciences, mathematics, statistical subjects, and to a lesser degree law and economics, whose disciplines better resist such manipulations, the studies made by Chinese in Western subjects do not in general as yet give them, however perfect their command of English, that power of critical neutral examination and understanding which should be their prime purpose.

This is a sufficiently sweeping generalization, but it is not likely, I think, to be disputed by anyone who has taught in China and has been a witness, in the Chinese scene, of the defeated struggles toward the peculiar Western critical attitude of men often, in other respects, of the first order of intellectual capacity. This detached and critical attitude is obviously much easier to maintain in the atmosphere of a Western university than at home in China.

Such a charge may well seem offensive, but I believe that those

Chinese who are exceptions and escape it will agree with me that it is justified, and that this tendency to accommodating interpretations is indeed a formidable obstacle to understanding. Expositions of Chinese philosophy in Western terms we will naturally expect to be full of such manipulations. I have, for example, seen two accounts, given in detail, of the thought of Chu Hsi (the great schoolman who reinterpreted Confucianism in Sung times). The first displayed him as a mixture of Aristotle and Kant; the second as an out-and-out Platonist. Neither account made any attempt to analyze either the thought of Chu Hsi, or of Aristotle, Kant, or Plato, or to give an apparatus by which interesting and relevant comparisons might be made. They merely borrowed the Western vocabularies. "Nothing peculiarly Chinese in this!" we may think, recalling the exploits of those Western thinkers who used to derive Plato from Moses. But my contrast is with post-Royal Society scholarship. These accounts of Chu Hsi came from two of the foremost scholars in comparative philosophy that China has produced. And Hu Shih's *The Development of the Logical Method in Ancient China* (this title alone tells us how strange logic was to Chinese scholarship, however sophisticated), though more frankly recognizing the perils of his venture, is a further case in point. He too found in his Chinese texts mirrors in which what he had learned of Western philosophy at Columbia (Pragmatism, Theory of Inference, and Evolution) could be reflected. He too showed the same tendency to accommodate his material to a pre-formed system rather than to examine it for its own sake.

The peculiar elsewhere-directed responsibilities of the Chinese attitude to meanings, even in the case of quantitative and comparatively precise concepts, has been well shown in the struggles of the various committees which have been set up to prepare standard Chinese terms with which to render Western technicalities. Some of these committees—that on Terms in Psychology for example—were in existence for years without venturing any report, though their personnel was as eminent as possible. The wisdom of such delay is evident, since no satisfactory recommendations can be made without a labor of analytic comparison between Western uses of these terms, which has not yet been anywhere carried out. But the attitudes governing some of the recommendations that have been made are what are of interest here. In the Introduction to *Some Statistical and Measurement Terms Standardized in Chinese,* by Dr. J. P. Chu (issued in 1923 under the auspices of the Chinese National Association for the Advancement of Education and published by the Commercial Press) we read: "During the process of translation, Dr. McCall has greatly helped in interpreting the English terms in their functional meanings and many times in suggesting *entirely new but nevertheless appropriate meanings. . . .* Thanks are expressed to Professors X and Y for translating a few very subtle terms and to Professor Z for *giving a literary touch* to many of the words." (My italics.) If we realize that what was being discussed is a word-list, in which terms such as *frequency, subjective, intelligence,* or *mentality* were being given single Chinese "equivalents," we shall feel the strangeness (to our conception of such work) of the remarks I have italicized. I have not the knowledge required to judge the merits of these proposed standard terms, and I cite this introduction only because it reflects assumptions I have encountered too often in other translation work, into and from Chinese, not to feel them as most formidable obstacles to the naturalization of the more abstract statements of the social sciences in the Chinese language. All Chinese who have done such work have, I believe, learned their scientific specialty in English, or in some other foreign language, and do their thinking in it.

There are in fact practical difficulties of a very grave kind in the way of any extensive introduction of scientific terms into the present Chinese language and thus of any *widespread* teaching, *in Chinese,* of science as a precise intellectual discipline. New words and character-groups can, of course, easily be made up; they have been introduced at a rate which has rarely, if ever, been equaled in the history of any people. Where their meanings can be directly controlled by facts of observation and experimental technique, the difficulties are, with care, rapidly overcome. But the case is different with words that must take their meanings not from observation of fairly unambiguous situations, but from explanations and definitions in terms whose meanings are part of the ancient Chinese tradition of thinking. Most terms in psychology, ethics, logic, sociology, aesthetics, criticism, grammar, politics, economics come under this head. *Instinct, emotion, attention, knowledge, truth, justice, socialism, condition, character, quality, concept, abstract, cause, discrimination, responsibility, value* are examples.

We ourselves know how ambiguous such words are and how difficult it is, with all the resources of our own traditional, historical and analytic technique, to keep them in control. When they are rendered into Chinese "equivalents" the risk of their generating a new crop of ambiguities, *not* parallel to those with which they are already afflicted, becomes excessive; and there is only too good reason to believe that this miscegenative proliferation has been happening on a very great scale. It has been noted often by foreign observers with such words as *democracy* and *justice*. Those who have taught out there realize that it is happening as disastrously with less conspicuous, but intellectually as important, verbal instruments also.

The group of words over which radical misconceptions can be most dangerous are those which, for the West, convey—and to many almost embody—their key political principles. Among such are: *State, Constitution, Rights, Freedom, Liberty.* (I put them in capitals because of what they have to deal with.) It is not a matter that can be realized with any comfort in the West, or that should be taken in any carefree spirit in China, that the manifold meanings of these words have proved *untranslatable* in Chinese.

In an exacting and minutely critical study, Dr. Fo-ch'üan Chang [3] has for years been tracing in detail the attempts to introduce these major Western political terms and concepts into Chinese. Such an account entails of necessity a reciprocal attempt to represent Chinese modes of political thinking in English. What results is a display of as yet unresolved divergencies formidable beyond brief description. The study is, I should insist, no piece of politics itself but a purely linguistic inquiry unconnected with the division of China or with world divisions which may increasingly stem from that. He is describing as simply as he can how the various terms which have been tried out by Chinese translators for our Capital Words have *had* to be understood by their readers, ever since accounts of the West began to appear in Chinese. What emerges is this: Any detached but persistent inquirer will have to conclude that the means of political reflection available to the Chinese-using and the English-using peoples are too different for thought in the one to present anything better than a blurred and twisted image of the thought of the other. A bilingual scholar such as Dr. Chang, deeply and discerningly read both in Western political theory and in Chinese discussions of questions of government, can, more or less and with difficulty, make piecemeal comparisons. He can record in one or the other language how a Chinese term fails to correspond, in this or that of its components, with the English term it might try to represent, and vice versa. With scholarly reserve and due uncertainty he can take stock of the resources within each language for treating what are—by the nature of the case—only imprecisely analogous topics. He can note how, for example, the usage of a Chinese term through eighteen centuries gives it a pejorative force which makes it inevitably represent *license* rather than *liberty*. And he can show too why this term was the preferred choice of the translator, and he can report that no better term in Chinese is available. He can show, more fundamentally, that Chinese terms which may be offered as equivalents for *state, government, rights, liberties* are interwoven, through contrasts and connections with other Chinese expressions, in ways which prevent them from presenting to Chinese readers anything but a travesty—and it may seem a malicious travesty, but isn't—of what Western users hope they would want to say. In brief, these terms are all examples of what I have labeled as ^{di}_____^{di} handling. Every term offered, as an equivalent to the Western word, has as its unavoidable outcome a way of bringing in other expressions from other contexts jointly reflecting a social-ethical-political system deeply different from those within which the English words operate. These themselves have their own complex multiplicities of meaning, which English users attempting much precision find hard enough to order. The Chinese expressions have another multiplicity and in all probability different principles of ordering. All this an able-enough bilingual can explore and thereby protect himself and a few specialist readers, in some measure. But the general Chinese reader and the English reader is left undefended from even extreme misconceptions—of the situations his opposite number may be trying to cope with, of the ways in which he is trying to take account of what is happening and of how he in his turn uses his opposite number's endeavors. All this quite apart from the continuous intensely motivated propagandist efforts on both sides to misrepresent the opponent's every motive and action.

It is a truly awakening, alerting and summoning thought that while the linguistic-semantic barrier is perfectly permeable to the technicalities of the missile and of biologic warfare—at the mass-murder level—vast segments of mortal humanity are so separated by it on the moral-political front that they must still deeply misconceive one another's characters, one another's intents, and one another's devoted, dedicated, hope-impelled efforts to be of service to mankind.

There is reason, then, to doubt the wisdom of urging that Western subjects should be studied in Chinese. The report of the League of Nations Mission of Education experts, entitled *The Reorganization of Education in China,* illustrates this insistence. After observing that "to penetrate the consciousness deeply . . . an adequate mental representation of the world about us . . . should be largely based on the entire living and familiar experience of the child," it goes on:

> Another consequence, and a still more important one, concerns the language in which, especially at the beginning, the teaching of science ought to be given in secondary schools. If it be agreed that new ideas are deeply assimilated by the mind of the child and cling so that they later become truly and efficaciously his own, then these ideas must be imparted in his own language, by means of symbols around which all his anterior knowledge has been organized. Hence the necessity absolutely to proscribe the use of manuals in foreign languages in secondary teaching.

The intention behind this simple application of a commonplace of out-of-date French pedagogy is no doubt excellent, but it entirely overlooks the practical objections. For "the symbols around which all his anterior knowledge has been organized," are, for the Chinese child, vigorously recalcitrant to the purposes of science, both as regards the separate meanings of these symbols and his attitudes in them, and as regards the mode in which they will have organized his "anterior knowledge." The educational experts do indeed remark that "There ought to be a preliminary determination of the new vocabulary which is special to each discipline." Indeed there ought! But they evidently had had no experience of the problems that this determination, for Chinese, brings up.

Moreover, as Owen Lattimore has pointed out in *Manchuria: Cradle of Conflict,* p. 173:

> An enormous proportion of the technical terms that are currently being incorporated into the Chinese language are not directly created; they are either artificially translated, or taken over through the Japanese. The fact that such terms are written in the Chinese character tones down the fact that they are nonetheless in a foreign language, and a language far more foreign to the existing body of Chinese thought than are, for instance, the technical terms created from Latin

or Greek roots that are commonly used in the West. It is difficult for
foreigners to appreciate that such terms have a sort of unreality which
keeps them alien from the body of the language, and that the processes
of thought behind these terms are so alien to the language itself that
many of them cannot be expressed in terms naturally evolved from
the language, but must be dealt with in a language within the language. . . . [In the West] the major part of the jargon of medicine,
of engineering, even of chemistry and physics, can also be expressed
clearly, without loss of scientific clarity in the vernacular of each
nation, for the antecedent processes of thought are native in each
nation. In this lies the great handicap of Chinese technical phraseology; for many terms either cannot be expressed in locutions under-
standable by the people, or have to be expressed with such a burden of
circumlocution that the thought which it is intended to convey is
borne down and smothered, becoming in the end meaningless and
absurd; for the thought . . . which it is desired to express is alien to
the modes of thought inherent in the language itself. Consequently
a terminology which is thought of in the West as merely a *specialized*
language remains in China a *foreign* language. The final proof of this
is in the fact that it is better for a Chinese to learn a foreign language
as a means to the mastery of advanced technique than to attempt to
study it in Chinese.

These conclusions are, I think, supported by all who have
given special attention to this problem.

Thus, at present, the invasion of new terms into Chinese is
not making so quickly and directly for a Chinese understanding
of Western thought as may be supposed. Skewed new blends
of meaning which accompany them are not, however, accessible
to Western inspection so readily as the not a whit stranger interpretations of English, as taught in China, which form the
other side of the picture. I will turn to some examples of Chinese "appreciation" of Western literature.

Imagine a course of lectures on English Literature delivered
on the assumption that any pair of male and female characters
left by a novelist alone together must be supposed to misconduct
themselves. The well-known Anglo-Saxon prudery explains why

the novelist does not indicate this. These lectures are not the invention of a satirist, but were given annually by a Chinese Professor of English Literature who ranked as a scholar in Chinese among the most eminent there are.

Or consider this extract from an able examinee who has been studying *Tess of the D'Urbervilles* as a large part of his year's work in English:

"The plot of this novel is quite good. He clearly sees in Tess all that is irresponsible for good and evil in a woman's character, all that is untrustworthy in her brain and will. Yet he still not wished such a woman free from punishment, so he made her to be tormented under the hard works and at last punished to death. All these things he managed very well, they flow naturally and artistically and they are of everyday life."

The explanation of this is that Tess was an unfilial daughter, and so deserved all that she got. This was not a stray individual's interpretation, but the view also of the Chinese teacher who conducted the class.

Before we smile complacently at such absurdities let us remember what misdirections of effort are still acquiesced in by departments of Literature and of Linguistics in many of the universities of the Western world. That such distortions occur, and countless lesser ones which are more serious (since they are more difficult to detect and to correct), is not the fault of the individuals in whom they take place. It is the fault of the piteous misdirection of labor that the programs of Western Studies all over the world entail. At present the curricula push the students into extensive literary studies before they have acquired more than a very few glimmerings of insight into Western meanings. And the avid curiosity of the students, their tireless industry and brilliant ingenuity complete the disaster. Literature, as it comes to them through their defective equipment as readers, gives them nothing, as a rule, of those powers for which we value it. It offers little more than an unrestricted opportunity for misconceptions; its alien content becomes for them a vast exercise ground for *disorientation*—an opening into all the sinister possibilities which the pun suggests.

In all this I am using and reappraising an essay written in 1934, when I came back to Cambridge fresh from some years of teaching English literature to the best students in the universities of Peking. I have to confirm what it says from the widened viewpoint of an observer of education, from a Harvard angle, in India, in Peking again (1950) and in Africa. My experience of my first Chinese students stands out: partly because I was younger then, more impatient, readier to acclaim and to reject; partly because of the magnificent intelligence, industry and resolve of my Chinese students; partly because the view, which this book is attempting to present, of the real dangers of mutual miscomprehension was formed then. Neither the missile nor the computer was needed to make one realize what the gulf between China and the West could lead to, how perilous the contact must be between two equally inordinate vanities so opposite in grounds. The coming of such ever-increasing capacities to destroy and to create turns current history into a race between them. In these years we may well be haunted by Coleridge's lines:

> Like strangers sheltering from a storm
> Hope and Despair meet in the porch of Death.

Meanwhile, the new super-human powers, carrying with them super-human responsibilities, are about to *spray* the planet (by the record the image is dreadfully just) with ˢʷinstructionˢʷ via satellite distributors. And this through channels that could, if only the designers of the instruction knew how, convey much that would help with the prime problem. But alas, through the thirty-odd years that could have been given to preparations *in design* for this challenge most of those competent have preferred to busy themselves with other things. The world supply of examinations in English, for example, is much as it was in the thirties, as inappropriate and frustrating; and the *advice*—to

Africa, India, Indonesia, Pakistan, in fact to the majority of the
human race—on how they can best acquire the necessary means
of world cooperation has remained (as distributed by governments and foundations) about as routine, as vacuous and vision-
less, as it was then. China, meanwhile, through an inexplicable
fit of pique, has been conjurerwise ¹vanished¹, sent to stand in
the corner for bad behavior, treated as non-existent by the
English-speaking country that most prides itself on its concern
with education.

The point deserves to be put with energy. The urgency of the
need for better policies will be not denied by anyone who
watches what is happening. This is the unparalleled moment of
the meeting and mixing of cultures. In China, India, Africa,
America, and in Europe, the best minds are everywhere flounder-
ing toward clarity of will and thought through labyrinths of
confusion that are mainly avoidable. There is no one who is
working seriously toward the increase of intelligence in himself
or his fellows who does not waste a great part of his energy from
the lack of systematic devices for remaking necessary distinctions.
It may be held that a general technique of explanation is an im-
possibility, that the common starting points required are just
what are unavailable. Such an opinion has not taken account of
recent gains and present resources. What was formerly too difficult (I remind myself here that these paragraphs were written
in 1934, before computer possibilities were in sight) has become
today a matter mainly of industry, acumen and cooperation—
just in time to meet the enormous increase in the need for new
explanatory apparatus, which mechanical communications have
brought about.

A university of China is a good place in which to realize what
the oncoming world situation will entail. So is an Indian university—where students are still offered Anglo-Saxon and Gothic
as a preparation for what is before them! But any place where
active minds are trying to think clearly will do as well. They

have to deal with more ideas, belonging to more varied traditions than ever before; ideas more dependent upon the words
that represent them and less supported by experience and the
social milieu in which the thinkers live. And they must for the
most part receive them from, and handle them with, a language that is not their own, or after the distortions of translation into languages for which these ideas are aliens. With whatever admiration we regard those who succeed, is not an equal
obligation to improve the agents of transmission imposed upon
us? If we were to change places with them and more often become learners rather than teachers we should feel this more
strongly. We in the West are the product of several mixtures of
culture, to which mixtures the richness of our resources, as of
our potential confusions, may be due. We are participating now
in a greater mixture and we can neither transmit the best that
we have achieved nor develop what we so badly need without
better instruments of apprehension and ordering than we possess.

But to return to China, to India, to Africa, to Indonesia . . .
to the billions who are about to suffer beyond our easy imagination for lack of knowledge that can come to them only through
English. What is required, what must be achieved, if the rising
generation in these countries is to come into wide and sane and
effective contact with one another and with the West, is a way
of access to Western meanings and thereby to other meanings of
whatever origin, which will break right through the linguistic
barrier of literary English without, in so doing, endangering the
values it has for those who thereafter turn, better prepared, to
its study. The majority of these students are *never* going to learn
to understand much literary English. It forms no natural part
of their life-needs. But they do need an understanding of an
enormous number of ideas, feelings, desires and attitudes that
they can only gain through some form of Western language. In
practice this means some form of English. Literary English is
being used today to give them this—although it is recognized to

be a noise-engendering and unsuccessful medium. It is being used because no more effective medium has been available. With the introduction of a more suitable medium, Literary or Complete English will take its proper place—an important but a restricted place. It will become the concern only of those whose life's work is to be devoted to its study.

A better medium should, from the beginning, recognize the disparity between Western and Other attitudes to language and its meanings, discussed above. It should aim at giving the African or Chinese learner of English what his own language does not provide him with (and perhaps never will), an instrument for controllable comparisons. It should be a medium inviting and requiring a clear and explicit definition of the matter that it conveys. This not only because a lack of habits of discriminating reflection is the chief disability of the non-Western student— but because the Western ideas, feelings, desires and attitudes which the medium is to convey differ, for better or for worse, from their ideas, feelings, desires and attitudes chiefly in different articulations with one another in complex sentiments. To use a handy metaphor, the particles in the two cases may be the same but the molecules of meaning with which the languages operate are for the most part not the same. The only way to avoid travesties of Western units of meaning through other-language ¹equivalents¹ is by giving these meanings through, and together with, an apparatus for comparing complex meanings— through an explicit analytic language.

The prototype for such languages is Basic English. But to judge of these possibilities a Western reader will do best to consider them in connection with those aspects of our own problem—the teaching of English at home, in our schools and universities—which show most analogy with the troubles of the Chinese student. Montesquieu, Voltaire and Goldsmith knew one way of using the East to display the West. But there are others, and the reader will have noticed that only a part of the Chinese student's or any other foreign student's difficulties with

English is peculiarly his. Inability to consider meanings *critically,* lack of training in systematic comparison and discrimination, a tendency to accommodate a passage to a preformed view rather than to examine it for itself, these are not unknown anywhere. Let us then examine them in the field in which we can most hope to understand them thoroughly.

Sources of Conflict

(1)   *versions:* of *Republic,* 1966, and of *Euthyphro, Apology, Crito, Phaedo:* my *Why So, Socrates?*—a dramatic rendering suited for performance in schools or on TV—and of the *Iliad: The Wrath of Achilles* (New York, Norton, 1951). Of these the last is the simplest and may well precede the others, which are in so many ways a commentary on the *Iliad.* All three are experiments in the controlled—maximal gain, minimal cost—English discussed in the final essay. Between them they could do more, for an African or a Chinese coming into English, to make Western culture intelligible to him than any miscellany of contemporary reading.

(2)   *what had better be accepted:* Compare "Their idea of Order derives from a healthy country feeling for *good understanding.* . . . This feeling . . . always rested . . . upon a kind of passion for autonomy, and upon a need, no less strong, for comradeship and friendship. State, Dogma, Law, were powerless as compared with Order. Order was conceived as a Peace which no abstract forms of obedience could establish, no abstract reasoning impose. To make this Peace reign everywhere, a taste for conciliation was necessary, involving an acute sense of compromise, spontaneous solidarities and free hierarchies. . . . To understand and to induce understanding is to create Peace in oneself and around oneself." M. Granet, *La Pensée Chinoise* (Paris, Albin Michel, 1934). Quoted by Needham, *op. cit.,* p. 338. We may wonder if dissatisfac-

tion with conditions elsewhere may not have contributed to Granet's fine picture.

(3)   *Freedom and Human Rights in Modern Chinese Political Theory.* A treatise in course of preparation by Dr. Fo-ch'üan Chang of Tunghai University, Taiwan, now at the East Asian Research Center, Harvard.

10

Toward a World English

This final essay offers the proposals to which the previous essays have led. The chief premise is that every possible means should be tried to avoid the too probable outcomes of current courses. Among these means, the opportunities opened by a major world-wide demand for a common auxiliary language should no longer be neglected. And among these opportunities is the feasibility of so teaching English that new levels of mental capacity are induced. No doubt many if not most aspirants to effective English see it as a ladder to relative wealth and prestige. Many of those promoting English see it, no doubt, in terms of commercial profit. No matter. If the presentation is well enough designed what is presented will take over—to the development of those concepts and sentiments: methodic, economic, moral, political, on which the continuance of man's venture depends.

We of the West have somehow—out of a strangely unself-regardful, indeed a regardless, impulse of benevolence—committed ourselves to universal education as well as to universal participation in government, nominal only though this last can be. We have been selling this program for man—in which the gaps between the meanings and the actualities are everywhere horrendous—as though it could be in itself a cure-all. But is it not plain that this incalculable venture, as noble as it is perilous, cannot possibly succeed without such a liberation of human capacity and good will as few but Shelleyans have imagined? The alternative is chaos on a scale which will compel the sacrifice of very much more than ideals.

Such is the frame of reference within which the following essay looks back to proposals, made over a third of a century ago, for a common-sense instrument with which to work for a common-world education.

No doubt we can see now, as the proposer of Basic English hardly could, that an auxiliary world language will have to be (as with the automobile and the airplane) a developing design, redesigned as performance data indicate. But since no more significant model for a World Auxiliary has appeared or seems to be on the stocks, I have put my points in terms of probable successors to Basic English. It may be that the obstructions of which earlier pages have spoken at perhaps too much length will prevent their development. But, at least, an awakening plan for helping with what matters most will have been put forward again.

Governments today have a far harder task than any of their predecessors: the problems that come to them are far more complex and the outcomes of their decisions carry risks not known before. This grim reason [1] for a great immediate attempt to improve world-wide intellectual communications can speak for itself. If it is not to be listened to, words here will not help.

At present—whatever may happen later—the task of serving as an elucidatory world auxiliary, of helping more people to understand themselves and others more clearly, falls upon some form of English. Why not say simply "upon English"? The question goes to the heart of the need. There are any number of highly proficient speakers of English who understand themselves and others very little. No adaptation of English, of course, no restriction, no special design, regimen or discipline can ensure discernment, can automatically secure understanding. Nonetheless there are means, in the mode of acquisition and cultivation of English and in the appraisals induced through its discriminations, which can increase the probability of clear, self-corrigible comprehension.

The possibility of devising a restricted form of English (an expanding series of restricted forms rather) effective toward this aim depends upon a remarkable fact. A relatively small selection from its vast vocabulary is capable of representing the rest, of saying—not perfectly, of course, but still to an extraordinary degree—what the rest can say. This selection, this language within a language, can thus serve as a sort of caretaker, an inspectorate, a maintenance, repair and remedial staff, able to examine, criticize, deputize and demonstrate where needed: in brief be a control upon the rest. And not a control merely over its lexical performance, the efficiency of its vocabulary in use, the choice, justice and comprehensibility of its terms. The possible control covers the implications, the requirements and exclusions mentioned in preceding essays. This capacity of a small segment of the language to exercise such a wide and deep supervision over the rest is the ground for believing that an effective heightening in men's ability to understand one another can—given an adequate attempt—be brought about.

No one, it is to be hoped, will suppose that this can be a light and easy undertaking. The devising of the means of cultivating and refining the work of this caretaker, this instrument of reflection,[2] will call for high, devoted, open-minded and many-sided ability, much new design, experimentation and redesign. But the tools for much of this, with the development of the computer, are at hand. What is needed, if they are to be usefully set to work, is searching and imaginative consideration of purposes and principles. It would be well to be as clear as we may be about what is needed and what can be done before we get caught up in finding the people, spending the money, and in promoting the schemes.

The demonstration of the existence and of the extraordinary powers of this caretaker core of English was the work of C. K. Ogden, inventor of Basic English. My own part in its design ended early—very soon after we had noticed, in some joint work on Definition, that a comparatively few words were doing most of the work whatever the word being defined might happen to be. *The body of words which together are capable of defining all the rest in all their senses* [3] would be a brief formula for what I have been calling the caretaker selection.

The essential comparisons between things we might say, and between different ways of saying what we call ᵂᵗthe same thingᵂ, are not, of course, necessarily made *through* these words; but if we come to discussion of such comparisons, distinguishing and relating the meanings we are comparing, then these words, we will find, can do most of the job. Cultivation of our use of these words, increase of our skill, our resource, clarity, discrimination, flexibility and common sense in the handling of them, is thus the readiest way of improving our understanding of meanings.

Ogden's Basic English was in several ways both more and less than a proposal for the cultivation of these words. It was to be an all-purpose auxiliary language suited for Business, Administrative, Scientific, Instructional and Commercial uses.[4] It was also to be an adequate channel through which the world's great literature—the Bible, Homer, Plato, Mencius, Shakespeare, Tolstoy—could be presented to all peoples whether they had a literature of their own or not. It was to carry news, gossip, social exchanges, including what Ogden's friend Malinowski called "Phatic Communion." It had, moreover, to be learned as quickly as possible, both as a medium that might be for many learners enough in itself for their needs and as a stage on their way to whatever more English their interests and activities called for. These last considerations, together with what I may describe as the promotional aspects, had a deep influence on the form Ogden finally gave it. So too had his highly original views on the nature of the verb, theories developed largely from his regard for Jeremy Bentham.

Economy in learning effort, compactness of presentation, the separation of the "functional" from the "content" words [5]—these three converged to recommend to him the format of the celebrated "Basic English Word List," with its nine columns: the 100 Operation Words, the 600 Things (400 General and 200 Pictured), the 100 Qualities and the 50 Opposites. Ogden had an attachment to this presentation, "a list able to be printed on one side of a bit of business notepaper" which perhaps reflected the prolonged pains of coming to his decision about it. Once established and promulgated, its layout, those shapely round figures, the absence of room, the compression of the rules . . . these things gave a rigidity to the system it might otherwise have escaped. On the other hand there can be no doubt of the Word List's success in gaining attention.

There may well be lessons to be learned. One of them Ogden pointed out himself in the remark that if an English-speaking user kept within 90 per cent of pure Basic that would be good enough.[6] It seems likely that proposals toward restricted languages for whatever purposes will do well to adopt such a tentative, relaxed and tolerant posture.

There are perhaps other lessons.

It is a disturbing if a salutary thought that those who have paid much attention to language should so often be conspicuously unable to understand or be understood by those who have done likewise. Bacon, in a charitable mood, observes that "The true atheist is he whose hands are cauterized by holy things." It is hard to see why linguists so often have to behave so. It should be mentioned, however, because it belongs, alas, to the elementary strategic considerations of those who will have to try to improve communications between peoples.

What Churchill's and Roosevelt's experiences were with Basic English is mentioned in "Computer-Conveyed Instruction." Its reception by professional linguists was naturally mixed. Some few saw it for what it was, commended it but felt it was all a little remote, their awareness then of the human situation being average. Others, as soon as it became a "movement," grew hostile. I tried to tell Ogden that "movements" in such matters get nowhere; but that did not help him. And then soon after Churchill and Roosevelt had given Basic English their push, there developed a series of misrepresentations: accounts of it from "specialists" who had not read Ogden's expositions, charges from people who did not know (and could not see) which words were on his Word List or not. Any good graduate student will have little difficulty in finding and exhibiting these failures to be fair. He will learn useful things about human nature and the tactics of controversy. But the lesson can be learned without those details.

There is a more important reason for mentioning these attacks. They can easily give quite false impressions of Basic English to designers who might learn from it much that would be valuable in their work. With the forthcoming reappearance of Ogden's own chief expositions enriched by his pioneer study in phrasal lexicology, *The Basic Words,* most of what is most relevant in his work to theory and practice in language restriction will be again available. No other restricted English has been tried out so variously and on such a scale.

It will be useful then to offer a summary account of the aims and the design of Basic English as a preliminary to discussing some modifications which a rather long and varied experience with it has suggested.

The aims were four:

(1) It was to be such that everything that anyone wishes to say might be said—so far as the plain sense goes—as clearly and explicitly in Basic as in Complete English.

(2) It was to be acceptable to the eyes and ears and minds of users of Complete English; to be a selection from Complete English allowing nothing in vocabulary, phrase-building or

syntax contrary or foreign to what we often, somewhat obscurely, call the "genius" of English.

(3) It was to be capable of being learned with the minimum of labor by speakers of other tongues, including Far Eastern and African tongues as well as those Indo-European tongues from which other proposed auxiliary languages (Esperanto, Ido, Novial, Interglossa, etc.) have chiefly drawn.

(4) It was designed to give automatically as much insight into the structure and articulations of our meanings as could be contrived.

As so stated all these aims need comment.

(1) *Plain sense.* Basic can handle more than that, as the *Basic Bible* well shows. But it is, on the whole, at its best when it sticks to factual matters. Attempts to put the Gettysburg Address into Basic are only useful as a way of bringing out the merits of the original. Unfortunately, people often get attached to their versions.

(2) Sentence by sentence this can be so. Long stretches of Basic inevitably grow monotonous and feel *flat* to an English speaker. But this is correspondingly an advantage to a learner of English.

(3) Learners rarely, if ever, learn the whole of Basic, if by that we mean that they acquire a command of all the 850 words in their chief uses, and without picking up a lot of other English as well. Ordinarily they learn a certain amount—what is in the texts or films through which they learn it—and then branch out as their interests lead them. Most early discussion of Basic focused on *readers'* use of it. Not very many English speakers have become able to converse freely in pure Basic, though prepared speeches and technical talk can readily be managed by those who keep in practice. Learning to write in Basic is far easier. It is while doing so that its success in its fourth aim becomes prominent.

Experience has shown that there is a general expectation that learning to write easily in Basic must be extremely difficult for users of Complete English. It has even been said that to learn

Basic must be harder for those to whom Complete English is their native tongue than for foreigners. This, as was long ago demonstrated overwhelmingly by the experience of many, is simply a mistake. An English speaker can learn to write in Basic *in a day*. But, as in other kinds of learning, he must set about his work in the right way. If he merely takes the Basic Word List and attempts virtually to reinvent for himself the whole technique of its use, he is likely to be defeated and to become discouraged. Basic cannot be easily learned from the Word List or from a rapid perusal of a few specimens. But it can be both quickly and easily learned by a ready writer who takes *The Basic Words* and *The ABC of Basic English* (the books of the Rules) and works for a short while under their guidance.

The principles underlying Basic (they are at the same time the technique of its use) are extremely simple. They derive from the observation that the number of ideas we actually use in explaining or defining any meaning is surprisingly small. Their exact number cannot be settled unless we first settle on how we are to count them. This is partly an arbitrary matter depending upon how we set up our scales of precision. But the important point is that our key *general* ideas are not many, though the rich variety of our vocabulary makes us suppose that they are innumerable. To take an analogy that is useful if not pressed too far, the chemist is prepared to give in terms of a very small number of elements an exact description of innumerable compounds for which any ordinary language would require an indefinitely large vocabulary. So Basic, with a small apparatus of terms, is prepared to give an account, as exact as circumstances require, precise enough for the purpose in hand, of innumerable meanings for which Complete English has its immense resources.

The parallel with chemistry must not be taken too far; the second aim of Basic, listed above, prevents it from being a purely logical analytic notation. It is a good thing that this is so, for very much work, of the kind which led to Basic, would have to be done before a universal logical language of the kind that

Leibniz dreamed of could be created. It is no longer, however, out of sight. But its uses would be by no means similar to those of Basic. It would require, for example, much more knowledge and intellectual energy in its users than a world auxiliary language can possibly call upon—at any rate during the next few centuries. Basic is in fact a partially analytic language adjusted to the level of experience and intelligence that already exists and is available in its users. The larger part of its Word List consists of names (*camera, card, neck, reading, doubt,* for example) which are not ultimates of analysis. With enough ingenuity we could always replace them by descriptions in terms of an irreducible minimum of words, descriptions which would better show the ingredients and the structure of the meanings these names carry. But these descriptions would as a rule be very inconvenient. They would often be long and clumsy, and would not do the work in the practical affairs of the world for which Basic is designed.

Nonetheless the briefness of the Basic Word List and the comprehensiveness of its covering power derive entirely from an analytic principle of the language, used though it is with discretion. No other word list, which does not employ the same analytic method, has any chance of being of the same service. The interval in efficiency between Basic and other "simplified English" word lists (of which many have been proposed) is too wide to be bridged—unless they become Basic in essentials themselves. This analytic descriptive principle, on which the powers of Basic both as an auxiliary international language and as an instrument in education depend, is a technical innovation in the deliberate control of language. What it makes possible could not be done without it—any more than an airplane could fly the Atlantic without the theoretical engineering behind its design. It is important, therefore, to keep the theoretical aspects in mind.

Basic, whenever it needs to, uses a *description* of a thing or event in place of the name of the thing or event which Complete English would use. It can give a description because it has in its Word List names for the chief ingredients which are required in such descriptions as well as an adequate apparatus for putting them together in any way that is required. A learner of Basic very soon discovers that he has not one but a number of alternative ways of saying anything he wishes to say in Basic. It is thus unnecessarily powerful, redundant in its resources, as a medium of expression; but the advantages of this for its general purposes, social as well as logical, are very great. It gains a suppleness which allows it to take note of factors in the situation which are not being explicitly mentioned; it follows its parent, Complete English, in being a language in which two speakers need not, unless they wish to, always use the same phrases. Stylistic differences between different writers of Basic are, in fact, surprisingly marked. Basic, furthermore, is like every other language; there is *good* and *bad* Basic writing, a point it is well to remember in studying specimens of Basic. Judges who are not familiar with it are apt to treat any Basic passage they come across as though it must represent the only possible Basic version of the thought. But this is a mistake; we do not consider that a backward schoolboy's essay shows that Complete English is a poor language!

The close relation of Basic to Complete English—that of a part to a whole without any change of essential nature between them —gives it its opportunities. It is, however, also the ground of a very frequently expressed doubt or fear: the doubt, namely, whether a foreign learner of Basic can go on to learn Complete English, whether Basic may not become an obstacle to the learning of Complete English and, further, whether the learning of Basic in schools in English-speaking countries might not tend to a corruption of Complete English.

Half of this doubt turns on the question of vocabulary. There is a very prevalent belief that good use of any language is a matter of the *quantity* of the words in it which are available and employed. For a non-generalizing and non-analytic language (could there be such a thing) this view would be correct; the number of the words we know would be a measure of our command of the language. But, as we all know, it is not the quantity of the words we are acquainted with, but the quality of our understanding of them, which matters. The chief vice of foreign-language learning (and indeed of much native-language learning) is picking up words without learning quite what they mean, accepting them with indefinite and vague meanings that thereafter obscure their real uses from us. Basic, through its analytic procedure, can avoid this danger more thoroughly than any other mode of introduction to Complete English. For the Basic learner's understanding of the next 10,000 words grows out of his understanding of the first few hundred. He thus follows a natural course—that largely followed in his learning of his native language. The new words come to him through their meanings as explorable through the words he already knows, not as supposed equivalents to words in his native tongue which may, too often, be only very remotely and occasionally equivalent.

The other half of the fear that Basic may be an obstacle to Complete English concerns syntax. The best answer to it that I know is in the words of Confucius: "In hewing an axe handle, the model for it is in our hand." In going on to the whole range of English syntax, the Basic user has the model for it in his mind, he has all the essential types of construction already at his command. I have not seen any argument to show that the Basic learner, here, has any greater difficulty to face than, say, a pupil who has done First Year French going on to Second Year French! And though this fear has been vigorously proclaimed in some quarters, the fearers have not yet made any attempt to point out wherein the Basic learner is in any different position from that of any learner of any other language whose complete mastery must go by stages. In point of fact the transition from Basic toward Complete English has now been made very smoothly and comfortably by countless learners.

Let us turn now to consider the kind of strict critical examination and questioning of meanings that translation into Basic tends to promote. I will take a short passage of prose, about the meaning of which for the average reader I have more than usual information since I have at various times obtained Non-Basic paraphrases of it from some 200 students at Harvard or at Cambridge. Although, when carefully examined, it is seen to be discussing a point of importance, a bare four per cent of my paraphrasers, though invited to comment on its content, found anything there to remark on. From a similar set of Basic paraphrasers, however, I got plenty of severe-enough comments. The passage is from an article in *The New Republic* thought sufficiently weighty to be reprinted in China, where I first read it. Here it is:

In brief, the educational significance of modern social development is to emphasize the need for a liberated intelligence. This in turn requires, first, a reorganization of educational agencies so that theory may operate freely on the level of practice, and, secondly, a consideration of the question of whether and to what extent we are willing to accept the principle of a free intelligence as a basis for our social outlook or philosophy of life.

Now let us see what happens with a Basic translation:

To put it shortly, the effects of developments in society on education make clearer (greater) the need for minds which are free (which have been made free).

These we will not get without, first, a new organization of the ways (instruments, workers) in education, by which theory may be put into use (may become a guide to our acts) without trouble (being stopped, waste). And second, it is necessary to give an answer to take up the question: Are we ready, and how far are we ready, to take the free operation of thought as the general rule controlling our outlook on society (as men in society) or our theory of what is right (our beliefs, our ideas, and acts).

I chose the passage in part to show the peculiar *resolving power* of Basic applied to a confused utterance. It does not so much reproduce any one meaning as offer us a selection of possible ingredients in the meaning. I hope that this specimen will further show the extent to which the writing of a Basic version of a passage of Complete English is an exercise in Complete English—not merely in Basic. So, the process of learning Basic, for native English speakers, is, from the beginning, work—of a kind which no present-day school-tasks provide—*on Complete English*. After a very little practice, the difficulty of writing Basic versions ceases altogether to be a difficulty in finding Basic turns of phrase and becomes a difficulty in deciding just what the original is, may, or might be saying. The work becomes, that is, very nearly a pure exercise *in interpretation*. From this point of view it is useful to compare it with those exercises which have in the past been of the most service as training in interpretation—I mean translation from and into Latin.

The chief effect of having two or more alternative modes of expression for almost the same meaning together before the mind and of pondering them is, of course, to heighten and clarify our sense of both; which is why translation is such a valuable educative device. But where one language (say Latin) is very imperfectly known—merely as a syntactic system quite apart from any more recondite ways of knowing it—this effect is apt to be lost. So translation from and into Latin, in the earlier stages of learning Latin, is not an ideal way of learning English. The two purposes of the exercise, (1) as a means of studying the meanings and (2) as a means of learning the Latin, get in one another's way.

Where both languages—as with Basic and Complete English— have once been mastered, as far as concerns control of their superficial syntax, the work of translation soon becomes almost wholly a training in examining and comparing meanings, and it can be made to bear directly and undistractedly on the question "Just what is being said?"

Despite an opinion that used to be widely entertained, the struggle to acquire command of strange and difficult syntaxes is not in itself an especially valuable exercise. The "insight" into the forms of thought that it was supposed to give is nowadays thoroughly discredited. Mill's view that Greek and Latin are uniquely valuable disciplines to the intellect, as being so complicated and regular, with his notion that grammar is "the beginning of the analysis of the thinking process" [7] were already out of date when he put them forward. Far from being valuable initial disciplines, the acquisition of strange syntax patterns by the rule and rote application of grammatical distinctions are probably, for numerous types of learners, actively stultifying—as many teachers have maintained. At the least they distract attention from the more important work of discriminating between meanings.

The value of translation into Basic varies with the type of passage translated. Apart from its use for the normal needs of international communication, travel, business, etc., translation is most instructive with passages of expository or argumentative prose dealing with semi-abstract subjects. And it is least helpful with passages of emotional evocation concerned with special local objects and activities which employ large numbers of specialized means. Thus a sentimental reverie over a cricket match would be about the worst example we could choose, and to put into Basic even a simple remark about a linnet fluting in a myrtle bush would not be a profitable exercise. It could be done, but the effect of the Basic version on the bird-lover's ear would not be that of the original remark. Descriptions of local activities, however, belong to a type of writing in less need of improvement in regard to composition or interpretation than any other. No one runs much risk of misunderstanding perceptual descriptions—if he has had the necessary experience—and without it he will fail to understand in any case. But we all run some risk of misreading any semi-abstract argument. And the breakdown will not, commonly, be due to the difficulty of the thought *as thought*. It will come from the indefiniteness, the embarrassing richness and variety of the possible meanings that may be borne by the medium, and our lack of practice in taking conscious account of them in interpretation. No educational instrument can be equally effective in all fields. Basic is aimed to assist at the weakest points, at the points where interpretation most needs to discriminate, to clarify and to increase control and order.

I have been outlining some of the reasons for thinking that a limited analytic language on the model of Basic may have a peculiarly important future before it both as a medium by which Western thought may be introduced to Chinese and other students in the East and in Africa more successfully than at present and as an instrument in clarifying thinking in schools everywhere. These two uses may be taken together because the essential problem is the same in both of them: how to induce and to maintain a discriminating examination of meanings. Local conditions in China, the circumstances touched on above, enormously magnify the difficulty of this problem, but they do not fundamentally change its nature. The juxtaposition of the two illuminates them both. We shall not see the perils that would come from the breakdown of traditional Chinese culture, and the powers of the possible remedies, unless we make every effort to see them in terms of our own problems and our own experience at home. And to have seen our own troubles enlarged and exaggerated in the Chinese scene may help us in turn.

As a teacher of English at Cambridge, with decades of experience of similar conditions at Harvard, I feel some confidence in saying that our most careful and expensive methods of teaching people how to read are, judged by their results, at present almost ludicrously inefficient. This is no place to present evidence in quantity to show that a large proportion of candidates for Honors in English have not learned to read.[8] The fact can, however, be demonstrated without the least difficulty. I printed a large collection of representative evidence some decades ago in *Practical Criticism* and, more revealingly, in *Interpretation in Teaching* for prose; and F. L. Lucas, on the basis of his extensive examination experience, added valuable corroboration in his essay in *Cambridge University Studies.*

In saying that these products of our present methods of studying English have not learned to read, I am not taking some impossibly high standard of impeccable intelligence and discernment, by which a reader would know how to interpret everything he read. I have no "fluent speaker" (p. 97) in mind. I mean no more than this: that they have not learned how, when they sweep perusing eyes over a passage of prose or verse, to ask themselves whether or not they have understood it, to ask reasonably relevant questions about its meaning in order to arrive, rightly or not, at an interpretation that can be defended by reference to the text. Something seems to be missing in Literary Education, some training in careful interpretation which would accustom readers to distinguish between guessing at the meaning of a passage and looking for it seriously.

Most school or university study of English literature is controlled—as we know to our grief—by more or less distant examinations. This, we must for the moment assume, is unavoidable. Our problem is how we are to make the examination influences as little pernicious as possible. Examinations are of one or other of two types:

They are either tests of information about authors, books, tendencies, influences and so on—in other words a specialized form of history, in itself by no means so valuable as other kinds of history and only worth acquiring as an aid to intelligent reading.

Or they purport to be tests of capacity to read intelligently. And this is the weak point; for it is in practice extremely difficult to devise questions about a student's reading which are not an invitation to him or her to expatiate in original or recollected judgments on the merits and qualities in general of the works in question. As Mr. Lucas feelingly observes, "One grows tired of reading denunciations of Meredith's prose (not that I wish to defend much of it) by writers who, on their next page, will attribute to him a piece by Sir Philip Sidney." He remarks, "The great and outstanding difference between a paper in English and a paper in Classics remains that the first asks for opinion after opinion—estimates of Burke, estimates of Johnson—from people who a year or two ago were still at school. What wonder if maundering is the result?" Again "Imagine a young person called on to acquire in two years, or often in one, a knowledge of English Literature from 1300 to the present day, including certain set books of prose, poetry and criticism; a knowledge to be tested largely by his or her ability to extemporize, in thirty-five minutes each, opinions of given books or authors, or opinions of someone else's opinions of them."

Lest it be thought that the mere haste under which examination answers are scribbled will account for the misinterpretations and the maunderings, and that the defect does not lie much deeper in a lack of proper training in reading, let me cite a few, alas! not unrepresentative, passages from a student who has had ample time to consider what he is saying. I will take them from a recent book, which is typical enough to remain anonymous. It was published by a famous university press in a series of studies in comparative literature, with a preface adorned by distinguished academic names to whom the author offers his thanks "for reading the manuscript" and supplying "valuable criticism and advice" as well as "inspiration and encouragement." The book is about the interactions of Science and Poetry; and this is part of his account of what seventeenth-century Science did to seventeenth-century Poetry:

If the spirit of the age tended to make some of the poets analytical, they desired, nevertheless, to bring a certain order out of chaos. Note William Walsh's questioning analysis of love:

> 'Love is a medley of endearments, jars,
> Suspicions, quarrels, reconcilements, wars;
> Then peace again, Oh would it not be best
> To chase the fatal poison from our breast?'

Lest it be supposed that I have merely picked out a place where something has gone wrong with the page, here is another example:

Along with the growth of science in the seventeenth century went an increasing tendency to question many values which had merely been accepted before. About the middle of the century Robert Herrick declared:

> 'Putrefaction is the end
> Of all that Nature doth entend.'

Values which had merely been accepted before! And here, from the philosophic preliminaries, is a third specimen:

"Many of the Romanticists . . . feel—and surely not without cause —that the analytic method of the scientist tends to destroy beauty of expression, while the procedure of generalizing and abstracting deprives poetry of its concrete and sensuous qualities. This is also the attitude of the philosophers Schopenhauer and Croce."

They might as well be invoked to maintain that boiling vegetables deprives them of their freshness!

The point I have to make with these quotations is, briefly, this: That the difference between a mind that can solemnly pen them, or read them through without agreeable spasms of irony and malice, and a mind that can see what they are saying is a life and death difference. The writer is a product of a certain kind of training in literature. We catch him at a moment when he is passing (with a Ph.D. thesis) through the gates that let him in to a lifetime's work in giving the same kind of training to a succession of other minds in their most susceptible years, and it is demonstrable that he does not know how to read even fairly simple writing. He treats of the most serious matters. The first sentence of the first extract seems fit indeed to stand as an epigraph to any study of poetry in any changing age— pre-eminently our own. But as we read on we see that the words do not even make up such a platitude as may be mistaken by a tired research worker for a discovery. By the example we are invited to note, they are reduced to a string of dominoes, mere phrases which the rules of the game permit to be placed end to end. And the example! No suspicion that love-squalls are a perennial human interest that no spirit of any age could alter. The writer cannot possibly have thought that the shock of science was required to make a poet perform such "a questioning analysis of love." He was not thinking about the meaning of the verses at all, nor about what he was saying, otherwise the remedy by which the poet proposes "to bring a certain order out of chaos,"

> Oh would it not be best
> To chase the fatal poison from our breast?

would have struck him as at least queer.

The "fatal poison" in this critic's breast is the same as that in the breast of the average examinee and of the Chinese student. As I said before, it is psittacism, the habit of using words without attention to their meanings.

"I used to think it the object of English to make people well read," Mr. Lucas says. "I have come to see that its aim must be to teach them how to read. They have the rest of their lives to read in." Alack! Thirty years have shown us that, unless they become teachers or publishers or editors or reviewers, students of English don't read more than they can help. Yet the aim of *teaching them how to read* remains what it was. What are the possible lines on which this aim may proceed? All, I believe, who are aware of the extent to which both prose and verse are currently misread even by seemingly well-qualified readers are agreed that training in some form of paraphrase or gloss is the best remedy for it. But the use of paraphrasing in schools is often so unsatisfactory that we may well feel that the remedy brings in as many evils as the disease.

Paraphrases in general divide into two types. There is the paraphrase that merely replaces the words in the original with rough synonyms, leaving all the doubtful parts of the meaning unillumined. This exercise of shuffling synonyms about is merely deadening to whatever germs of interpretative capacity may exist in the student. It may be agreed that the less he is subjected to it the better.

But the alternative is almost as bad. Here to write a paraphrase is to compose another passage made as nearly as possible a rival to the first. Rarely tried with a prose original, with poetry it is an invitation to write another poem—in prose—on a partially similar theme. As such, it is an exercise whose effects are often very far indeed from an improved comprehension of the original. This is the kind of paraphrase the more promising kind of pupil usually produces and he deserves our sympathy. For the terms of the task set him are something of an outrage on his sensibility. He is given an original which presumably he respects; he is asked—under the unfair condition that he may use none of the best words because these have been used already by the original poet—to build up a cluster of words, which will, so far as he can contrive, be an equivalent. The better reader he is, the more closely will he realize that what he is being asked to do is something not only presumptuous but impossible and absurd.

The exercise of writing a Basic paraphrase escapes all this. We are there playing a game: giving under strictly binding rules and conditions as accurate a representation as we can of the meanings of the original. But no one will expect our version to achieve a perfect translation. It is *not* claimed that a passage of Ruskin or Shakespeare can be reproduced without loss in Basic, or with that (rather remote) fidelity with which a good French version will render it. Sometimes, indeed, and with a frequency which is to many people at first surprising, passages of great English writing will be found to be already almost in Basic. A comparison of the Basic version and the Authorized Version of the Book of Ruth provides a striking example. But in general our poetry and our more ornate and elaborate emotive prose are not reproducible in Basic. Shakespeare has single lines in Basic:

Making the Greene one Red

for example, but the line above that

The multitudinous Seas incarnadine

defeats a Basic version, if from that version we expect anything like the integral effect of the line. But, and this is another point at which a misunderstanding of the purpose and use of a Basic version is extremely likely to occur, no such expectation is invited. Its use is quite other. Though it cannot reproduce the total effect, it can, item by item, display as many of the ingredients of sense which go into producing that total effect as any other analytic medium, and as clearly. The space, the notion, the expansion, the coming on of the waves without number and without end; the shock when the idea of blood is joined with that of water, "water, water, everywhere," and the way the Seas seem not only to be colored with the blood but themselves to become Seas of blood; all this with the suggestion in *incarnadine,* so full of fear and so deep-rooted in the part of the mind which is not conscious, of a living existence that is suddenly given to the waste of blood; all this may be put (I have been writing in Basic since the word *medium*) as completely, if not as delicately, as in any other language.

What are difficult to describe in Basic are not the *ideas* which may be divined in and extracted from the original but the nuances of feeling which result from them and from such other factors as the rhythm. But in any exposition these are difficult to display; and there is, I believe, a very strong case to be made for saying that the exercise of attempting to describe them is not a valuable one. It too easily becomes a debauch, an outflow of unregulatable sensibility. The valuable exercise is the analysis, the tracing out of the sense items, the ideas and their articulations—for these are a main part of the springs of the effect. To study them is to penetrate to the body of poetry; to describe effects is to play with shadows.

The typical instruction for a Basic exercise, I may accordingly suggest, should be this: "Make a Basic version; then, in normal English, point out where and how your Basic version fails (if it fails) to do justice to the original, and if it distorts it, say how." By such an instruction we should avoid the danger of the Basic version being supposed by the more weak-minded or ill-advised pupils to be "just as good" or "really what the poet ought to have written, or meant to say, if he had not been wanting to make it look pretty."

We may now consider what changes in the design of Basic English are likely to be proposed as a result of the varied and extensive use it has received. The chief of these concerns Ogden's treatment of verbs. Basic English is not the only instance of a design for which it is the very feature that most appealed to the designer, as his best contribution, that later seems most to need changing. His policy with verbs was to Ogden his master stroke, the step which made Basic English possible. On many copies of the Basic English Word List he even managed to squeeze in his NO 'VERBS' claim with the following model statement: "It is possible to get all these words on the back of a bit of notepaper because there are no 'verbs' in Basic English." Naturally enough, it was this claim which most of all drew attention to Basic and this feature which more than any other aroused opposition.

What Ogden did was this: Guided by some suggestions from Jeremy Bentham, he selected a minimal set of verbs, *come, get, give, go, keep, let, make, put, seem, take; be, do, have; say, see, send; may, will,* which could—in conjunction with other words in Basic—*substitute for* (take the place of) all the other verbs in the language. As the punctuation suggests, these verbs fall into four groups. The first ten (*come* to *take*) are names of irreducibly simple acts. *Seem* somewhat resists this classification or indeed any description. It is easiest to think of it as complementary to *be.* (We *seem* wise and good perhaps; we *are* perhaps foolish and bad.) But the others name what we do, or what things do, and between them they cover our doings, and the doings of things, in a peculiarly comprehensive fashion. Into the meanings of other verbs comes some component able to be carried by one or more of these operators (as *enter,* for example, has a meaning of *come in,* and *meditate* has a meaning which may be carried by *give thought* or *take thought*). And this is what has been meant by the claim that Basic has "no verbs." Its use of these super-verbs or operators allows it to dispense with the rest.

Next come *be, do* and *have,* which get such a lion's share of the work in English either as full verbs or as auxiliaries. Then come *say, see, send.* These are luxury conveniences in Basic and not strictly indispensable. We could cover their uses with other Basic words. When we *say* something, we *put* it into words; when we *see* something it *is* in view or we *have* it before our eyes; when we *send* someone we *make* him *go,* and so on. But these peri-phrases would be awkward, and these three words are of such general utility that it is better to have them on the list. Lastly come *may* and *will,* auxiliaries of possibility and permission, and of futurity.

An immensely strong case can be made for this extremely drastic restriction of verbs *as a design for early stages in learning English as a second language.* These are the verbs which can do most work in the language. They are verbs which must be mastered in any case if the learner is to attain any real com-petence. This plan gives them early an extraordinary amount of exercise: at first in situations which make their meanings en-actively, visibly and pictorially clear and unambiguous. Later come extensions. It is here that the argument for revision arises. Why not, both for paraphrasing purposes and—after a certain stage—for the foreign learner, use *as verbs* all the general words on the Basic List that admit of such use? There are some two hundred that may be so used though in strict Basic they are nouns only: *account, act, air, answer, attack, attempt.* . . . And there are useful verbs contained in Basic nouns: *add*ition, *adjust*-ment, *advertise*ment, *agree*ment, *amuse*ment. . . . There are others still, such as *argue* (argument), *attend* (attention), *behave* (behavior), *believe* (belief), which are no trouble to the English speaker—though they give a learner something further to note and remember.

What results from this redesign is of course a language much nearer than Basic to standard English, a language easier to speak in and to write (for the native), but harder, to an undetermined degree, for the learner. It is commonly proposed further that *can* and *must* (not Basic words) be added, along with varying numbers of others: *ask, bring, buy, find, think*, and so on . . . to yield a language which would still be restricted but would seem until analyzed to have almost the full powers of normal English.

It is not hard to see that in terms of the four aims above, this suppled-up Basic would differ little in coverage (1). It would be far more acceptable (2). As to ease of acquisition (3), it might well cost more than double the toil for equal coverage. This last point could without great trouble be determined by experiment. Appraisal as to (4): Insight into meaning, on the other hand, is a far more tricky matter, not in the least so readily settled. Those who have done most work upon this question and had most opportunity to compare pure Basic and verbed-up Basic as media for paraphrase are far from certain about the balance of advantages. Judgment in the matter turns on a very great number of minute analyses made with varying success by students of varying ability. What seems to emerge is that while it is undoubtedly easier to write paraphrases in verbed-up Basic, the degree of *insight into the original* which results often seems to be markedly less. The higher cost in time and toil of the more restricted Basic version seems for many to be repaid in superior understanding.

A policy that on the whole seems recommendable may be stated as follows:

(a) For the learner entering English, when a secure command of the Basic eighteen verbs has been *attained in their physically enactable, depictable uses,* go out from Basic into verb uses of other words through already acquired Basic phrases: start saying "He changed it" for "He made a change in it" or "He got it changed." A habit of explaining the new through paraphrase in the old can thus be built into the expansion of the learner's English.

(b) For the English speaker, joint use both of verbed-up Basic and of pure Basic with as much comparison between the versions as can be undertaken.

(c) Another step of redesign for Basic seems desirable. It goes along with much-needed cultivation of pictorial literacy. There seems no reason to attempt to limit the intake of words for which a simple picture, or sequence of them, can unambiguously present the meaning. Ogden's category of pictured things, his 200, would thus lapse. Many of them would, of course, come in early for a beginner as means of expanding and exercising his sentence-situation command. But there would be no attempt to make him learn them ahead of his need for them in his *use* of the language.

As a medium for paraphrase, the vocabulary resulting from this last enlargement would seem to have great advantages over pure Basic. In place of the question, "Is this word on the List or not?" we have "Is this thing depictable?" The gearing of language into actuality is thereby increased. And the responsibility of deciding whether or not the paraphraser sufficiently *understands* is put where it belongs, *on him.* Attention is directed to where it is most needed in controlling the structure of the meaning in place of being dissipated over points of no consequence, which nonetheless can waste much time and trouble.

Paraphrase—though I have given it here such prominence—is only one of a wide range of exercises which the use of a selection from English on the model of Basic suggests. The detail of the study of the advantages and disadvantages of one type or another of limitation; the arguments for the inclusion of this or that word or family of words, of this or that construction; sorting games with the Word Lists; the collection and classification, for example, of nouns that work as adjectives too; hundreds of investigations into what words can and cannot do; how they support and control one another; the varieties of opposition; the limits of analogy . . . there is no end to the invitations to exploration set on foot by this representation of a whole language through a part. Nothing more naturally prepares the mind to cultivate its powers of systematic reflection than these word-games which are in fact nothing less than inquiries into how meanings serve one another and how they serve and are constrained by reality.

The dissatisfactions with customary "English" studies touched on above are *bitterly* felt the world over. They are reflected in the fluctuations of pedagogic views of ?grammar? as well as in much energetic searching for new curricula for "English" to match those, from which so much has been hoped, for Science and Mathematics. It may be that what has been sought, as Socrates discovered of justice (*Republic,* 432D), "has been rolling under our feet from the start" and that we have been "like people hunting for what they hold in their hands."

But the new curricula to be designed have duties more ambitious and more exacting than those they must replace. It is not only ?English? that is failing us; the roots of an elementary school ˢʷMental and Moral Philosophyˢʷ have been left unwatered and the real sources of our cultures starved. As the preceding essays have tried to suggest, our thought and our means of thinking, though distinguishable, are interdependent. The way to recover a truly *elementary* education (one which provides, nourishes and liberates the elements) is through the same experimental curiosities as to how language works which give the child speech. But when he comes to writing let us give him sequenced explorables—to sustain and encourage in him the concept of an intelligible world.

In closing this discussion of the design of a World English we may remind ourselves again both of the growing scope of man's powers and of the need for clear and firm decisions as to what such powers should be used for. There is an analogy between the conception of a world order and the design of a language which may serve man best. The choice of words for that language and the assignment of priorities among their duties can parallel the statesman's true tasks. And it is through what language can offer him that every man has to consider what should concern him most. If rightly ordered, and developed through a due sequence,[9] the study of English can become truly a humane education.[10] May not such a language justly be named "EVERY MAN'S ENGLISH"?

Toward a World English

(1) *This grim reason:* There are those, of course, who say that the more understanding rises and spreads, the greater will be the world's danger, and perhaps we all may have moments when these voices seem to be speaking in our hearts. It was to ventilate these sorts of treason that the discussion of "the empires of the future" was included in "Meanings Anew." In brief, his new powers have made traditional man, of any of the major cultures, too dangerous. He is no longer viable. We need a new model capable of global organization and equipped to handle current and oncoming tensions.

(2) *instrument of reflection:* ' "And man became a living soul." He did not merely *possess* it, he became it. It was his proper being, his truest self, the man *in* the man. . . . Nothing is wanted but the eye, which is the light of this house, the light which is the eye of this soul. This *seeing* light, this *enlightening* eye, is Reflection. It is more, indeed, than is usually meant by that word; but it is what a *Christian* ought to mean by it, and to know too, whence it first came, and still continues to come—of what light even this light is *but* a reflection.' Coleridge, *Aids to Reflection,* Aphorism IX, in my *The Portable Coleridge* (New York, Viking Press, 1950), p. 395.

(3) *all the rest in all their senses:* The dawn of this dream for Leibniz is thus described (c.1679) by him, as having in his early youth been "scratched down on paper to be laid before my astonished teachers.

"Upon making the effort to study this more intently, I necessarily arrived at this remarkable thought, namely that a kind of alphabet of human thoughts can be worked out and that everything can be discovered and judged by comparison of the letters of this alphabet and an analysis of the words made from them. This discovery gave me great joy, though it was childish, of course, for I had not grasped the true importance of the matter." "On the General Characteristic," G. W. Liebniz, *Philosophical Papers and Letters,* Leroy E. Loemker, Ed., Vol. 1, p. 342 (Chicago, University of Chicago Press, 1956).

(4) *Commercial uses:* Ogden's own acrostic read "British, American, Scientific, International, Commercial."

(5) *separation of the "functional" from the "content" words:* On this see *English Word Lists: A Study of Their Adaptability for Instruction,* prepared for the Committee on Modern Languages of the American Council on Education, by Charles C. Fries with the cooperation of A. Aileen Traver, 1940, especially Chapter VIII, "Notes on Seven English Word Lists." For a critique of these authors' discussion see *Basic English and Its Uses,* by I. A. Richards, Routledge, 1943. "The separation of the 'operations' from the rest of the vocabulary as is done in Basic English seems to us," they remark, "a fundamentally important contribution to the solution of this problem of teaching a foreign language" (p. 89). "To classify the verb as an 'operator' and therefore to use only a minimum number of verbs in a *first* vocabulary list seems not only theoretically sound but helpful from a practical point of view" (p. 90). The impact of Ogden's Word List on all such work is well shown in their Table I (p. 74).

(6) *Basic English: International Second Language,* by C. K. Ogden, edited by E. C. Graham (Harcourt, Brace & World, 1968), includes his *Basic English, The ABC of Basic Eng-*

lish, and *The Basic Words.* Dr. Graham's *Basic Dictionary of Science* (New York, Macmillan, 1966), published in England as *The Science Dictionary in Basic English* (Evans Brothers, Ltd.), and *The General Basic Dictionary* (London, Evans Brothers, Ltd.), are invaluable resources in work with restricted forms of English.

(7) *analysis of the thinking process:* from his Inaugural Address at St. Andrews, 1866. As Henry Sidgwick said: "Translation is continually straining and stretching our faculty of language in many ways, and so necessarily imparts to it a high degree of vigor; but the precise power that will be of most use to us for the purposes of life, it does not, by itself, give, and it even causes us to form habits adverse to the acquirement of that power." (*Miscellaneous Essays and Addresses,* pp. 281–297. Quoted by Sir Philip Hartog, *The Writing of English,* p. 88.) This objection, valid against translation from or into foreign languages, lapses, I believe for the reasons given, as against translation from and into Basic. See further my *Interpretation in Teaching:* on Mill's view, Chapter 17; on Basic, Chapter 11.

(8) *have not learned to read:* "*Cicero* in his second Booke de Oratore, bringeth in one Lucilius, a pleasant and merie conceipted man, who saith, that he would not have such things as he wrote to bee read, either of those that were excellently learned, or of them that were altogether ignoraunt. For, that the one would think more of his doinges, and have a farther meaning with him, than ever the aucthour selfe thought: the other taking the booke in his hand, would understand nothing at all, being as meete to reade Aucthours, as an Asse to play on the Organnes." (Sir Thomas Wilson, *The Arte of Rhetorique,* 1560.)

(9) *due sequence:* As an example of the power of a developing **sequence to enhance** expectations of intelligibility in lan-

guage, in meanings and in actuality, see the last forty pages of *English through Pictures,* Book 2 (New York, Washington Square Press, 1961).

(10)   *humane education:* I feel that these Notes and Glosses cannot close better than with a quotation from one of the greater utterances of our times: "The uneven division of power and wealth, the wide differences of health and comfort among the nations of mankind, are the sources of discord in the modern world, its major challenge and, unrelieved, its moral doom." P. M. S. Blackett, President of The Royal Society, in his address as President of the British Association, Dublin Meeting, Sept. 4, 1957. (*The Advancement of Science,* No. 54, Sept. 1957.) We may add now, ten years later, not only its moral but in drear likelihood its actual doom as well.

Index